Oxford Studies in Gender and International Relations

Series editors: J. Ann Tickner, University of Southern California, and Laura Sjoberg, University of Florida

Windows of Opportunity: How Women Seize Peace Negotiations for Political Change
Miriam J. Anderson

Women as Foreign Policy Leaders: National Security and Gender Politics in Superpower America
Sylvia Bashevkin

Enlisting Masculinity: The Construction of Gender in U.S. Military Recruiting Advertising during the All-Volunteer Force
Melissa T. Brown

The Politics of Gender Justice at the International Criminal Court: Legacies and Legitimacy
Louise Chappell

Cosmopolitan Sex Workers: Women and Migration in a Global City
Christine B. N. Chin

Intelligent Compassion: Feminist Critical Methodology in the Women's International League for Peace and Freedom
Catia Cecilia Confortini

Complicit Sisters: Gender and Women's Issues across North-South Divides
Sara de Jong

Gender and Private Security in Global Politics
Maya Eichler

Scandalous Economics: Gender and the Politics of Financial Crises
Aida A. Hozić and Jacqui True

Equal Opportunity Peacekeeping: Women, Peace, and Security in Post-Conflict States
Sabrina Karim and Kyle Beardsley

Gender, Sex, and the Postnational Defense: Militarism and Peacekeeping
Annica Kronsell

The Beauty Trade: Youth, Gender, and Fashion Globalization
Angela B. V. McCracken

Rape Loot Pillage: The Political Economy of Sexual Violence in Armed Conflict
Sara Meger

From Global to Grassroots: The European Union, Transnational Advocacy, and Combating Violence against Women
Celeste Montoya

Who Is Worthy of Protection? Gender-Based Asylum and U.S. Immigration Politics
Meghana Nayak

Revisiting Gendered States: Feminist Imaginings of the State in International Relations
Swati Parashar, J. Ann Tickner, and Jacqui True

Gender, UN Peacebuilding, and the Politics of Space: Locating Legitimacy
Laura J. Shepherd

A Feminist Voyage through International Relations
J. Ann Tickner

The Political Economy of Violence against Women
Jacqui True

Queer International Relations: Sovereignty, Sexuality and the Will to Knowledge
Cynthia Weber

Bodies of Violence: Theorizing Embodied Subjects in International Relations
Lauren B. Wilcox

WOMEN AS FOREIGN POLICY LEADERS

National Security and Gender Politics in Superpower America

Sylvia Bashevkin

OXFORD
UNIVERSITY PRESS

Oxford University Press is a department of the University of Oxford. It furthers the University's objective of excellence in research, scholarship, and education by publishing worldwide. Oxford is a registered trade mark of Oxford University Press in the UK and certain other countries.

Published in the United States of America by Oxford University Press
198 Madison Avenue, New York, NY 10016, United States of America.

Library of Congress Cataloging-in-Publication Data
Names: Bashevkin, Sylvia., author.
Title: Women as foreign policy leaders : national security and gender politics in superpower America / Sylvia Bashevkin.
Description: New York, NY : Oxford University Press, 2018. |
Series: Oxford studies in gender and international relations |
Includes bibliographical references and index.
Identifiers: LCCN 2017055645 (print) | LCCN 2018000702 (ebook) |
ISBN 9780190875381 (Updf) | ISBN 9780190875398 (Epub) |
ISBN 9780190875374 (hardcover : alk. paper)
Subjects: LCSH: Women diplomats—United States. | Women cabinet officers—United States. | Kirkpatrick, Jeane J. | Albright, Madeleine Korbel. | Rice, Condoleezza, 1954– | Clinton, Hillary Rodham | National security—United States. | United States—Foreign relations—Decision making. | United States—Foreign relations—1981–1989. |
United States—Foreign relations—1989–
Classification: LCC JZ1480 (ebook) | LCC JZ1480 .B37 2018 (print) |
DDC 327.730092/52—dc23
LC record available at https://lccn.loc.gov/2017055645

9 8 7 6 5 4 3 2 1
Printed by Sheridan Books, Inc., United States of America

CONTENTS

PREFACE

Beyond the sleek lobby and gift shop, visitors enter a wide gallery. It's the last day of the Denver Art Museum exhibition in 2012 called "Read My Pins," showcasing hundreds of brooches Madeleine Albright wore when she served as the first woman secretary of state and, before that, as US ambassador to the United Nations. The rooms are full of mature women and young girls who recognize Albright as a local daughter who made it very big. The biographical note on the wall informs us that Albright lived in this city from adolescence—when she arrived with her parents from Czechoslovakia—until she graduated from high school.

Large color photographs hang above row after row of pins, like posters for an American Dream movie. One shows Albright descending under blue skies from a white jet, dressed in a dark coat and black Stetson hat. For Coloradans, there's no mistaking the local content in the choice of head gear. A larger message is also clear: the new "sheriff" on the world stage in 1997 was a woman (Dobbs 1997).

Lines of display cases extend in all directions. One pin on a tuft of blue velvet features a gold snake with a diamond in its mouth, wrapped around a long branch. Albright chose it for her meetings with Iraqi leaders in the era of Saddam Hussein. The brooch plays off a phrase by the dictator's official poet that described Albright (2009, 17) as "an unparalleled serpent." The pin signaled her view as to the identity of the real snake. Another brooch symbolizes breaking the glass ceiling. It holds fused translucent shards overlaid by a gold stripe to represent the entry of women to decision-making roles.

For me as a political scientist, the exhibition raises important questions. Did Albright's presence and that of other women make a meaningful difference to the conduct of international affairs? How might decisions made by these leaders illuminate assumptions about women as gentle seekers of peace and consensus? To what extent have female decision-makers acted in ways that advance women as a group?

Albright's career recalls an older debate about the consequences of more females on the international stage. In a controversial article, Francis Fukuyama (1998) argues that the confident and aggressive behavior of young male leaders in the developing world demands uncompromising elites in Western countries. In his view, the clout of the United States and other liberal democracies is in jeopardy if lots of women—whom he portrays as largely pacifist and conflict avoidant—attain senior foreign policy positions.

The track records of three prominent women cross my mind as I examine Albright's collection. During the early 1980s, Margaret Thatcher dispatched soldiers, ships, and aircraft to a remote location in the South Atlantic. Other British leaders opposed sending a military task force to defend the Falkland Islands (Campbell 2008, 132, 137; Steinberg 2008, 223). Yet history tells us that Thatcher prevailed. When she served as India's prime minister, Indira Gandhi offered military support to secessionist interests in East Pakistan (Steinberg 2008, 36). By the end of 1971, what had been Pakistan split into two countries: Bangladesh and Pakistan. The actions Gandhi took aided not just the fracturing of the neighboring state but also India's emergence as a major power. Although she was criticized for failing to prepare her country for conflict, Golda Meir ordered a full-scale mobilization of Israeli troops in 1973—despite competing pressures from American allies and her defense minister, Moshe Dayan (Steinberg 2008, 142). Israel's ability to survive surprise attacks by Syria and Egypt in the Yom Kippur War reinforced Meir's reputation, dating back to her service in the cabinet of David Ben-Gurion, who described Meir as "the best man in the government" (Ranta 2015, 84).

Like these cases, "Read My Pins" suggests that Albright was ready to defend national interests with vigor and decisiveness—including the use of military force. Yet unlike Thatcher, who questioned what the women's movement had ever done for her (see Sanzone 1981, 44), the display in Denver shows that Albright identified closely with pro-equality efforts.

I return to Toronto, where a student frames his seminar presentation around a tongue-in-cheek essay titled "Is America Ready for a Male Secretary of State?" John Norris's (2012) subtitle is at least as memorable: "Running Foggy Bottom Is a Tough Job—Maybe Too Tough for a Man." The text portrays foreign policy leadership as requiring interpersonal talents usually associated with women, plus a level of dedication that any "family-minded man" will find onerous. According to Norris (2012), Madeleine Albright, Condoleezza Rice, and Hillary Clinton devoted not just "time, energy, and focus" to their work. All demonstrated unusual willingness "to stand up to tyrants" and, Norris (2012) concludes, "[w]e just hope a man would be up to the task."

The timing was fortuitous. I realized that once Clinton completed her term as secretary of state, scholars would be able to assess multiple women in senior foreign policy jobs in Republican as well as Democratic administrations, in a country with a powerful military and a history of feminist activism. *Women as Foreign Policy Leaders* pursues the fascinating questions that emerged on my journey to Denver.

ACKNOWLEDGMENTS

This manuscript has benefited enormously from the generosity of many different people and organizations. Their support is most appreciated given that what began as an intriguing research idea has since taken multiple twists and turns.

Colleagues and friends offered valuable advice as the project unfolded. They include Gary J. Bass, Amanda Bittner, Giulia Calvi, Louise Carbert, Sarah Childs, Marjorie Griffin Cohen, Drude Dahlerup, Shir Daphna-Tekoah, Natalie Zemon Davis, Linda Silver Dranoff, Maya Eichler, Katie Engelhart, Cynthia Enloe, Sian Evans, Lenita Freidenvall, Bailey Gerrits, Dorit Geva, Galia Golan, Ayelet Harel-Shalev, Mary Hawkesworth, Steven Hermans, Hanna Herzog, Ran Hirschl, Anne-Marie Holli, Mala Htun, Henry Jacek, Carolyn James, Genevieve Fuji Johnson, Jacqueline Krikorian, Mireille Lalancette, Ruth Linn, Timothy Lynch, Laurel MacDowell, Helen McCarthy, Ken McGoogan, Deborah Moskovitch, Carla Norrlof, Ilana Pardes, Louis Pauly, V. Spike Peterson, Elizabeth Riddell-Dixon, Diane Sainsbury, Marian Sawer, Claire Schneiderman, Ayelet Shachar, Yael Shomer, Glenda Sluga, Jean Edward Smith, Miriam Smith, Melanee Thomas, Ann Towns, Deborah Trouten, and David Wolfe.

Earlier versions of the study were presented at the Women, Diplomacy and International Politics conference at the European University Institute; Women and US Foreign Policy conference at the University of London; Mothers and Others Workshop at the Banff Centre for Arts and Creativity; Women in International Security workshop at Queen's University; Listening to Narratives of Security and Insecurity workshop at Ben Gurion University; Dalhousie University; the DEMDI Nordic network conference; McMaster University; Memorial University of Newfoundland; Simon Fraser University; Stockholm University; Tel Aviv University; University of Arizona; University of Bristol; University of Gothenburg; University of Haifa; University of Helsinki; University of New Mexico; University of

Toronto; as well as at meetings of the American Political Science Association, Canadian Political Science Association, International Studies Association, NATO Association of Canada, and Social Science History Association.

At the University of Toronto, I have benefited from the wisdom of colleagues and staff members who have reviewed my research plans and offered perceptive comments on them. Students in a variety of courses opened my eyes to many different perspectives on questions that rest at the heart of this project. For their crucial research assistance, I am grateful to graduate students in the Department of Political Science, notably Megan Dersnah, Emma Gill-Alderson, Vivian Hua, Lama Mourad, Alesha Porisky, Erica Rayment, Daniel Sherwin, Ethel Tungohan, and Jason VandenBeukel.

The study would not have been possible without the support of the Social Sciences and Humanities Research Council of Canada.

At Oxford University Press, Angela Chnapko and Alexcee Bechthold have guided me through the publication process with grace and skill. I thank them as well as the series editors, J. Ann Tickner and Laura Sjoberg, and two anonymous assessors whose insights made this a better book.

Finally, no writer can survive, let alone thrive, without the love of family. I dedicate this book to mine.

Women as Foreign Policy Leaders

CHAPTER 1

Introduction

How have women, both as individuals and collectively, engaged with international politics? In particular, what consequences follow from the appointment of "firsts," such as Madeleine Albright, to top foreign policy posts? Inspired by recent work in the field of feminist diplomatic history, this discussion responds to each question in ways that challenge and extend the existing gender and politics literature.

Women as Foreign Policy Leaders offers a comparative account of women's presence in senior national security positions in the American political executive. It examines four high-profile appointees in the United States since 1980: Jeane Kirkpatrick during the Reagan years, Madeleine Albright in the Clinton era, Condoleezza Rice during the George W. Bush presidency, and Hillary Rodham Clinton in the first Obama mandate. The study explores the ability of each decision-maker to insert herself in a domain long dominated by men, focusing in particular on the extent to which these women shaped foreign policy in meaningful ways during a series of Republican and Democratic administrations.

The chapters that follow probe two specific and, as yet, not widely excavated research tranches: first, the influence of female decision-makers, notably their ability to make a measurable difference to the understanding and practice of national security policy; and second, leaders' actions with respect to matters of war and women's rights. Given that standard histories of diplomacy tend to ignore women's involvement, feminist scholars have begun to document a long record dating back to the early modern era (see Sluga and James 2016). The current project reinforces the efforts of feminist historians to identify and assess these contributions, albeit with a spotlight on contemporary foreign policy rather than the salons and state-craft of the sixteenth century and following.

Like history, the discipline of political science has largely neglected women's participation as decision-makers in international affairs (for exceptions, see Hudson and Leidl 2015; McGlen and Sarkees 1993, 2001). To the extent that scholars address this subject, they tend to start with a view that female elites will mirror the relatively pacific preferences of women in the general public as well as the claims of progressive women's movements. When their findings diverge from these expectations, authors suggest that upon reaching higher office, women feel pressure to conform to existing norms and thus adopt stereotypically masculine perspectives (see, for example, Koch and Fulton 2011).

This chapter proposes a competing thesis: since 1980, women leaders in the United States have made diverse and transformative foreign policy contributions during a series of presidential administrations. Taken as a group, their track records reveal (a) a consistent willingness to pursue mus-cular, aggressive approaches to international relations, contrary to "pacifist angels" theories of gender and conflict; (b) widely divergent views about feminism, in contrast to assumptions that elites will uniformly repre-sent the interests of progressive women's movements; and (c) patterns of assertive behavior that pre-date recruitment to senior posts, suggesting that the repertoires of foreign policy leaders are in place before they reach executive office.

The following text develops the main contours of this argument. We begin with a review of key insights from feminist diplomatic history that anchor our examination of contemporary decision-makers. The next sections consider the gender and politics literature, showing how the field's emphasis on legislative institutions creates valuable opportunities to ex-plore cabinet-level office and the consequences of presence in the polit-ical executive. From these starting points, we develop a research design that facilitates the comparative analysis of recent foreign policy leaders. The final section presents an overview of the subsequent chapters and summarizes the methodology employed in the empirical discussion.

PERSPECTIVES FROM DIPLOMATIC HISTORY

Feminist historiography opens a promising door for exploring the circumstances under which international leaders can potentially make a difference. It poses such questions as the following: What structural patterns permit or, conversely, restrict women's influence? Have female diplomats historically endorsed either pacifist or feminist positions? How has their presence been received by others?

In addressing each query, historians highlight a core normative or political project for feminist scholars across the academy. At the same time, their research suggests important thematic markers to guide inquiry in fields beyond their own (see McCarthy 2014; Sluga and James 2016). To begin with the first pivot, historical scholarship reminds us that feminist academics are, by definition, deeply committed to the task of recovering women's agency as social actors. Whether that agency is best revealed in the actions of individual diplomats dating back to early modern times, or collectively in the work of groups that emerged in the interwar years such as the Women's International League for Peace and Freedom (WILPF), researchers stress that women have largely been erased and continue to be erased from what Glenda Sluga (2016, 129) terms "grand historical narratives."

What are the implications of this erasure? As Helen McCarthy (2016, 168) observes, the tendency of mainstream scholarship to downplay or ignore what women do not only marginalizes them within the historical record, but also renders "invisible the gendered power relations on which that history has rested." Failing to address women's contributions means that we ignore the significance of gender relations as flagged early on by writers such as Joan Scott (1999, 6), who describes them as "meanings of sexual difference [that] are invoked and contested as part of many kinds of struggles for power."

Feminist diplomatic historians examine how gender and power have interacted inside the shifting parameters of international affairs. They probe how women were accepted, marginalized, or ignored in this domain, asking how female actors navigated a realm in which they were frequently viewed with hostility and treated as outsiders (see James and Sluga 2016, 9). Historians admit in explicit terms, however, that this work carries the risk of further obscuring women's engagement. As Laura Santaliestra (2016, 69) writes in her account of seventeenth-century Spain, "Ironically the application of gender analysis to the history of diplomacy has contributed to reaffirming the paradigm of masculinity in foreign affairs due to an underestimation of the potential of individuals and a very narrow conception of diplomatic activity, limited to the formal channels of power."

On one plane, researchers have addressed this challenge by insisting that individuals do matter—a point to which we return shortly. On another, they probe such informal realms as family, courtship, friendship, and social networks associated with women's salons of the early modern era and later, in order to showcase these venues as sites of influential diplomatic interaction and as loci deserving of academic attention (see Sluga and James 2016). At least with respect to this second response, feminist historians resemble feminist international relations scholars in their emphasis on widening the intellectual terrain that is implicated in a shared political project (see, for example, Enloe 1989; Tickner 2001, 2014).

What broad avenues does feminist diplomatic history suggest for political science and international relations? Four main themes stand out, each of which provides useful grounding for research on the contemporary era. They involve (1) how the institutionalization of diplomacy has restricted women's opportunities; (2) sustained differences of opinion among women about matters of war and peace as well as about feminism; (3) diverse negative tropes that revealed a deep discomfort with juxtapositions of women and diplomatic power; and (4) varied responses adopted by female emissaries to these narratives of discomfort. The next paragraphs summarize each direction in order to situate our study of the contemporary period.

The first theme highlights a gradual shift away from older familial and especially dynastic patterns of informal diplomacy in which women with valued social connections could participate as credible and legitimate actors, toward more scientific, formal, and professionalized practices that elevated "reasoned discussion among men" (James and Sluga 2016, 6). Under the latter rubric, male diplomats could represent either monarchs or sovereign states in a newly institutionalized diplomatic realm. By contrast, women were systematically squeezed out of the authoritative practice of international relations—consigned, for example, to the status of wives of professional foreign service officers.

Historians date this transition from multiple chronological moments and settings, including mid-fifteenth century Italy (see James 2016), the sixteenth- and seventeenth-century Habsburg era (Marini 2016, 51), the eighteenth century in Britain (James and Sluga 2016, 6), and the interwar years that produced WILPF and the League of Nations (see Herren 2016). Even though the timing of this process seemed to vary depending on context, the outcome was effectively the same: an increasingly masculine, institutionalized diplomatic regime emerged that limited women's opportunities—such that the restrictions affecting women of privilege under the newly professionalized regime were tighter than under the older informal one.

By training a spotlight on the evolution of diplomacy, historians illuminate the ways in which assets such as education and social networks permitted some females to be extremely active beyond the so-called private sphere as far back as the early modern period. As James and Sluga

(2016, 2) write, "it is misleading to assume that there was a concordance between male and public, or female and private" as far back as the 1500s. Processes of institutionalization meant that men from privileged backgrounds could ascend the diplomatic ladder, while similar women were increasingly excluded from the formalized realm of international affairs. In the Victorian era in the United Kingdom, as McCarthy (2014, 21) shows, the combination of a "proper" family class background and an individual's Oxbridge education opened doors for men to the "clubbish" and highly masculine world of state-to-state relations. Females with high social status "continued to enjoy much latitude" through the early twentieth century— notably as the convenors of influential salons and tea tables. Yet only a tiny handful became official diplomats (McCarthy 2014, 32).

The work of feminist historians in charting how diplomacy has evolved directs our attention to the broader context in which contemporary decision-makers operate. Analysts of US foreign policy argue that from the initial postwar decades, the US State Department was increasingly eclipsed by the Pentagon in staff size, budget, and political influence (see Clinton 2014, 24; Lindsay and Daalder 2001; Navarro 2016). From this perspective, recent investments in expensive, sophisticated tools of intelligence-gathering and warfare (such as drone aircraft) only widen an already yawning gap between the resources and prestige attached to traditional American diplomacy versus those commanded by the Department of Defense. Women "firsts," beginning with Jeane Kirkpatrick, therefore arrived as older diplomatic institutions were themselves in retreat; female elites needed to struggle not only for personal legitimacy in a historically masculine setting, but also for the structural relevance of the units they served.

Second, historical research unsettles essentialist and homogenizing notions of women as pacifists in the realm of conflict, feminists in the domain of gender relations, and progressives with respect to other policies. Laura Beers (2016) reveals one origin of these assumptions that dates from the interwar years, when veterans of the struggle for suffrage promoted the pacifist, democratic, anti-colonial, and redistributive agenda of groups like the Women's International League. Beers (2016) notes that some WILPF activists rejected not just elite control of foreign policy, but also national sovereignty in general. As one of them proclaimed, "I have no sense of nationalism, only a cosmic consciousness of belonging to the human family" (Rosika Schwimmer, as quoted in Beers 2016, 209). During an era of growing institutionalization, as McCarthy (2014, 120) points out, lapses of imperial sentiment in such groups as the League helped to justify the assignment of British women diplomats to stereotypical roles as "international social-workers-cum-saints." Their remits included refugees, orphans, and alcoholism, rather than mainstream security considerations.

The historical record also reveals that official envoys and movement campaigners frequently held diametrically opposing views. McCarthy (2016, 177ff) demonstrates how female diplomats operating from the interwar period through the 1970s not only were deeply committed to advancing British interests, but also were ambivalent toward—and, in some instances, vigorously opposed to—women's movement claims. Philip Nash (2016, 234) indicates early American women diplomats identified more with feminist causes than their British counterparts. He links this pattern to the willingness of US presidents to recruit appointees from partisan backgrounds rather than from the professional foreign service.

This is not to suggest that all American diplomats during the 1930s and following endorsed pacifist, feminist, or progressive positions. Instead, as Nash (2016) reports, their perspectives were mixed and, overall, were more sympathetic than those of British representatives. Historical analysis thus underlines the range of views that characterized women doing similar work for similar countries in the same period. It confirms that roughly a century ago, neither unanimity nor homogeneity characterized the views of female diplomats. This material suggests a broad spectrum along which scholars can evaluate varied positions toward international conflict, feminism, and other subjects. We explore this continuum in greater detail in Chapter 2.

A third theme pertains to multiple and, in some instances, contradictory criticisms. Historical research demonstrates that men of diverse ranks and backgrounds have long voiced hostile views toward women's practice of diplomacy. As Natalie Zemon Davis (1993, 170) notes, women monarchs in the sixteenth century confronted "the usual suspicions," including "that women would be subject to male favorites and would be changeable and irrational." In more recent times, these assertions saw women as poorly equipped for international relations, disruptive to the diplomatic service, and not worth investing in because they frequently left the profession (see McCarthy 2016, 169, 179). As McCarthy (2016, 176) observes, this last claim was tautological given that through the 1970s, rules prohibiting married women from working in Anglo-American foreign services constituted a major reason why so many resigned their positions.

In 1936, for instance, members of an interdepartmental committee released a report on admission to the British diplomatic corps. Their verdict was clear and direct, concluding, in McCarthy's (2014, 149) words, that "the government was doing women a favour by denying them access to a profession for which they were genuinely unsuited." This decision echoed the views expressed by a Foreign Office undersecretary during the same period. He described appointing women as "a deeply distasteful notion" that would damage "a profession founded on fine masculine qualities—character, integrity, loyalty, clubbability" (Charles Howard Smith, as quoted in McCarthy 2014, 87). The undersecretary was supported by the wives of prominent British diplomats, who were prepared to testify in favor of his argument (see McCarthy 2014, 141–143).

Speaking in the House of Commons in 1943, Labour Party Member of Parliament (MP) Harold Nicolson extended general claims about inappropriateness by emphasizing not just the qualities women lacked, but also the traits they possessed in excess. In his words,

> The special virtues of women are singularly ill-adapted to diplomatic life. These virtues, I should say, were first, intuition and secondly, sympathy. Intuition is absolutely fatal in diplomacy. It tempts people to jump to conclusions. Sympathy is equally fatal because it leads people to identify themselves with causes or personalities with which or whom they feel sympathy. That is fatal to that very balanced attitude which it is the business of the Diplomatic Service to preserve. (Nicolson, as quoted in McCarthy 2014, 235)

Whether women were defective because they were insufficiently masculine or overly feminine, the upshot of the generalist criticism was that they did not make good diplomats.

Reinforcing these broad assertions was a set of more specific ones. Probably the most damning charge employed by proponents of exclusion in Britain as well as the United States said women would not be accepted or taken seriously in a given location (see McCarthy 2014, 86–87, 108–110, 137–140). China, for example, was historically seen as unprepared for a woman emissary from the United Kingdom, as were most countries of the Middle East and South America (see McCarthy 2014, 236–237). According to this view, sending females to regions where they were unwelcome risked national interests and deprived men of valuable career opportunities.

Litigation initiated by an American diplomat exposed this position as a convenient cover for the home country to impede women's careers and pay them less than men, while blaming outsiders for the problem. Alison Palmer began working at the State Department as a clerk typist in 1955 and, after passing the requisite entry exam in 1958, reached the status of junior Foreign Service officer. In 1960, Palmer became vice consul in Leopoldville, Congo, just as crisis engulfed the country. Her efforts in that job, according to McKenzie (2015, para. 1), helped to save the lives of "several young American men," as well as a number of citizens of other nations. Palmer went on to gain experience in other US embassies but was turned down for higher posts (McKenzie 2015, para. 22). Hired by the ambassador to Ethiopia, Palmer found she was expected to serve as his wife's social secretary (Alison Palmer papers 2010, 2 of 20).

Palmer challenged claims that it was reasonable to restrict her upward mobility because white North American women were vulnerable to sexual advances and possibly assault by African men. Instead, she argued, the main sources of "harassment and sexual threats" came from other Americans employed by the US government (McKenzie 2015, para. 25). She filed an internal grievance against the State Department alleging sex discrimination.

In 1969, the Equal Employment Office in the department concluded its investigation in her favor, although the decision was neither made public nor noted in her personnel file (Alison Palmer papers 2010, 2 of 20). Palmer then appealed in 1971 to the Civil Service Commission, which held hearings that resulted in her receiving a promotion as well as a retroactive salary payment (Alison Palmer papers 2010, 2 of 20). Palmer initiated a class action suit in 1976 together with eight other plaintiffs; it alleged that the department discriminated against women at the point of recruitment, offered them less promising career assignments after they joined, and rewarded them with weaker performance ratings and honors once in rank. Although a federal district court in 1985 rejected the suit, it was upheld in subsequent appeals and district court rulings (see Alison Palmer et al. 1986).

At the point of the initial judicial decision, according to Gamarekian (1989), "41% of the men in the Foreign Service were political officers and 16.2% were consular officers. Only 22.9% of Foreign Service women held political jobs, while 36.9% were in consular positions. Just 3% of senior officers were women." Other 1985 data indicate that the US Foreign Service was composed of 20 percent women and 80 percent men, with the males overwhelmingly white (72 percent) and only low percentages African American (5.4 percent), Hispanic (3.4 percent) or Asian American (0.7 percent; Association for Diplomatic Studies and Training 2015).

By mid-1989, Palmer had spent about $150,000 of her own funds as lead litigant in the anti-discrimination suit (Gamarekian 1989). Costs for the class action proceedings later exceeded $200,000 and half of Palmer's pension (McGlen and Sarkees 1993, 289). Her campaign achieved at least two major objectives: first, a court ruling required the State Department to undertake corrective action, which meant 600 women were notified that they might be eligible for "court-ordered relief," including reassignment to higher positions; and second, public acknowledgment that women failed sections of the Foreign Service examination at higher rates than men, which led the department to cancel the test entirely for 1989 and then redesign it (Gamarekian 1989).

Since the US government appealed sections of the 1989 decision, litigation dragged on for decades. In late 2009, Palmer and her attorneys announced they were terminating the lawsuit. The US District Court for the District of Columbia then dismissed the case on the grounds that all parties agreed the State Department had met the terms of earlier judicial orders. Actions that constituted compliance with court decisions included offering restitution (including retroactive pay) to women who had been denied promotions, opening prestigious political (as opposed to administrative or consular) positions to women, and reforming recruitment practices in ways that diversified the composition of the professional diplomatic corps (see Alison Palmer papers 2010).

What Palmer and her fellow plaintiffs experienced followed from a portrayal of women as weak, vulnerable, and hence underpowered candidates for diplomatic responsibility. These claims echoed older descriptions in the historical literature of females as indecisive and incompetent (see James and Sluga 2016, 8); unable to keep order (Mitchell 2016, 89); meddlesome (Sluga 2016, 127); vacuous (Ghervas 2016, 157); and too delicate and sentimental for the demands of international negotiation (McCarthy 2016, 169).

Tropes suggesting that women are overpowered for diplomatic work present an intriguing contrast to underpowered arguments. The former can be discerned in accounts dating from the Renaissance and Napoleonic eras that stress the romantic as well as other-worldly bases of women's closeness to power (see Ghervas 2016, 163; James 2016, 23; Woodacre 2016, 31). These highly sexualized narratives sometimes present females as dangerous and cunning sorcerers who conspire with mystics. In other cases, they suggest sly, conniving tricksters who use feminine wiles to charm and deceive. Corina Bastien (2016, 113), for example, writes of allegations in early eighteenth-century France of "overweening ambition, curiosity, indiscretion, passion and an avid desire for domination." Overpowered claims thus contrast women's backroom intrigue with men's professionalism, a comparison that helped to justify consigning women to the margins of an increasingly institutionalized diplomatic regime (see Sluga 2016, 129–131; McCarthy 2016, 170).

Taken together, overpowered and underpowered narratives on the historical record since 1500 serve to demean women's contributions. They not only cast doubt on the suitability of females to diplomatic engagement, but also impugn their ability to succeed in any endeavor that demands intellectual rigor, sustained concentration, and balanced judgement. Each trope offers a discourse of discomfort or unease that is worth probing with respect to the careers of contemporary women leaders. In particular, the sexualized and often dominatrix-like images of Condoleezza Rice as national security advisor and secretary of state evoke earlier overpowered portrayals documented by historians such as Bastien (2016; see also Alexander-Floyd 2008).

A fourth theme underlined in feminist historiography involves varied responses to exclusion. Pioneering emissaries sent by the United States to Northern Europe during the 1930s and following, for instance, developed a populist brand of diplomacy. It reached over the heads of individuals who resented women's participation, whether they were the leaders of host governments or fellow diplomats. As the chief of mission to Denmark and Iceland, Ruth Bryan Owen engaged in people-to-people diplomacy by traveling extensively and becoming the first American minister to visit Greenland (see Nash 2016, 225). Florence Jaffray Harriman stood out for her willingness to join Norwegian cod fisherman on their annual Arctic expedition (Nash 2016, 226). This populist approach was later employed by British women diplomats in the early years of World War II, when they tried to convince skeptical Americans to join the Allied effort. According to McCarthy (2014, 202), their campaign "focused primarily on winning hearts and minds, rather than the more conventional diplomatic work of influencing power-brokers in government."

A related strategy portrayed stereotypically feminine characteristics as useful and beneficial for diplomats. During the interwar years, British MP Nancy Astor maintained that women's intuition would assist imperial interests (see McCarthy 2014, 117). In 1945, a male diplomat told his superiors in London that women were "discreet, reliable and intelligent and a woman's instinctive or even emotional approach to the problems of a strange country or foreigners, or again of British subjects in need of help, is sometimes more practical than a man's logical and analytical approach" (memo from John Price, UK consul in Geneva, as quoted in McCarthy 2014, 228).

Yet another response saw individual women cultivate area specializations and social networks that made them recognized experts on one slice of the earth's geography (see McCarthy 2016, 168). Gertrude Bell's close familiarity with the Middle East, for example, meant that she stood out during the interwar years as a British diplomat who possessed "unrivalled specialist knowledge and the personal support of powerful allies" (McCarthy 2014, 75). Bell's case reveals the advantages of being both substantively immersed in a given region, as well as a consummate networker whose support among influential men mitigated the effects of discrimination.

Finally, historical research shows that while diplomats like Alison Palmer organized a class action lawsuit to contest discrimination, others rejected pro-equality movements and issue positions—thus creating a clear distance from other women. Gertrude Bell, for one, was "hostile to feminism," including the extension of the franchise (McCarthy 2014, 75). During the period of International Women's Year in 1975, women diplomats in the United Kingdom "did not, as some feminists had predicted they would, work collectively to bring questions of particular interest to women into the purview of British foreign policy" (McCarthy 2014, 253). As McCarthy (2014, 285) concludes, "If Women's Liberation called for revolution, female diplomats preferred evolution."

Each of these broad strategies employed in the past can be discerned in recent American foreign policy. During the first Obama term, Hillary Rodham Clinton practiced a highly visible form of people-to-people diplomacy. Much like women who reached ambassadorial posts in the 1930s and following, she responded to doubts about her aptitude for the role by reaching over the heads of the doubters in order to make a mark independently. Albright's knowledge of Central Europe and, during the first Reagan administration, Jeane Kirkpatrick's familiarity with Latin America offered a valuable substantive edge inside the cabinet—one that reinforced the strong relationships they built with the presidents who appointed them. During the 1990s, Madeleine Albright wore an extensive collection of brooches to communicate forceful messages about US positions on the Middle East and elsewhere (see Albright 2003, 436). The pins demonstrated in visual terms the argument that being a woman can constitute a crucial advantage in the realm of diplomacy. Finally, the critical views of both Kirkpatrick and Condoleezza Rice toward women's movements echoed the perspectives of earlier diplomats such as Gertrude Bell.

In short, feminist diplomatic history opens our eyes to multiple constraints facing women in international affairs, and to the varied strategies they have employed to survive in the field. For students of contemporary politics, this literature identifies important patterns of exclusion, as well as routes toward gaining acceptance that foreground present circumstances, and illuminates the push and pull of actors inside changing structures.

Although the field of feminist diplomatic history is relatively new, thirty years have passed since Antonia Fraser (1988) published *The Warrior Queens*—a popular account of leaders from Cleopatra and Boudica through Margaret Thatcher. Her study, like the work of McCarthy (2014) and Sluga and James (2016), shows that while females were far from usual either near or at the apex of power, they were also not unique. An ongoing pattern of neglect helps to explain how women active at senior levels of international responsibility continue to be treated as "exceptional" (McCarthy 2014, 144; Santaliestra 2016, 81; Sluga 2016, 121ff.), "exemplary" (McCarthy 2014,

171), "extraordinary" (Santaliestra 2016, 81), and "anomalous" (McCarthy 2014, 144), rather than as individuals whose contributions merit systematic comparison and evaluation.

CONTOURS OF POLITICAL RESEARCH

In the discipline of political science, a lack of attention to foreign policy leaders is consistent with emphases since the 1980s on the role of structures (see Evans et al. 1985; Krook and Mackay 2011). Given that an institutional approach by definition privileges social forces rather than personal agency, this perspective has stimulated strong interest in such matters as the stability of parliamentary practices and norms. As the literature on women's presence inside institutions makes clear, far less study has been devoted to questions of whether, when, and how actors manage to alter circumstances (see Phillips 1995).

Compounding these preoccupations is the sustained interest of gender and politics scholars in legislative participation. Empirical research has barely begun to probe more senior levels of public office, where opportunities for individuals to "be agentic" likely eclipse those available to lawmakers. To the extent that existing studies address involvement in the political executive, they reach two main conclusions. First, proportions of female presidents, prime ministers, and cabinet ministers have tended to increase over time but continue to vary widely across countries, parallel with trends showing women's generally rising but still highly variable numbers in parliaments (Annesley et al. 2014; Atchison and Down 2009, 8; Jacob et al. 2014, 333; Krook and O'Brien 2012, 841). Second, women who attain cabinet office are more likely to hold portfolios in feminine or "soft," often lower prestige, social and cultural fields than in masculine or "hard," generally higher prestige, domains such as foreign policy and finance (see Atchison and Down 2009, 6; Borrelli 2002, 57–63; Davis 1997; Escobar-Lemmon and Taylor-Robinson 2005, 2009; Hoogensen and Solheim 2006, 17; Jacob et al. 2014; Krook and O'Brien 2012, 842; Siaroff 2000; Studlar and Moncrief 1999; Tremblay and Stockemer 2013). The only longitudinal study to date of the foreign policy field finds considerable cross-national and within-case variation among advanced industrial systems, but an overall trend since the mid-1970s toward more female appointees in senior positions (Bashevkin 2014, 417–420).

Considerably less is known about the consequences of women's presence in executive office. The origins of this gap are explored in the following section in greater detail. They range from core normative and methodological preferences to theoretical orientations that direct attention toward group representation and away from individual influence. Taken together, these trends mean that since the formative era in the field, coinciding with the rise of second-wave feminism, key texts have stressed structural barriers between women as a collectivity, on one side, and positions of major policy responsibility, on the other. In particular, conceptions of group mobilization as the best hope for challenging women's marginalization directly shaped the body of knowledge known as gender and politics. One practical result is that few academic accounts consider the impact of individual actors (exceptions include Genovese 1993).

This study seeks to reorient the gender and politics literature in three significant ways. First, building on the social science consensus since Marx's time, which sees agents and structures interacting in dynamic, co-constitutive ways (see Sewell 1992), I maintain that the study of individual decision-makers is both theoretically justified and empirically necessary. Second, as detailed in the following paragraphs and in Chapter 2, this study proposes a more nuanced treatment of political representation than is typically used in empirical studies. Third, it posits that elite representation forms one piece among many within the larger puzzle called leadership. If political representation entails claims-making (or, alternatively, an unwillingness to engage in such action) on behalf of a larger group, then our understanding of representation is best advanced within a more generalized consideration of executive influence. The empirical core of this book in Chapters 3 through 6 widens the purview of gender and politics scholarship by interrogating the impact of political executives, including at a representational level, on the broad substantive directions of the country they served.

Overall, this study seeks to extend gender and politics research such that studies of cabinet ministers, prime ministers, and presidents address more than their willingness to carry forward (or not) the interests of organized feminism or the modal priorities of women in the general population. We suggest a critical view of representation that is embedded in larger questions about the willingness and ability of individuals to recast policies and reshape institutions. By calling for a rebalancing at conceptual as well as empirical levels, this account advocates "bringing the actor back in" to gender and politics scholarship, as a counterpoise to disciplinary attempts in the 1980s to restore the primacy of state structures (see Evans et al. 1985).

The domain of international affairs offers a promising context for this reorientation. Foreign offices form a sturdy centerpiece in the annals of world history, notably as places where crucial decisions about conflict as well as cooperation were developed and implemented. As Madeleine Albright notes, however, diplomatic leadership was so long the domain of men that Henry Kissinger told an audience in 1997 that he wanted to welcome her to the "fraternity" of secretaries of state. Albright (2003, 432) responded, "'Henry, I hate to tell you, but it's not a fraternity anymore.'" The arrival of meaningful numbers of women in senior positions remains a relatively new phenomenon, and corresponds roughly with the growth of second-wave feminism (see Bashevkin 2014, 420).

Above all, global diplomacy constitutes among the most politically significant and empirically relevant locations for probing the difference that individuals make. Foreign policy leaders in systems including the United States hold the ability to go to war, impose severe sanctions, or make peace with adversaries. They face fewer constraints from legislatures, public opinion, and courts than do elites with responsibility for domestic policy (see Auerswald 1999). In short, a reasonable possibility exists that agents with diplomatic portfolios will act from time to time upon structures, rather than simply being acted upon.

For gender and politics researchers, bureaus tasked with shaping a country's external affairs provide among the only venues where it is possible to probe simultaneously two promising and, as yet, not widely explored areas: first, the power of women decision-makers, in this case their ability to make a measurable difference to the understanding and practice of foreign policy; and second, their actions with respect to matters of international conflict and gender politics, where existing accounts suggest that female decision-makers will operate in ways consistent with the relatively pacifist preferences of women in the general public, feminist movement claims, or stereotypical masculine norms that they confront upon reaching elite office.

An unprecedented series of "firsts" in top international positions in the United States since 1980 makes it possible to study newer actors in older executive institutions. The fact that multiple women have held senior foreign policy responsibilities in one country means scholars can control for within-system variation more than they could in the past. It is no longer necessary to compare leaders from vastly divergent places including Argentina, India, Israel, and the UK simply because each country had only a single woman in a position of influence (see Genovese 1993, Steinberg 2008).

Moreover, the career trajectories explored in this study unfolded during an era of superpower dominance, when the scope of action available to US leaders was wide and, in particular, when recognized foreign policy options included the unilateral use of military force. Examining Northern

European countries such as Sweden, Finland, and Norway during the same period offers valuable insights, since multiple females reached senior foreign policy posts in that region (see Bashevkin 2014, 417). Yet Nordic decision-makers rarely pursue armed intervention, and even more rarely do they wage war outside a larger coalition.

The arrival of a series of American appointees, however, stands alongside a remarkable silence in the academic literature. Whether one sifts through US and comparative studies of gender and politics where matters of representation inside public institutions form a major research pivot, or the literature of feminist international relations—known for its attention to the gendered dynamics of peace, conflict, and transnational social mobilization, the inattention to US pioneers is nothing short of startling. Except for a few studies of individuals such as Madeleine Albright and Hillary Clinton—written in some cases by historians rather than political scientists—the shattering of thick glass ceilings in the realm of diplomacy has largely passed unnoticed, much like the proverbial tree falling in a distant, uninhabited forest (exceptions include Alexander-Floyd 2008; Garner 2012; Hoff 2007; Hudson and Leidl 2015; True 2003).

This book presents a comparative assessment of four path-breaking American leaders, two appointed by Republican and two by Democratic presidents. Each held a senior foreign policy position during a pivotal moment in international affairs, when a seat in the top ranks of the US executive branch brought with it the real possibility of shaping world politics. Jeane Kirkpatrick, the first American woman to attain cabinet rank in the field of foreign policy and the first to represent the United States at the United Nations, served as a member of Ronald Reagan's initial administration during the twilight years of the Cold War. Madeleine Albright, whose exchange with Henry Kissinger was quoted earlier, held the UN ambassadorship and became the first woman secretary of state during the Clinton years, shortly after the fall of the Berlin Wall. Condoleezza Rice, the first woman to hold the position of US national security advisor and the first African American woman to become secretary of state, served George W. Bush in the period of the attacks of 9/11 and subsequent military actions in Afghanistan and Iraq. Finally, Hillary Rodham Clinton, the first to move from president's spouse to elected politician to America's chief diplomat (and later to presidential candidate), faced major changes in the Arab world as well as China's rise to prominence during the initial Obama mandate.

We consider each pioneer with reference to two key questions related to foreign policy leadership in the United States since 1980. First, to what degree were these appointees transformative decision-makers who made a measurable difference to the understanding and practice of international relations in a global superpower? Second, how did they operate with respect to matters of political conflict and gender equality?

Empirical material presented in Chapters 3 through 6 demonstrates that female elites not only played significant roles in shaping the foreign policies of four disparate presidential administrations, but also that their contributions were inconsistent with prevailing assumptions. Women decision-makers, we report, were neither pacifist angels averse to military intervention, nor sudden converts to masculine norms of aggression and belligerence following their arrival in executive office. Despite their vastly different backgrounds, all four women advocated a forceful defense of US national interests on the global stage. They stood out both before and after joining their respective administrations for a willingness to act decisively and to press back against stereotypical understandings of women as cooperative, nurturing consensus-seekers who try to avoid conflict (see Keohane 2010, 134; Steinberg 2008, 4–9).

With respect to matters of gender equality, material presented in the core empirical chapters indicates that Democratic appointees championed progressive feminism more than their Republican counterparts. Using a revised concept of representation, we demonstrate in Chapter 7 not that Republican elites were "defective" trustees of American women, but rather that leaders from both parties resembled their respective political constituencies. From this perspective, the actions of Republican decision-makers were consistent with the views of moderate and conservative Americans who did not share the more leftist outlook of Democratic leaders and their supporters. In short, we conclude, women decision-makers in the domain of international relations after 1980 were not only powerful and assertive shapers of national security policy, but also normatively good representatives of the country's population.

The next section considers how the gender and politics field evolved and, in particular, probes its emphasis on institutions and especially legislatures. We then examine a key theoretical pivot of the field, political representation, and suggest ways in which the concept can be reconceived.

QUESTIONS OF AGENCY AND REPRESENTATION

Jo Freeman's (2013) influential article, titled "The Tyranny of Structurelessness," helps to explain the primacy of institutions over individuals in the gender and politics literature—including well before mainstream political science embraced "bringing the state back in" (see Evans et al. 1985). Freeman (2013) maintains that feminist campaigners resented those activists who stood above the collective crowd, treating them as "stars" who unfairly hogged the limelight. From a sociology of knowledge perspective, Freeman's piece identifies a central predisposition that migrated from women's liberation politics toward academic scholarship.

Circulated widely in a number of formats beginning in 1970, "The Tyranny of Structurelessness" probes the hostility directed by early second-wave militants toward the few women who spoke publicly on behalf of a movement that claimed to be leaderless, without structure, and opposed to masculine power hierarchies. Freeman's (2013) description of the vitriol directed toward "stars" of the feminist galaxy—spokeswomen who usually hesitated to step forward and only did so in the absence of other volunteers who were prepared to articulate movement claims for a larger audience—captures in colorful language the negative loading of the terms "star" and "elite" during the formative years of gender and politics research. As Freeman (2013, 238) writes, activists who reached beyond their local consciousness-raising groups to become publicly recognized as movement leaders "often find themselves viciously attacked by their sisters." The opprobrium heaped upon these individuals meant, she observed, that "'[e]litist' is probably the most abused word in the women's liberation movement. It is used as frequently, and for the same reasons, as 'pinko' was used in the 1950s" (Freeman 2013, 238).

This normative predisposition was reinforced by subsequent methodological developments in American as well as comparative politics. Efforts to secure legitimacy for a nascent research area encouraged gender and politics scholars to adopt the dominant quantitative techniques of the discipline in which they sought faculty positions and their emerging area of specialization sought credibility. Counting behavioral phenomena, conducting regression analyses, and, in this manner, demonstrating facility with the tools of the political science mainstream could confer academic respectability upon the predominantly female practitioners of gender and politics. From this perspective, the larger number of women holding legislative office during the 1970s and following loomed as a more fruitful and, in particular, more quantitatively tractable focus than the few who reached presidential, prime ministerial, or cabinet positions in that period (exceptions include Annesley et al. 2014; Atchison and Down 2009; Borrelli 2002; Genovese 1993; Genovese and Steckenrider 2012; Jacob et al. 2014; Jalalzai 2013, 2014; Krook and O'Brien 2012; Martin 2003; Murray 2010; Reynolds 1999; Skard 2014; Steinberg 2008).

These legacies help to explain how the gender and politics literature became heavily weighted in favor of structures such as legislatures, where numbers and proportions of women were relatively high, and considerably less focused on a few named individuals in domains such as the political executive. The same background also helps to elucidate why, decades after the peak of radical feminism and the initial circulation of Freeman's article, scholarship continues to pivot around a concept that echoes older movement preoccupations with collective rather than individual action. To wit, when analysts treat structure and agency in tandem, they typically frame their inquiries with reference to Hanna Pitkin's (1967) theory of political representation. Roughly a half-century after its release, Pitkin (1967) remains a referential norm in single-case as well as comparative investigations of women's public engagement (see, e.g., Bashevkin 2006; Carroll 1994; Childs 2004; Lovenduski 2005; Phillips 1995; Squires 2007; Swers 2002, 2013).

Pitkin (1967) conceives of representation as the process by which political actors take forward, or represent, the shared views of other citizens to a policymaking forum. Her distinction between "standing for" or descriptive representation, referring to the numbers of a given category such as women who are present in an institutional setting, versus "acting for" or substantive representation, meaning the willingness and ability of those participants to promote policies relevant to the larger group by "acting in the interest of the represented, in a manner responsive to them," has formed the main conceptual grounding for studies of multiple deliberative arenas (Pitkin 1967, 209). They include the US House of Representatives, US Senate, US state legislatures, British House of Commons, and many other bodies (see, e.g., Childs 2004; Dodson 2006; Reingold 2000; Sawer et al. 2006; Swers 2002, 2013; Tremblay 2010).

Scholars use the idea of substantive representation to frame their evaluations of how and when lawmakers carry forward (or not) an issue agenda associated with women's collective interests. They gauge the latter either by studying legislators' support for feminist positions—which may include opposition to war—or by assessing the congruence between actions taken by elected members and attitudinal patterns among women in the general population (see Celis et al. 2008, 105–106). Analysts thus ask what priorities elected members raise in caucus, committee, and floor debate settings; how they vote on specific bills; and whether patterns of behavior vary according to party affiliation, gender consciousness, and other factors.

Two issue areas have attracted close attention. The first involves specific women's rights, including legal equality, child-care services, family leave provisions, and access to abortion, which stand as central claims animating feminist mobilization in much of the advanced industrial world since the late 1960s. A second pertains to the use of military force and patterns of government spending, where women's groups have tended to favor peaceful methods of conflict resolution and have opposed military intervention in international crises. Consistent with the latter, survey research reports stronger public support among women than men for government expenditures on domestic social programs such as health care and education, and less approval for spending on armaments—a pattern that is known colloquially as the guns/butter trade-off (see Eichenberg 2003; Fite et al. 1990; Gidengil 1995; Shapiro and Mahajan 1986).

Arguably the most striking finding in the small empirical literature that considers political executives is that generalizations drawn from legislative scholarship do not hold at more senior levels. Especially on matters of international conflict, investigations of parliaments and executives yield starkly contrasting results. We explore this disjuncture between theoretical expectations and research results in the following sections.

LEGISLATIVE VERSUS EXECUTIVE OFFICE

Before she joined the Reagan cabinet, Jeane Kirkpatrick was a political science professor at Georgetown University. Her 1974 book, titled *Political Woman*, presents some of the earliest data ever gathered on legislators' issue priorities and views toward gender equality. Kirkpatrick (1974, 164–167) reports women members of US state houses expressed more pro-feminist attitudes than either the men with whom they sat in the legislature, or men and women in the general public. As well, Kirkpatrick (1974, 153) finds that female lawmakers showed greater interest in traditionally feminine or motherly matters related to education, health care, and children's welfare than their male counterparts.

The patterns Kirkpatrick observed more than forty years ago have since been confirmed by extensive research on the United States, Canada, Western Europe, and elsewhere. Scholarship from the late 1970s through the present shows that women legislators as a group tend to voice more support for pro-equality issue positions than their male colleagues, whether measured by attitudinal surveys, votes cast, bills introduced, or verbal interventions in floor and committee debates (see Celis and Childs 2012; Dodson 1991; Frankovic 1977; Leader 1977; Sinkkonen and Haavio-Mannila 1981; Tremblay 1992, 1998). This general pattern is sustained across time and political systems, regardless of whether the empirical focus is support for legal reform including the US Equal Rights Amendment, access to abortion, policies to address violence against women, child-care services, or other initiatives likely to broaden the scope of women's well-being and independence (see Reingold 2000).

Yet, as any introductory textbook makes clear, legislators do not create public policy on their own. In one of the only studies to compare parliamentary with executive influence, Atchison and Down (2009) consider family-leave provisions in eighteen parliamentary democracies between 1980 and 2003. They find that countries with higher percentages of women in the political executive offered more generous state-guaranteed parental leave than those with lower levels. As to whether allowances for time at home were better explained by numbers in political executives or legislatures, they conclude that "having women in cabinet is of *greater* importance than having women in parliaments" (Atchison and Down 2009, 17, emphasis in original).

Less straightforward results follow from studies of the link between elite presence and policy outcomes at the international level. Breuning (2001) concludes, based on data from seventeen Organisation for Economic Co-operation and Development (OECD) countries between the late 1980s and late 1990s, that women parliamentarians had a significant and positive effect on levels of foreign aid. Yet Lu and Breuning (2014) find that development assistance in twenty-one OECD states between 1990 and 2001 was positively associated with legislative and cabinet numbers but *negatively* correlated with the presence of a female foreign minister. In their words, female foreign secretaries "were associated with less generous aid policies than their male counterparts" (Lu and Breuning 2014, 326).

One of the only studies to consider targeted foreign aid reports OECD countries with relatively high numbers of women as UN ambassadors, ministers of foreign affairs, and government leaders since 1976 (notably Norway, Sweden, and the United States) spent more generously on equality programs in the global South than those with fewer females in top positions. In probing how party in power affects donor-state generosity, it finds that in some instances, the presence of women from left-of-center parties in senior foreign policy roles in the global North was positively associated with pro-equality aid to developing countries (Bashevkin 2014, 421–422).

Studies of heads of government further complicate this picture. They show that prominent political executives from right as well as left parties blocked or, at best, only partially supported equality initiatives. Sykes (1993, 219) summarizes the careers of Indira Gandhi, Isabel Perón, and Margaret Thatcher as follows: "none reveals the potential for women executives to provide transformational, feminist leadership." Bashevkin's (1996) study of relations between Thatcher and organized feminism finds that the first female prime minister in the United Kingdom strongly opposed women's movement positions on a range of issues, including maternity leave and the stationing of Cruise missiles on British soil. Jalalzai and dos Santos's (2015) account of the first term of Brazilian president Dilma Rousseff reveals a qualified commitment to equality positions, since Rousseff only advocated for lower-income women in ways that did not challenge conservative religious interests. In short, unlike the literature on legislators, studies of women foreign ministers, presidents, and prime ministers report that executives were not only inconsistent substantive representatives but also, in some cases, confirmed opponents of feminist policy claims.

Even larger differences between legislators and political executives emerge in the literature on international conflict. Caprioli's (2000) study of more than two thousand disputes involving about 160 countries between 1960 and 1992 finds that numbers of female lawmakers were inversely related to the probability that armed force would be used. As she writes, "a 5% decrease in the proportion of women in parliament renders a state nearly five (4.91) times as likely to resolve international disputes using military violence" (Caprioli 2000, 61). Overall, Caprioli (2000) identifies a statistically significant negative association between female parliamentary representation and a state's use of military force. Caprioli and Boyer's (2001) account of international conflict during the years 1945 through 1994 confirms this pattern, showing a significant negative correlation between legislative numbers and the severity of a state's violent crisis behavior. According to Caprioli and Boyer (2001, 514), "As the percentage of women in the legislature increases by 5%, a state is nearly 5 times (4.86) less likely to use violence."

Similarly, Regan and Paskeviciute's (2003, 295) study of violent interstate conflict during the years 1965 through 1992 finds that raising women's representation in lower houses of parliament reduces the chances that a country will engage in militarized forms of dispute resolution. Koch and Fulton's (2011) investigation of twenty-two established democracies in the years 1970 through 2000 also shows that higher numbers of women legislators were associated with reduced conflict behavior and lower defense spending.

Results for political executives diverge sharply from these patterns. Caprioli and Boyer (2001, 514) report that from 1945 through 1994, the presence of a female prime minister as top foreign policy decision-maker significantly raised the severity of violence in international crises—or the reverse of their findings for legislators. They caution that since only four women led countries facing serious threats in that period (Benazir Bhutto in Pakistan, Indira Gandhi in India, Golda Meir in Israel, and Margaret Thatcher in the United Kingdom), it is difficult to draw firm conclusions.

Yet Caprioli and Boyer (2001, 516) observe, based on their four cases, that "women leaders can indeed be forceful when confronted with violent, aggressive, and dangerous international situations."

Using more recent data, Koch and Fulton (2011) find that the presence of female political executives in democratic systems is positively and significantly correlated with the likelihood that a country will engage in armed action. They report higher numbers of women presidents, prime ministers, ministers of national defense, and ministers of foreign affairs serve to heighten levels of military spending and intervention such that females in executive roles "oversee greater defense spending and increases in conflict behavior than when men hold the same positions" (Koch and Fulton 2011, 13). By contrast, the presence of female parliamentarians tends to mute the hawkish behavior of leaders regardless of gender (Koch and Fulton 2011, 10).

In short, empirical studies thus far reveal a significant gap between findings about political executives versus legislators. The fact that concepts of substantive representation work reasonably well when applied to one level but fall short at another recalls Mackay's (2008) insight concerning the limitations of this prism. As she writes with respect to the study of parliaments, "Whilst it is plausible that women representatives may act for women, there are no guarantees: shifting identities, differences amongst women, partisan loyalties and institutional factors are all seen to play a part in shaping and constraining their inclination and capacity to 'act for women'" (Mackay 2008, 127).

The sources of variation cited by Mackay (2008) are arguably more relevant to comparisons of lawmakers with ministers than to studies of single legislative institutions. Patterns of socialization and recruitment to public office often differ dramatically for parliamentarians versus executives (see Annesley, Franceschet, and Beckwith 2014; Docherty 1997; Sanbonmatsu, Carroll, and Walsh 2009). The two levels hold widely divergent public mandates given that presidents and prime ministers are expected to appoint cabinets that rise above particularist concerns in order to advance national interests. Ministers hold cross-issue, country-wide, and, in some instances, international policy mandates rather than the sectorally focused, often geographic, issue-based, and partisan remits of parliamentarians. As a result, the experiences, outlooks, and commitments that individuals bring to each level of public office can lead them to think in highly divergent ways about the interests they represent. For these reasons, it is not surprising that studies of how legislators, as compared with cabinet ministers, prime ministers, or presidents, take forward or represent the views of other citizens have yielded disparate results.

Findings to the effect that female political executives have variously acted or not acted in concert with the views of women in the general public, that they have pursued or ignored feminist claims, or that some entirely rejected movement positions, cannot stand as the end point of gender and politics research. Instead, these results invite scholars to probe key corollary questions, including the following: Which executives acted in what ways, when, and why? How did each conceive of women as a collective unit?

In the next section, we suggest a refreshed line of inquiry that begins with the observation that political executives seem to be less consistent champions than legislators of conventionally defined gender interests. Chapter 2 expands this discussion by showing the wide range of views toward war and feminism that have been associated with women in Western cultures. It proposes treating group interests along a spectrum or continuum, as opposed to a dichotomous gauge.

RETHINKING SUBSTANTIVE REPRESENTATION

Among the most striking features of the literature on "acting for" representation is its conflation of responsiveness to women as a group, on one side, and advocacy for progressive feminism, on the other. As Celis and Childs (2012) argue, based on studies of British, continental European, and North American political systems, a left feminist substantive representation of women is not the only possible representational repertoire. Responding to the concerns of women as a group requires, they maintain, sensitivity to a range of perspectives, including anti-feminist positions (see also Chappell 2012; Klatch 1987; Schreiber 2008).

According to Celis and Childs (2012, 214), "An exclusive focus on feminist actors and policies creates both a blind spot and bias in our empirical research, and furthermore, limits our theoretical understanding of substantive representation and of what constitutes 'good' democratic representation." Since women in the general populations of most Western systems hold opinions that range across the ideological spectrum, gender and politics scholars need to acknowledge that "not all women are necessarily gender conscious, nor are they all feminists, and in any case, women's interests are not necessarily homogeneous . . . feminism simply does not speak for, or to, all women and, following from that, feminist substantive representation can only be considered to be part of the substantive representation of women" (Celis and Childs 2012, 215, 219).

This approach rejects essentialist conceptions and instead asks how leaders understand their own carrying forward of group interests. Rather than depicting elites who do not promote progressive feminist positions as failed substantive representatives, Celis and Childs (2012) offer a more inclusive understanding of political responsiveness. They conceive of elites who hold moderately feminist, critical, or anti-feminist views as acting for different but nonetheless legitimate women's interests. At a normative level, Celis and Childs's (2012) recasting of substantive representation recognizes the democratic linkage between leaders and citizens as not only extant but also beneficial—regardless of where it occurs along the ideological spectrum.

This reorientation encourages scholars to focus on specific actors. As Childs and Krook (2008) note, gender and politics research finds limited support for claims that rising descriptive representation automatically produces more feminist policy outcomes. In the words of Celis and Childs (2008, 420), "empirical studies have revealed multiple relationships between the proportions of women present in political institutions and the substantive representation of women. Any idea—or hope—that simply counting the number of women representatives will tell us very much about the likelihood of the substantive representation of women no longer looks to be tenable" (see also Beckwith and Cowell-Meyers 2007).

Following from Dahlerup's (1988) work on "critical acts," Childs and her colleagues highlight the rare individuals who are prepared to champion feminist policies. According to Childs and Krook (2008, 734), critical actors "initiate policy proposals on their own and often—but not necessarily— embolden others to take steps to promote policies for women, regardless of the number of female representatives present in a particular institution." Although the concept of critical actor has not been widely applied beyond the literature on legislatures (see Childs and Withey 2006), it holds considerable promise for research on political executives. We outline the bases for this claim in the following discussion.

How have researchers explained results that diverge from standard expectations? In probing the foreign policy directions of legislators versus executives, Koch and Fulton (2011) attribute variations between the two levels to disparate gender norms in each institution. Their account of national security decision-making, a traditionally "hard" policy domain with relatively few women appointees, maintains that pressures to reject typically female characteristics associated with softness and nurturing, and instead adopt male norms of assertiveness and belligerence, rise markedly in the transition from legislative to cabinet roles (see also Lu and Breuning 2014). According to Koch and Fulton (2011, 4), "women may confront credibility challenges in masculinized leadership positions, such as executive office" where efforts "to gain credibility may lead women to present themselves as more masculine, in an attempt to combat the stereotype."

This hypothesis presses beyond the treatment of women elites as either strong or weak substantive representatives, depending on how their actions meet or violate traditional understandings of collective interests. At the same time, however, it ignores the fact that political executives tend to reach cabinet office with firmly articulated outlooks. Instead of positing that pressures to conform inside peak institutions make a woman behave in stereotypically masculine ways, an alternative approach would see her attain ministerial office with a confirmed modus operandi and track record. Not only would her repertoire be well practiced prior to cabinet recruitment, it also would be well known to the chief executive responsible for her ministerial appointment.

By examining the careers of individual elites, researchers can evaluate the degree to which decision-makers are (a) agentic in that they hold clear views about such matters as war and feminism at the point they assume office and maintain those perspectives in senior posts, or (b) institutionally compliant in that they absorb prevailing norms after their appointment. The possibility exists under (a) that leaders might voice opinions critical of progressive feminism or inconsistent with the main currents of female public opinion long before they reach top positions. In empirical terms, then, the primary distinction between agency versus structure rests in evidence of the pre- versus post-recruitment origins of elite views, rather than the content of those perspectives.

In acknowledging that cabinet appointees might arrive in executive positions carrying feminist preferences, option (a) is consistent with the critical actor thesis proposed by Childs and Krook (2008); that is, some individuals may directly challenge gender norms and practices long before they arrive in executive office. This argument finds support in True's (2003, 381) account of efforts by Madeleine Albright to press for international action on sex trafficking during the 1990s, notably via a "strategic coalition" she created among female foreign ministers. The group, which resembled networks in which Albright participated before she joined the Clinton cabinet, ultimately shaped policies on the global trade in women and girls.

Similarly, Curtin's (2008) study of political executives in New Zealand stresses the impact of pre-recruitment background. According to Curtin (2008, 490), "an active and influential feminist reference group" shaped the policy directions of cabinet members in areas ranging from employment rights to child-care services to violence against women. In each case, the prior Labour Party experiences of female executives led them to act in ways that are inconsistent with an institutional compliance thesis. As well, Bashevkin (2014, 423) shows that foreign policy leaders from the United States, Finland, and Sweden who had backgrounds as progressive campaigners became outspoken equality advocates in senior office. Rather than acceding to existing norms, these decision-makers stood out from others in their willingness to challenge the boundaries of traditional international relations.

Taken as a group, these findings support the synthetic or co-constitutive understanding of agents and structures that has underpinned social science inquiry for more than one hundred years. In his assessment of the primacy of institutional forces versus the ability of human beings to alter or transform the conditions of their times, Karl Marx famously wrote, "Men make their own history, but they do not make it just as they please; they do not make it under circumstances chosen by themselves, but under circumstances directly found, given and transmitted by history" (Marx 1969, 15; see also Sewell 1992).

How do women make their histories, particularly inside well-established and, recalling Henry Kissinger's remark, fraternal institutions not of their own creation? The next section provides a road map to guide our response.

STUDYING EXECUTIVE LEADERSHIP

Arguably the most significant contribution that any study of women decision-makers can make is to situate intellectual inquiry at the crux of what animates politics—that is, power. As Keohane (2010, 26–27) writes, "a leader directs the activities of others and coordinates their energies, which is a basic form of power." If we define the term loosely as the authoritative capacity to act upon, shape, or accomplish meaningful objectives in the public domain, then the theoretical and empirical lens provided by a focus on power measurably extends the parameters of gender and politics research. Questions about responsiveness and representation that have preoccupied generations of analysts are, from this perspective, secondary to matters of clout within a decision-making group, since no minister who seeks to champion (or, conversely, undermine) a particular view of collective interests is likely to do so in the absence of power.

In asking why so few women reach influential positions, social scientists have posited that leadership in many cultures remains a stereotypically masculine concept. Eagly and Karau (2002), for example, show how perceptions of ambition and readiness to lead are gender-based such that (a) women are presumed to hold strengths in nurturing or communal as opposed to agentic skills, and (b) men remain more likely than women to be assessed as effective leaders. Niederle and Vesterlund (2007) employ experimental techniques to demonstrate how men's overconfidence advantages them, while women's aversion to competition has the opposite effect. In thinking about how women can advance as leaders, Eagly and Carli (2007, Chapter 10) conclude that blending traditionally masculine and feminine traits can prove beneficial. We return to this theme in Chapter 7.

The authority wielded by members of a political executive is clearly more complex than the title or rank attached to a given position. As Genovese and Thompson (1993, 1, emphasis in original) observe, "Leadership is a complex phenomenon revolving around *influence*—the ability to move others in desired directions. Successful leaders are those who can take full advantage of their opportunities and their skills." Scholars have distinguished between routine and exceptional leaders using a variety of metrics. Burns (2003), for example, contrasts the values-based impact of what he terms "transformational" versus merely "transactional" elites, while Hook (1943) separates individuals who make events from those whose influence could have been replicated by others.

Probing how elites wield influence illuminates the interplay of agency with structure inside cabinet institutions. This study employs a basic understanding of the verb "to transform" in asking whether women foreign policy leaders changed in meaningful ways the ideas and directions of the presidential administrations in which they served. A series of counterfactual questions point toward the conclusion that since 1981, women leaders indeed influenced policy in ways that transformed American international relations: Would the Reagan doctrine have been the same without the presence of Jeane Kirkpatrick? Is it likely the Clinton administration would have championed NATO intervention in Bosnia and again in Kosovo had Madeleine Albright not served in the cabinet? Lacking Condoleezza Rice's pre-emption doctrine, could the Bush administration have justified the invasion of Iraq to either domestic or international audiences? Would the first Obama administration have pressed for multilateral military action in Libya and made women's security the pivot of its foreign policy doctrine had Hillary Clinton not been secretary of state?

Chapter 2 foregrounds the discussion of policy impact by amplifying a key theme of feminist historiography, namely the varied perspectives toward war and equality that are associated with women in Western cultures. This review shows how efforts to present half of humanity as a homogeneous unit have fallen short—whether those attempts portray the group as consistently pacifist, feminist, or otherwise. I develop from this material a normative proposition that in liberal democratic systems, executives should ideally carry forward disparate outlooks that roughly approximate the distribution of policy views in the general population. At the empirical level, we conceive of positions toward war and equality along a spectrum or continuum of opinion.

Chapters 3 through 6 evaluate the actions of each appointee with respect to international conflict and gender equality. The chapters examine accounts of the administrations in which Kirkpatrick, Albright, Rice, and Clinton served, asking how each woman is portrayed in them. What role did female decision-makers play in shaping the foreign policy directions of the presidents they served?

Chapter 3 considers Jeane Kirkpatrick's influence during the early 1980s as the first woman ambassador from the United States to the United Nations, where she built a reputation as an outspoken diplomat with a visceral belief in America's greatness. Kirkpatrick supported a muscular but prudent defense of US interests well before her cabinet appointment, and helped to ensure that the foreign policy directions of the first Reagan presidency reflected her views. Critical of left feminism prior to her time in cabinet office, Kirkpatrick served a Republican administration that won office thanks to support from an electorate that held similar views.

Chapter 4 focuses on Madeleine Albright's contributions to the two Clinton administrations of the 1990s, when as UN ambassador and the first woman secretary of state she held key responsibility for the only armed interventions to that point in NATO's history. Her support for military action in Bosnia and Kosovo was consistent with an assertive outlook that pre-dated her cabinet appointments. Unlike Kirkpatrick, Albright engaged in feminist networks both before and during her time in top office, and supported pro-equality claims that resonated with the support base of the Clinton administration.

Chapter 5 assesses Condoleezza Rice's contributions in the George W. Bush era as the first female national security advisor and first female African American secretary of state. In the wake of the events of 9/11, Rice developed a pre-emption argument that said the United States could not wait for attack before defending itself. This view, which underpinned the Bush administration's decision to invade Iraq in 2003, was consistent with an aggressive approach to leadership that pre-dated Rice's time in senior foreign policy office. In contrast to Albright's sense of group consciousness, Rice was long committed to a "no victims" approach to discrimination— whether bias was based on race or sex. In that way, she amplified the conservative individualism of many Republican voters.

Chapter 6 evaluates the trajectory of Hillary Rodham Clinton from the roles of first lady, senator, and presidential candidate to secretary of state.

Clinton endorsed NATO intervention in Libya in 2011, which formed a crucial element of Obama's first-term foreign policy record and paralleled her support as a senator for military action in Iraq. Efforts by Clinton to make women's rights a major pivot of her international doctrine echoed the feminist perspectives she held since early adulthood, which in turn were integral to the Democratic Party support base of the 1970s and following.

Chapter 7 addresses the ways in which women leaders have made a difference in international relations and considers our main findings in light of themes from feminist diplomatic history, including the changing status of diplomatic, as contrasted with military, institutions in the United States. The discussion considers what personal traits assisted each leader and compares how Kirkpatrick, Albright, Rice, and Clinton dealt with matters of war and feminism. We return to concepts of political representation in order to juxtapose leaders' track records with the predilections of Americans generally. The chapter speculates as to what can be expected on the terrain of international affairs from an American woman who becomes US president—whether she is already operating in the public limelight or is someone as yet unknown.

Chapters 3 through 6 employ an inductive, qualitative, and ethnographic methodology drawn from two complementary research streams. First, we draw on the phenomenological approach developed by Geertz (1973) to understand the influence wielded by actors from new demographic categories inside well-established, traditionally masculine structures of the political executive. This stream of research uses memoir, biography, and other sources to probe how social reality is perceived by those living it. As a perspective that highlights human experiences and reflections upon them, ethnographic analysis permits scholars to study the importance that individuals attach to their own backgrounds. In particular, it sheds light on the ways in which actors alternately shape and are shaped by institutional environments.

This orientation dovetails closely with a second pivot, that of feminist international relations and feminist security studies, which encourages scholars to address human beings and not simply states on the world stage (see Cohn 2011, 583). As Wibben (2011, 592) writes, feminist researchers "counter the prevalence of bodiless data . . . by highlighting personal stories." Taken together, phenomenological and feminist tools of analysis provide promising vehicles for examining both the power that individuals wield over substantive policy decisions and the gender representation practices they employ. In turn, these perspectives inform our more general understanding of the contributions made by women leaders to superpower foreign policy.

As one of the first accounts of political executives in a single system, this study is necessarily heuristic (see also Borrelli 2002; Martin 2003). Within those limits, it suggests at a conceptual level that preoccupations with obstacles imposed by structures can be usefully balanced by consideration of opportunities to transform that are available to human agents. Examining foreign policy—a domain where the purview for elite action is relatively wide—permits us to demonstrate how and when individuals indeed changed the circumstances of their times. In empirical terms, this narrative extends gender and politics scholarship by probing the consequences of presence in national political executives. Given the pronounced centralization of power in the hands of presidents, prime ministers, and cabinets across the advanced industrial world, greater attention to this dimension of public leadership is long overdue (see Howell 2003; Richards and Smith 2006; Savoie 1999).

Above all, by treating executive influence as its main theme, this discussion shows how four women made a measurable difference to foreign policy outcomes in a global superpower. As feminist diplomatic historians remind us, staking out presence on the international record constitutes not just a worthy task, but also a crucial antidote to erasure.

CHAPTER 2

Interpreting Women, War, and Feminism

Feminist diplomatic history highlights the diversity of women's perspectives toward matters of armed conflict and gender equality. Research on the interwar era, for instance, shows that British and American activists in the Women's International League for Peace and Freedom (WILPF) advanced a range of pacifist and feminist positions. Female diplomats representing the United Kingdom and the United States in the same period disagreed both with the WILPF and with each other (see Beers 2016; McCarthy 2016; Nash 2016).

This chapter probes an intellectual stream that contrasts with feminist historiography: namely, homogeneous or essentialist thinking about women as a group. This tradition can be discerned in older as well as contemporary accounts of war versus peace as well as gender equality. In each domain, writers have for centuries been tempted to generalize about roughly half of humanity and to draw conclusions that, while often tidy and sometimes comforting, hold limited value as guides to empirical analysis.

Our discussion explores in broad, impressionistic terms the large canvas of women, war, and feminism. Given space limitations, we present a selective summary of the main lines of argumentation and evidence. Tracing the history of thinking about women as a unified group permits us to show how contemporary writers—including influential social scientists—adopt perspectives not unlike those of classical and liberal political theorists. In particular, we argue, recent accounts that portray female decision-makers as averse to using armed force unless pressured by men around them to do so mirror narratives of the ancient Greek *polis*, as well as later studies in Western philosophy and psychology. Each of these strands relies on a dichotomous view that identifies one side of the gender divide with norms of pacifism, serenity, and remoteness from sites of battle and contestation, and the other with a decidedly belligerent and combative public repertoire.

At the level of popular culture, a May 1999 issue of *Time* magazine neatly illustrates the durability of older views. The cover photograph in Figure 2.1 shows an intently focused US secretary of state speaking by field telephone from a NATO military base in Germany. The secretary wears a brown leather flak jacket with the bright insignia of US Air Forces in Europe. Above the insignia spills a bold headline in cautionary yellow type: "Albright at War." The text of the lead story, excerpted in the following, signals a clear

Figure 2.1. *Time* magazine cover from May 1999, with lead article by Walter Isaacson titled "Madeleine's War."

discomfort with Madeleine Albright's role in international conflict—thus reinforcing the imagery on the magazine cover:

> The Kosovo conflict is often referred to, by both her fans and foes, as Madeleine's War. In a literal sense, of course, that's not true these days. Now that it's become an armed conflict, she plays a supporting role to the President, National Security Adviser Sandy Berger, Defense Secretary Bill Cohen, and the military brass. But more than anyone else, she embodies the foreign policy vision that pushed these men into this war. And she is the one most responsible for holding the allies— and the Administration—firm in pursuit of victory. (Isaacson 1999, 1)

For general readers, the article promises to explain how one woman could cause so many powerful men to go to war in an obscure corner of Central Europe. For gender and politics scholars, the deeper puzzles are at least as fascinating. Why the unease with Albright's role? How should she have responded to events in the former Yugoslavia?

Closely connected to treatments of conflict are expectations that waves of feminist mobilization in Western industrial systems cause female leaders to carry forward pro-equality positions. While this view contradicts a construction of women as pacific souls who hover above public debate, the two approaches share important commonalities. Among the most troubling is a tendency to ignore crucial nuances and variations, many of which are well documented on the public record, in an effort to reach spare, often reductionist conclusions.

Drawing on a variety of sources, this chapter casts doubt on notions that women leaders will "act for" women in general by defending either (a) typically feminine perspectives that evoke images of heavenly seraphs floating above the terrain on which men fight, or (b) progressive feminist outlooks as champions of a particular set of social movement demands. Boldly stated, the assumption that female elites will echo a specific view is questionable because the weight of evidence shows that women as a group are not uniformly or even overwhelmingly antiwar or pro-feminist. Instead, data pointing toward a polyvalence or diversity of attitudes are too fulsome to support sweeping generalizations about substantive representation.

Our discussion posits that views toward conflict and gender equality are best understood with reference to a spectrum of opinion, defined as a dynamic continuum that embraces widely disparate positions. We revisit theories of democratic representation that were introduced in Chapter 1 in order to reconcile the carrying forward of public claims by leaders with the varied views of citizens. The concluding section of this chapter presents a normative argument that in liberal democracies, it is appropriate for political executives to defend views resembling those of the citizens who brought them to public office. We return to theories of normative representation in Chapter 7, where we compare the track records of women leaders.

This chapter opens with a look at how theoretical texts from the classical period and following present the relationship between gender and military force. Our attention then turns to the empirical evidence, where we show how interpretations of women as antiwar are highly contestable. The next parts consider left/right and feminist positions; they demonstrate why definitions of the substantive representation of women as "acting for" left and pro-equality interests are particularly problematic in research on contemporary American politics.

WOMEN AND CONFLICT

The claim that women are less inclined toward the use of force than men can be traced at least as far back as classical Greek philosophy. Women, like slaves, were not full members of the ancient political unit known as the *polis*. Instead, women's sphere was defined as the motherly, nurturing space of the private household—a quiet refuge distant from the rowdy public forum in which men debated and resolved civic issues.

This divide forms the basis for a foundational public/private dichotomy in political theory as well as practice, one that imputes specific qualities to each side of the split. Classical philosophers elevate the importance of the public domain in which strong, articulate men advance their positions on matters of general consequence and, in some cases, exchange physical blows in order to defend those views. While women's role is viewed as weaker and, in most respects, inferior to that of men, its grounding in self-sacrifice and care for others yields some compensation—namely, a persistent association of the private sphere with serenity, caring, and moral virtue (see Elshtain 1974, 456, 461–466; Okin 1979, 86).

In *The Republic*, Plato advances an innovative, relatively egalitarian treatment of gender and politics that broadly foreshadows socialist theories of the nineteenth century and following. According to his scheme for an ideal polity, the family and private property are eliminated to the point that some women are allowed to join a ruling caste known as the guardians. Although female guardians are seen as physically weaker than their male counterparts, they benefit from the same educational and political opportunities as men, including preparation in mathematics, philosophy, and martial arts. While Plato at no point considers female fighters to be the equal of males, he recommends investing in their military training in order to provide greater protection for a city under threat. After reintroducing private ownership in *The Laws*, Plato reverts to traditional understandings of women's domesticity, purity, and dependence on men (see Okin 1979, 69).

Given Plato's inconsistency on this point, the beginnings of a firm public/private divide are generally dated from Aristotle (see Elshtain 1974, 454–455; Okin 1979, 86). In *The Politics*, women's reproductive, sexual, and caregiving activities are central to the life of the family—which Aristotle presents as an institution essential to the existence of the *polis*, but not an integral political structure. The dominant male in his rendering participates fully in society by circulating openly in public life. By contrast, the subordinate female is effectively contained, confined to what Elshtain (1974, 455) terms "a lesser association, the household." The private family thus forms for Aristotle a bounded domain such that women's contact with the public realm is entirely mediated by male relations who hold full citizenship.

Defining women according to the terms of a "natural" association with the private sphere and its innately apolitical, system-supporting qualities proved extremely durable over the centuries. During the late medieval period, this approach found expression in the work of Christine de Pisan, among the most prolific European writers of the era. She remarks on "the pacifying potential of 'the good princess,'" given that "women, who are physically weak and timid, are therefore more inclined to make peace and avert wars" (de Pisan, as quoted in Fraser 1988, 7).

Liberal philosophers expanded this depiction of dichotomous spheres. In *A Discourse on Inequality*, Rousseau lays out each woman's responsibility to promote social and political stability, albeit in a quiet, behind-the-scenes manner. He charges her as follows:

> It is your task to perpetuate by your insinuating influence and your innocent and amiable rule, a respect for the laws of the State and harmony among the citizens. . . . Continue, therefore, always to be what you are, the chaste guardians of our morals, and the sweet security of our peace, exerting on every occasion the privileges of the heart and of nature, in the interests of duty and virtue. (Rousseau 2005, 8)

Rousseau treats women's activity in the home as highly purposive, both to create new generations and to inculcate within them a sense of ethical values as well as deference to the status quo. Rousseau's arguments helped to foster a long-standing conceptualization of women as preternaturally peaceful and, as discussed later in this chapter, politically conservative.

According to Elshtain (1995, 4), Western thinkers since the eighteenth century built on these precedents by assigning women a collective image as "beautiful souls." The framing of females as private creatures defined by little more than an innocent maternal identity meant that political philosophers could conceive of a partial citizen best typified by the virginal Madonna of Renaissance portraiture: calm, modest, life-giving. By comparison, theorists present men as society's bellicose combatants, the "just warriors" who would typically end rather than offer life. In Elshtain's (1995, 4, 166; italics in original) words,

> We in the West are the heirs of a tradition that assumes an affinity between women and peace, between men and war, a tradition that consists of culturally constructed and transmitted myths and memories. . . . Popular understandings of female givers, male takers, loft upward, becoming narrative truth for many, including contemporary scholars, male and female, and (some) feminists. Women and *men's* wars; we are reassured. Whatever women may finally do once wars have begun, women don't start them. Men are the first cause, the prime movers, of war.

This cultural legacy shaped understandings of peace and conflict long after the passing of the classical Greek *polis*. Using force in crisis situations, for instance, remains closely linked not to women, but rather to men. As Steans (2006, 48) notes, "If historically war has been associated with men and masculinity, peace has long historical associations with women and the 'feminine.'"

In an unusual twist in the history of ideas, Anglo-American suffragists adopted the "beautiful souls" concept in the late 1800s and following. Social or maternal feminists proposed what became a popular claim that female voters would, en masse, purify the public realm. They maintained that the best way to end international conflict, along with domestic challenges (including corruption at city hall), was to apply the cleansing hand of maternal experience to the sordid mess known as politics. Antisuffragists, by contrast, condemned what they saw as a loss of moral virtue inherent in extending women's influence beyond the private household (see Buechler 1986; Holton 1986; Kraditor 1965; Lemons 1973; O'Neill 1971; Phillips 2003).

Efforts to apply women's moral suasion to the civic realm underpinned not only social feminism, but also much of the broader Progressive project. As abolitionist Harriet Beecher Stowe (1967, 281) explains, the purpose of female political engagement is "to introduce into politics that superior delicacy and purity which women manifest in family life." As time passed, this perspective proved less threatening to members of the general public and more conducive to success in legislative debates than equal rights claims—which cited fundamental justice as the main rationale for enfranchisement (see Kraditor 1965; O'Neill 1971).

Divisions between public and private, masculine and feminine, remained in use long after the Progressive era. As Stoper and Johnson (1977, 193) write, the claim "that women are superior to men and therefore the world would be a better place if women were given their full share of power and public influence" remained alive and well through the late twentieth century. Whether expressed in radical feminist prose or more mainstream National Organization for Women (NOW) platforms, movement activists of the 1960s and following believed compassion and lack of egoism made females "saviors on whom the salvation of the world depended" (Stoper and Johnson 1977, 193). Feminist historian Joan Kelly echoed these views in expressing confidence that in the future, "women will struggle for a social order of peace, equality and joy" (Kelly, as quoted in Fraser 1988, 7).

What distinguishes second- from first-wave perspectives, however, are heightened demands that women's attributes infuse not just Western electorates but also the corridors of power. For example, Gloria Steinem (1970, 1) calls for heightened involvement by women as a counterweight to the belligerent masculinity most men carry into public life; she recommends increased female engagement as a promising route toward "tempering the idea of manhood into something less aggressive and better suited to this crowded, post-atomic planet."

Most notably, the idea that women carry particular features that reduce the likelihood of human conflict permeates multiple academic studies. In her text titled *In a Different Voice*, psychologist Carol Gilligan (1982) posits that girls grow up with an understanding of strength as emanating from interpersonal ties and, in particular, from showing emotional care and concern toward other people. This socialization process means that the lives of girls and women are shaped directly by expectations of nurturing and protective behavior. By comparison, male socialization experiences typically stress individual autonomy and physical prowess—a background that not only permits but also justifies the use of force to defend self and community (Gilligan 1982).

Philosopher Sara Ruddick (1995) extends Gilligan's position by pressing generalizations about care and nurturing beyond the category of women who bear and care for children. Ruddick claims that the maternal values girls learn while growing up are imprinted upon them for decades to come, and create ripple effects through the life cycle. For Ruddick, women without offspring absorb norms that emphasize empathy and caring for other people such that they become indistinguishable from females who experience motherhood.

In a volume called *The Better Angels of Our Nature*, psychologist Steven Pinker (2011) asserts that increasing numbers of women leaders will make the world a more serene place. He grounds this claim in concepts of maternal protection and, in particular, a view that holding motherly roles throughout history encourages females to favor calm, stable conditions in which to nurture the next generation. Pinker maintains that clear incentives have led women to avoid the alternative path—which is an evolutionary dead end of seeing sons and daughters traumatized, wounded, or killed in war.

To be sure, scholars are far from unanimous in endorsing a "beautiful souls" thesis. Elshtain (1995) lays out its limits from the perspective of political philosophy, showing how dominant tropes that portray women as pacifist and men as belligerent are not just simplistic, but also often inaccurate. International relations analysts cite the damaging consequences of this approach for the conduct of global affairs. Ann Tickner (2001), for example, questions the tendency of antiwar groups to evoke traditional stereotypes. She maintains that the extensive use of maternal imagery by international peace movements "allows men to remain in control and continue to dominate the agenda of world politics, and it continues to render women's voices as inauthentic in matters of foreign policymaking" (Tickner 2001, 60; see also Enloe 1989; Peterson and Runyan 2010, 243–255).

SUPPORT FOR "BEAUTIFUL SOULS" ARGUMENTS

If we set aside these critiques for a moment, it is important to acknowledge a large body of evidence that supports views of women as more pro-peace and less supportive of violent approaches to conflict. Since the beginnings of survey research and stretching through the first decades of the current century, a sustained flow of data shows women in the United States and most other Western countries are less likely than men to endorse military intervention to solve international disputes, and less supportive of higher spending to finance those conflicts. As the editor of *Public Opinion Quarterly* summarizes this durable, cross-national trend, women respondents typically lean toward "the antiforce option" at the same time as men choose the opposite (Smith 1984, 385).

While it is difficult to compress eighty years of poll data into a concise overview, the overwhelming pattern dovetails what emerged after the Roper Organization entered the field in early 1936. The firm asked Americans, "Would you be willing to fight, or to have a member of your family fight, in case a foreign power tried to seize land in Central or South America? Would you be willing to fight, or to have a member of your family fight, in case the Philippines were attacked?" In response to the first probe, about 22 percent of men and 12 percent of women answered yes. On the second, roughly 30 percent of men and 17 percent of women replied in the affirmative (Smith 1984, 386).

A year before the attack on Pearl Harbor, Roper found that 56 percent of men versus 42 percent of women in the United States believed "the time has come for us to take strong measures against Japan" (Smith 1984, 387). Between 1950 and 1953, polling by both the National Opinion Research Center (NORC) and the Gallup organization reported that American women were more likely than men to believe the United States had erred in sending troops to Korea, with differences reaching as high as 15 percentage points (Smith 1984, 388).

During the Cold War, Roper asked whether the United States should "adopt an even tougher policy dealing with the Russians," a proposition with which 60 percent of men, compared with less than half of women, agreed in 1960 (Smith 1984, 388). The next year, Gallup pressed Americans to "suppose you had to make the decision between fighting an all-out nuclear war or living under Communist rule—how would you decide?" Among men, 87 percent chose the "better dead than Red" option, while three-quarters of women expressed that choice (Smith 1984, 388).

Beginning in 1964, the University of Michigan's Survey Research Center posed the question of whether "we did the right thing in getting into the fighting in Vietnam or should we have stayed out?" American men were significantly more likely than women to support military involvement, in some polls by as much as 15 percentage points. Gallup asked respondents during the same period to categorize themselves as hawks "if they want to step up our military effort in Vietnam," or doves "if they want to reduce our military effort in Vietnam." In 1968, half of males versus less than a third of females described themselves as hawks (Smith 1984, 389).

This same pattern held when pollsters queried Americans about conflict in general, hypothetical military interventions, or levels of defense spending. According to 1975 Gallup results, women were far more likely than men to view war as "an outmoded way of settling differences between nations" (52 percent vs. 37 percent). Conversely, higher percentages of men saw war as still necessary (55 percent vs. 38 percent; Smith 1984, 389).

Surveys also found that American women were less willing to send troops to defend any number of allies in the event of a communist attack. In the case of West Germany, 37 percent of men versus 18 percent of women were willing to send troops (Smith 1984, 389). For Japan, 24 percent of males but only 9 percent of females approved of boots on the ground. For Canada, two-thirds of men versus less than half of women were prepared to defend the northern neighbors (Smith 1984, 390). When asked annually between 1973 and 1983 whether the United States was spending too much, too little, or "about the right amount" on military preparedness, men were consistently more likely to say expenditures were too low (Smith 1984, 390–391).

By 1980, results showing women's consistently lower support for defense spending and stronger endorsement for "butter" expenditures to underwrite domestic social programs began to hold significant electoral consequences (see Baxter and Lansing 1983; Conover 1988; Shapiro and Mahajan 1986). Multiple studies examine why Ronald Reagan won roughly 10 percent less support among female than male voters in 1980, and why Reagan garnered about 8 percent less in his 1984 bid (Bolce 1985; Chappell 2012; Frankovic 1982; Gilens 1988). Gilens (1988, 43, 44; italics in original) concludes that views about foreign policy and especially military expenditures were the central reason:

> The single most important factor in explaining gender differences in approval of Reagan is defense spending, which accounts for a 7.8 point gap between men and women. Adding respondents' evaluations of Reagan's handling of relations with the Soviet Union to attitudes toward defense spending shows that the military/foreign policy dimension alone accounts for a 10.8 point gender gap in overall approval. . . . Women *are* more liberal than men on these military/foreign policy issues, but more important, holding liberal attitudes produces a dramatically greater deficit in approval of Reagan among women than it does among men.

In short, Gilens (1988) finds that a robust gender difference held measurable implications for presidential contests in the 1980s.

Research since the Persian Gulf crisis of 1990–1991 reinforces these findings. Eichenberg's (2003, 112) assessment of nearly five hundred survey questions administered between 1990 and 2003 reports less support among American women for the use of military force for any purpose, largely because females are "relatively more sensitive to humanitarian concerns and to the loss of human life" than men. Haider-Markel and Vieux (2008) reach similar conclusions in their evaluation of American attitudes toward harsh interrogation tactics in the wake of 9/11. They find that women were less willing than men to endorse techniques that require detainees to be naked, face sexual humiliation, or have their heads held under water. During the Obama years, polls show that more than 60 percent of men and half of women supported a no-fly zone over Libya (CNN 2011). A Pew Research Center (2013) survey found that 39 percent of men and only 19 percent of women endorsed US military strikes against Syria.

These results resemble data from many other Western countries. British polls conducted between the mid-1950s and mid-1960s, for example, reveal an average gender difference of nearly 9 percent in approval for the use of force in a variety of hypothetical scenarios (Clements 2012). In subsequent years, men in the United Kingdom offered consistently stronger support than women for military involvement in Afghanistan, Iraq, and Libya, with differences as high as 19 percent in the case of a 2003 Pew Global Attitude Survey on intervention in Iraq (Clements 2012, Table 1). These trends are far from unique, since studies by Pew as well as Harris/Financial Times show differences in the 10 percent or higher range in Spain when surveys asked about intervention in Iraq in 2003, Afghanistan in 2010, and Libya in 2011; and in France, Germany, and Italy on involvement in Libya in 2011 (Clements 2012, Tables 1 and 2).

These survey findings parallel an extensive history of peace activism by women's organizations around the world. If we confine ourselves to North America and Western Europe during the past century, then a clear pattern emerges: many of the same campaigners who dedicated their energies to women's rights causes were high-profile advocates of alternatives to violent conflict. For instance, American members of what became the Women's Peace Party drew 1,500 demonstrators to a silent antiwar parade in New York City in 1914 (Stoper and Johnson 1977, 198). The party drew well-known feminists such as Jane Addams and Carrie Chapman Catt (see Alonso 1993). In the postwar decades, Eleanor Roosevelt and Alva Myrdal campaigned for both disarmament and women's rights (see O'Farrell 2010, 132; Stiehm 2005, 266). In the spring of 2015, Gloria Steinem co-chaired the International Women's Walk for Peace, a group of activist women who dressed in white to cross the demilitarized zone separating the two Koreas. In Steinem's (as quoted in Sang-Hun 2015) words, the campaigners' trek across the border was "a trip for peace, for reconciliation, for human rights."

A Canadian group known as Voice of Women formed in 1960 with the aim of promoting nuclear disarmament and world peace. Members included University of Toronto metallurgist Ursula Franklin, whose research showed how atmospheric testing of nuclear weapons led to an accumulation of radioactive substances in children's teeth. Voice of Women (VOW) pressed for greater Canadian independence from US foreign policy, and endorsed the country's withdrawal from NATO. In 1972, VOW helped to establish the National Action Committee on the Status of Women, a Canada-wide umbrella organization for second-wave feminism (see Macpherson and Sears 1976; Roberts 1989).

Greenham Common was the site of one of the largest peace mobilizations of the postwar period. From an initial effort by about 250 women to protest the Thatcher government's decision to station Cruise missiles at a British military base, the scale of activism increased to the point that one

Embrace the Base event in 1983 drew 70,000 demonstrators. The peace camp formed in the early stages of the protest continued until 2000, by which time the missiles were withdrawn and activists worked on creating a historic site to commemorate their campaign (see Harford and Hopkins 1984; Hipperson 2005).

A third stream of evidence that women are pro-peace follows from the careers of prominent female politicians. Jeannette Rankin, the first woman member of the US House of Representatives, opposed not only America's entry to World War I but also the declaration of war against Japan following the attack on Pearl Harbor (Woerhle 1995, 243). Ellen Wilkinson, among the earliest women to take a seat in the British House of Commons, stood out in Labour Party circles in Manchester as a vocal critic of World War I (Perry 2013, 223). The first female member of the Canadian House of Commons, Agnes Macphail, participated in international disarmament efforts and worked to close military academies (Crowley 1991, 147–148). More recently, Monica McWilliams and Pearl Sagar—founders of a pro-peace women's coalition of Catholics and Protestants—won seats in the Northern Ireland parliament (Cowell-Moyers 2014, 69, 72).

A fourth source comes from research on the relationship between women's legislative numbers and the probability of armed conflict. As discussed in Chapter 1, multiple analyses find that female parliamentary representation is consistently, and often to a statistically significant degree, associated with less likelihood of violent state action (see Caprioli 2000; Caprioli and Boyer 2001; Koch and Fulton 2011; Regan and Paskeviciute 2003). Furthermore, as Koch and Fulton (2011) report, numbers of women legislators are inversely related to levels of defense spending in Western liberal democracies.

Patterns showing lower approval among women for the use of force have created measurable unease in some quarters. Neoconservative author Francis Fukuyama (1998, 35), writing in the journal *Foreign Affairs*, worries that "increasing female political participation will probably make the United States and other democracies less inclined to use power around the world as freely as they have in the past." Fukuyama's key concern is not conflict among stable democracies—which he views as unlikely given that these countries share common legal norms and an emphasis on individual rights.

Rather, Fukuyama's (1998, 36) anxiety emanates from a feminized Western leadership facing "those parts of the world run by young, ambitious, unconstrained men." He cites the specific threats posed by "states in Africa, the Middle East, and South Asia with young, growing populations, led mostly by younger men" (Fukuyama 1998, 39). Those countries confront what he describes as shrinking Western societies, with a preponderance of small families unwilling to lose their single child to war, dominated in electoral terms by older women who oppose the use of force. According to Fukuyama, Western states seeking order in unstable times should embrace muscular and masculine foreign policies, rather than risk-averse, feminine approaches.

CONTRARY EVIDENCE

Feminist historians argue that public/private divisions were irrelevant to the lives of women leaders even in the early modern era, and question stark dichotomies between women/peace and men/war (see Fraser 1988; James and Sluga 2016). Fukuyama (1998, 36–37) admits that as prime minister of the United Kingdom, Margaret Thatcher refused to surrender in the face of armed force. This section considers a wide range of material that casts doubt on women's presumed aversion to conflict and support for pacifism. It concludes that sweeping generalizations are best avoided.

Significant sources in Western culture deviate sharply from "beautiful souls" expectations. In the visual arts, Caravaggio's painting of Judith beheading Holofernes reminds us of a dark biblical scene in which the Israelite widow wields the sword of her victim, focusing her gaze downward as blood splatters from his open neck. The expansive canvas shows us that Judith has visited the Assyrian leader in his tent, encouraging him to drink fine wine to excess. Once Holofernes collapses in a stupor, Judith decapitates him in order to ensure the defeat of his troops and the victory of her people. Holofernes' painful expression of surprise and fear contrasts with Judith's distant, remote look and her sense of wonderment as to how her hand has committed murder. Off to the side of the composition is the wrinkled, curious face of Judith's maid—a visage that contrasts starkly with the smooth complexion of the young Israelite.

Folklore contains many examples of actors who contradict the beatific concepts of docility and pacifism. Like Judith, forceful women in Celtic myths are often portrayed in highly sexualized terms, typically as seductresses. Fraser (1988, 11) observes that women who scheme for power are typically presented as voracious, licentious, and "preternaturally lustful" vixens. Given that they engage in public battles, these characters are denied the virtuous trappings of the beautiful soul. Yet the very existence of their stories suggests a far from sealed gender divide.

Social science data reinforce the case against a binary split between peaceful, risk-averse women and bellicose, risk-taking men. Surveys of mass publics show that considerable proportions of North American and European women were and remain sympathetic to assertive military action, just as they demonstrate that men were not and are not uniformly belligerent. For instance, Smith's (1984, 388) review of attitudinal data shows that when Americans were asked in 1960 how the United States should deal with Russia, 46 percent of women advocated "an even tougher policy than we have now—even if it means taking some risks." While this result is lower than the comparable level for men in the same survey (60 percent), it nevertheless represents the modal category for female respondents. Twenty years later, the presidential election of 1980 was widely seen as a watershed event that demonstrated weaker support among women for hawkish Republican candidates (see Bolce 1985; Frankovic 1982; Gilens 1988). Yet roughly half of female voters that year cast ballots for Ronald Reagan (see Davis 1991, 415; Roper Center 1980).

More recent data from the Pew Global Attitude Surveys show that many European women endorsed continued deployment of their country's military forces in Afghanistan. As Clements (2012) reports, 47 percent of British and Spanish, 46 percent of Italian, and 43 percent of French women questioned in 2010 favored having their armies remain in place until the situation stabilized. Although support for the same view among men was as much as 10 percentage points higher (in Britain, France, and Spain), the commitment of European women to retaining troops in Central Asia was substantial nearly a decade after the attacks of 9/11.

Research on terror suspects demonstrates that high percentages of women approved of forceful options. Haider-Markel and Vieux (2008, 31) find that 54 percent of American women questioned in 2004 endorsed not permitting detainees to sleep, 45 percent favored keeping a hood over suspects' heads for long periods, and 42 percent supported bombarding them with loud noise for long periods. Although approval for each tactic was higher among men, Haider-Markel and Vieux (2008, 27–28) emphasize that "not all men support harsh techniques and not all women oppose harsh techniques."

Like public opinion data, patterns of social movement activism reveal that women's mobilization was not always consistent with efforts to promote peace. In the run-up to World War I, for instance, the National American Woman Suffrage Association offered the US government the loyal patriotic services of its two million members—a group that massively overshadowed the size of the Women's Peace Party (Elshtain 1995, 186). In the same period, suffragists in the United Kingdom threw stones at windows in government buildings, set off a bomb outside the home of cabinet minister David Lloyd George, and slashed a stereotypically feminine portrait (the Rokeby Venus by Spanish painter Diego Velázquez) on display in London's National Gallery (see Phillips 2003, 255–256).

During the late 1960s and following, radicals such as Ulrike Meinhof and Bernardine Dohrn directed well-known, often violent protest factions. West German women who participated in the Baader-Meinhof Gang set fires in Frankfurt department stores to protest the Vietnam War (Rosenfeld 2010, 357–358). Dohrn and others who participated in the Weather Underground and its splinter organizations bombed the US Senate and detonated explosives in New York City, Chicago, and Washington, D.C., to condemn military actions in Vietnam (Churchill 2007, 31–33). In 1970, civil rights and prison rights advocate Angela Davis purchased guns used in a violent courtroom hostage-taking in California, which resulted in four deaths. Davis was charged with conspiracy in the case but eventually was acquitted (Shaw 2009, 101–102).

McGlen and Sarkees' (1993, 1995, 2001) research on US foreign policymakers also disconfirms claims about female pacifism. Interviews conducted in 1988 with about eighty men and women in senior State Department and Pentagon positions found that males and females held similar views on the use of force (McGlen and Sarkees 2001, 131; see also Holsti and Rosenau 1988, 288). Variations that did emerge reveal more hawkish views among women. In the Defense Department, for example, "women were more likely to disagree on the need to enlist the support of the United Nations in settling international disputes and to reject the desirability of giving foreign aid to poor foreign nations. Similarly, the women in Defense accepted the Cold War view that revolutionary forces are not nationalistic but rather controlled by the Soviet Union or China" (McGlen and Sarkees 2001, 131).

After dividing their sample between career civil service and political appointees, McGlen and Sarkees (2001, 142) report that careerists in the State Department were the most dovish and most unlike appointees from both streams at the Pentagon. Their analysis reveals widely varied attitudes among senior foreign policy officers, even during a conservative Republican presidency. As McGlen and Sarkees (2001, 142) conclude, "One thing is clear: The women in the foreign policy process, at least during the Reagan administration, were not a homogeneous group. There was no women's view adopted, even in part, by all women."

In terms of elected politicians, some parliamentarians who opposed World War I, including Ellen Wilkinson in the United Kingdom and Agnes Macphail in Canada, later endorsed decisions by their countries to enter World War II (Perry 2013, 220; Crowley 1990, 168). As noted in Chapter 1, quantitative studies report disparate results concerning conflict for parliamentarians versus political executives: women's presence at the latter level serves to increase the severity of violence, while legislative presence exerts the opposite effect (Caprioli and Boyer 2001; Koch and Fulton 2011).

The limits of a beautiful souls argument are arguably clearest in accounts of women who go to war. Goldstein (2001, 127) concludes his extensive review of this literature as follows:

> When women have found their way into combat, they have generally performed about as well as most men have. Women in combat support roles, furthermore, have had little trouble fitting into military organizations, and have held their own when circumstances occasionally placed them in combat (especially in guerrilla wars). They can fight; they can kill. . . . Most striking are the very rare historical cases in which larger numbers of women were mobilized into combat—a substantial number of the healthy, strong young women in a population. In the nineteenth-century Dahomey Kingdom and the Soviet Union of World War II, women made up a nontrivial minority of the military, and clearly contributed to the war effort. They were a military asset which, when mobilized, increased the effectiveness of the military in combat, in a few cases even turning the tide of battle.

Goldstein's account of the experiences of women under fire is consistent with Plato's initial view that training female guardians would benefit a besieged city.

What about women who command armies into battle? Fraser (1988) writes that although relatively few assumed this role in the centuries from Cleopatra to Boudica to Thatcher, their simple existence casts doubt on conventional assumptions. She reports that those who reached top positions did not hesitate to employ violent force when they faced serious threats and when other options failed; most conducted the wars they entered with courage, ferocity, and strategic insight. By contrast, ample evidence exists that some males failed entirely as "warrior kings." Goldstein (2001, Chapter 5, esp. 299–301) describes the travails of men who were seen as "wimps" or "sissies" precisely because they lacked typically masculine leadership skills.

In short, propositions about women's aversion to the use of force tend not to stand up to close empirical scrutiny. Although some data can be adduced to support "beautiful souls" claims, the historical record offers compelling grounds for rejecting binary ideas about gender and war/peace. Whether we consider patterns of public opinion, protest engagement, or action in combat, the idea of a preternatural aversion to violent conflict fails to describe the attitudes and behaviors of significant proportions of women.

The next sections trace questionable generalizations about ideological and, in particular, feminist preferences.

LEFT IDEOLOGY AND FEMINISM

Theories dating from classical antiquity, as reviewed earlier in this chapter, tend to associate men with the public world and women with the private realm. Rousseau's elaboration of this dichotomy assigns to females a specific and decidedly conservative task, one which holds significant consequences beyond each household: to defend the prevailing social order. Expectations following from Rousseau suggest that once women obtained the right to vote, they would endorse the status quo at the ballot box.

This view was confirmed for many decades in Western Europe—much to the chagrin of socialist theoreticians and party leaders who proffered multiple reasons for female voters to embrace political change. In fact, their understanding of women as logical partners in the progressive struggle contrasts directly with arguments advanced by Rousseau about women's conserving essence. In the paragraphs that follow, we summarize ideas and then data concerning gender, ideology, and feminism.

Utopian socialist Charles Fourier was among the earliest writers to posit an inextricable link between women, on one side, and progressivism and feminism, on the other. Writing in the early nineteenth century, Fourier presents human advancement, including sexual liberation, as directly related to improvements in the status of women. In his view, wider educational and occupational opportunities constitute the basis of generalized social progress. Fourier endorses the creation of communities called *phalanstères* in which a quarter of the female population voluntarily takes responsibility for domestic work, and where children are raised cooperatively to ensure women's economic independence (see Altman 1976).

These proposals presaged Frederick Engels's work (using earlier notes from Karl Marx) on the reorganization of domestic life under communism. In *The Origin of the Family, Private Property, and the State*, first published in 1884, Engels merges older notions of a natural attachment to the family unit with utopian concepts of community. As he explains,

> To emancipate woman and make her the equal of the man is and remains an impossibility so long as the woman is shut out from social productive labour and

restricted to private domestic labour. The emancipation of woman will only be possible when woman can take part in production on a large, social scale, and domestic work no longer claims anything but an insignificant amount of her time. (Engels 1970, 221)

Engels's version of the public/private divide thus eliminates private property, shares domestic work among women living on communes, and includes both genders in a socially organized system of production.

The rise of suffrage movements brought the question of whether women would endorse tradition or radical change into the domain of *realpolitik*. European parties of the left tended to support enfranchisement at the level of ideas, but dreaded the actual impact of female voters. By contrast, the Catholic Church and its allies were averse to changing gender roles, yet recognized the likelihood that as electors, women would support parties of the center and right (see Bashevkin 1985).

The initial decades of suffrage produced results favorable to conservative interests. On average more religious than males, females were vigorously courted by confessional parties including the Mouvement Républicain Populaire (MRP) in France and the Christian Democrats (CDU) in West Germany (see Goguel 1952; Klausen 2001). British Conservatives established a unit known as the Primrose League to recruit women, who over time became the backbone of the extra-parliamentary party (see Campbell 1987). Research indicates that the postwar dominance of the German CDU and the British Tories was directly attributable to loyal female support bases (Klausen 2001, 216).

Yet patterns of urbanization, industrialization, and secularization gradually undermined the advantage enjoyed by right-of-center parties. Younger cohorts of women who worked for pay were more open to "New Left" appeals of the late 1960s and following. As early as 1968, French surveys found that one-third of women voters overall and 46 percent of those under the age of thirty identified with the left. The passing of older generations, combined with concerted efforts by socialist groups to recruit female supporters, activists, and candidates, meant that by 1978 more than half of France's women voters and 62 percent of those under the age of thirty endorsed left parties (Bashevkin 1985, 94).

This trend crossed national boundaries. As Inglehart and Norris (2000, 459) demonstrate, women in six out of nine OECD countries tended by the 1990s to be "more left-leaning" than men—with younger females who came of age in the period of second-wave mobilization the most progressive, and older women the most conservative population segment. Similarly, in the United States, "women moved towards the Democrats since 1980 while men moved toward the Republicans on a stable, long-term, and consistent basis" (Inglehart and Norris 2000, 442).

Moreover, cross-national survey data from the 1970s and following show that support for pro-equality positions on such matters as legal rights, abortion, child-care provision, and equal pay formed part of a broadly left-of-center orientation that endorsed greater government intervention in the economy and higher levels of social spending (see, e.g., Conover 1988; Nevitte and Gibbins 1991). Most notably, younger women whose formative years corresponded with the peak of movement mobilization were found to be not only more progressive, but also more feminist than other citizens (Inglehart and Norris 2000).

These patterns help to explain the willingness of gender and politics scholars to define the substantive representation of women as elite advocacy for progressive, pro-equality claims. Considered even in narrow empirical terms, however, the conflation of women, left ideology, and feminism remains problematic for at least three reasons. First, as Inglehart and Norris (2000, 456) note, public opinion results show that women in many—but not all—advanced industrial systems tend to be more left-of-center than men. Gender differences in some nations are insignificant, while in cases such as Finland, women are more conservative than men.

Even in countries where females as a group are more progressive than males, considerable percentages of women nevertheless hold conservative views. As reported earlier, about half of American women who voted in the 1980 presidential election supported Ronald Reagan (Davis 1991, 415; Roper Center 1980). This finding is particularly significant given a Republican campaign platform that rejected feminist positions on constitutional equality rights, reproductive choice, and affirmative action (see Melich 1996).

A second difficulty involves the political coherence of organized feminism. Boldly stated, women's movements of both the first and second waves experienced deep internal schisms. Militant suffragists in the United Kingdom who chained themselves to the railings at the prime minister's residence and attacked a painting in the National Gallery were far more radical than moderate campaigners who held orderly public meetings and lobbied parliament for electoral reform. During the same period, rifts in the United States over constitutional equality show that first-wave activists fundamentally disagreed among themselves as to whether group interests rested in reinforcing traditional gender roles or challenging them. Serious internal divisions re-emerged in the 1960s and following, when second-wave streams of radical, socialist, and liberal feminism developed divergent agendas, and when cogent critiques from race, class, and sexual orientation perspectives challenged the priorities of affluent, white, straight women (see, e.g., Collins 1991).

Beginning in the 1970s, organized anti-feminism staked out a competing claim to represent the interests of American women—one which echoed attempts during the suffrage era to create a countermovement. In the period of World War I, that effort drew about 350,000 members to an organization opposed to enfranchisement (Marshall 1991, 51). Backlash mobilization against the second wave was less visible and less influential in countries such as Canada and the United Kingdom (see Bashevkin 1998, 45, 168), but in the United States the reality of a dissident conservative mobilization posed a third problem for analysts (see Critchlow 2005; Klatch 1987; Schreiber 2008). Simply put, it signaled that efforts to define the substantive representation of women as the carrying forward of left and feminist views offered at best a partial and, at worst, a distorted understanding of gender and politics.

How are variations in left/right ideology, within feminism, and between feminism and anti-feminism relevant to the study of political executives? We demonstrate in the following sections that each set of distinctions limits our ability to identify a bounded repertoire that constitutes "acting for" the category of women, to the point that no single cluster of claims-making activities since enfranchisement can be said to equate with "pro-women" representation. In fact, if we confine our review for reasons of space to the United States, it becomes clear that individual women in public life can defend any number of perspectives toward matters of left and right as well as group interests, and still can be considered representative in democratic theory terms of a palpable strain of female public opinion.

SPLITS OVER FEMINISM

Internal divisions during the first wave of feminist activism offer a helpful starting point for empirical discussion, since they helped to shape public attitudes in subsequent decades. The US movement contained two major streams that held competing understandings of women's status. On one side, social or maternal advocates affiliated with the Progressive movement proposed a range of policies to restrict child labor and impose controls (known as protective legislation) on women's paid employment. The latter typically barred female workers from night shifts, as well as jobs that involved heavy lifting or exposure to substances that could harm reproductive organs. Trade unions in sectors including the garment industry defended these initiatives as necessary limits on the already extreme exploitation of women—especially young girls and immigrants—in sweatshops (see Lemons 1973).

By contrast, equal rights feminists elevated the cause of pure justice above social reform and opposed sex-specific labor laws. In their place they promoted laissez-faire solutions that did not treat women either as weaker than men (and hence in need of special protection) or as irrevocably tied to caring roles. For Alice Paul and the National Woman's Party, the best route toward justice rested in constitutional language known as the Equal Rights Amendment (ERA), a short and simple clause first proposed in 1923 that remained controversial for decades afterward (see Kraditor 1965; O'Neill 1971).

While it is hard to gauge the resonance of traditional versus role-challenging ideas among the general public, research suggests that both streams exerted measurable influence. According to Rothman (1978), a strong social consensus through the 1950s viewed the primary place of the American woman as the domestic realm, and her priorities as the well-being of children and family. Yet early polling results also reveal the ripple effects of equal rights arguments. Sears and Huddy (1990, 251) report that "[i]n the 1930s and 1940s women were substantially more supportive than men of liberalized roles for women, particularly their suitability for paid work and political office."

At least initially, second-wave mobilization seemed to resolve the tension between traditional and role-challenging ideas in favor of the latter. The intellectual origins of activism in the 1960s and following rested in two change-oriented texts: Simone de Beauvoir's *The Second Sex*, first published in French in 1949, and Betty Friedan's diagnosis of "the problem that has no name" in *The Feminine Mystique*, released in 1963. Many second-wave recruits were young, progressive women with backgrounds in civil rights, student rights, and anti–Vietnam War activism (see Davis 1991). A sense that their contributions to those struggles had been ignored or trivialized provided valuable common ground for the consciousness-raising gatherings in which Jo Freeman and thousands of others participated (see Freeman 2013).

Yet established and more politically moderate formations dating from first-wave feminism, such as the League of Women Voters and the American Association of University Women (AAUW), remained active and proved integral to the legislative reform agenda of the National Organization for Women (NOW) after its founding in 1966 (see Davis 1991, 147). Moreover, older groups that focused on participation in mainstream institutions became springboards for many female legislators. In Jeane Kirkpatrick's (1974, 44) sample of state house members, "about forty percent were active in the League of Women Voters; affiliation with this group played a key role in the political careers of several." Lawmakers reported that they relied heavily on campaign volunteers from the League and the AAUW (Kirkpatrick 1974, 87, 89).

Once a series of US Supreme Court decisions deemed protective legislation to be unconstitutional, leading trade unions dropped their opposition to the ERA. They worked with NOW on pressing for a successful vote in Congress in 1972 and for state-level ratification. The fact that NOW allied with trade unions to alter the foundational law of the American polity underlined the left positioning of second-wave mobilization. Moreover, the assumption behind ERA advocacy in the second wave was unequivocally progressive: the regulatory and enforcement powers of government would be harnessed to the cause of gender equality (see Davis 1991, 61–64; Kenney 1992).

Anti-communist crusader Phyllis Schlafly claimed that the ERA threatened not just free and unfettered markets, but also conventional family organization. In the early 1970s, she launched a strong grassroots campaign against feminism that merged religiously based opposition to abortion and reforms to family law with a laissez-faire stance against expanding the state's reach. Schlafly saw the ERA as imposing a Soviet-style regime in the United States, one in which the small-state libertarianism she favored would be trumped by a large, heavy-handed, and highly bureaucratized government bent on making men and women equal (see Critchlow 2005).

Schlafly's vision of a moral order grounded in traditional Judeo-Christian values, with men as heads of household and women as wives, mothers, and keepers of the domestic realm, was thus tied to a rejection of political progressivism. Her influence was pivotal in practical terms, since she served as the lead catalyst for a conservative countermovement that placed American feminism squarely on the defensive (see Bashevkin 1998; Critchlow 2005). In the pitched battle between NOW and Schlafly's STOP ERA network, which reached its crescendo between 1972 and 1982, anti-feminists managed to slow and then reverse the momentum of pro-equality activism.

ATTITUDINAL DIVISIONS

Splits within pro-equality interests, as well as between movement and countermovement, help to explain why even at the peak of second-wave activism, American women were far from solidly behind either feminist or left positions. In an influential study of the major legal rights demand of US campaigners, Jane Mansbridge (1986, 27) concludes that NOW and its allies faced members of a general public who were ready to endorse the ERA "only so long as it did not change much in practice." Moreover, even though females were more likely than males to say they supported Democratic candidates and identified with the Democratic Party during the 1980s (Sears and Huddy 1990, 252), a higher proportion of women who voted in 1980 were opposed to or didn't have an opinion on the ERA than supported it (*New York Times/CBS News* exit poll, reported in Mansbridge 1985, 166).

Subsequent studies indicate that a trend toward greater egalitarianism that unfolded in the American public through the 1970s and 1980s had largely stagnated by the mid-1990s. Cotter, Hermson, and Vanneman's (2011, 261) analysis of data from 1977 through 2008 finds "quantitative evidence that the cultural attacks on feminist equality have had their impact on public consciousness." In particular, earlier shifts toward greater openness to female politicians and support for mothers working for pay reversed themselves in a decisive way.

Research on political elites further undermines the idea of a solidly pro-feminist consensus. Kirkpatrick (1974, 166) reports that about a fifth of the state lawmakers in her 1972 sample identified with radical strands of second-wave feminism. In her words, "Approximately 60% of the legislators expressed opposition to the women's liberation movement and many criticisms were leveled against the women's liberation movement" (Kirkpatrick 1974, 164). Lawmakers described the movement as "hostile to marriage and the family," "extremist in its criticisms and its proposals," and "partisan and sectarian" because it was too left-wing and overly wedded to the Democratic Party (Kirkpatrick 1974, 165). Kirkpatrick (1974, 166–167; italics in original) describes deep schisms among state legislators as follows:

Disagreements about the women's movement within this group of legislators illuminate the problem of uniting women in a single, political action group. Beyond agreement on some few, very basic beliefs about women's rights and women's place, these women see issues as Republicans and Democrats, liberals and conservatives, easterners or westerners. They did not at all agree with the proposition advanced by various speakers at the conference [at Rutgers University where the research was conducted] that *as women* they should support a particular child care bill, or health program, or welfare scheme. To most these seemed "political" questions, to be resolved by political philosophy and the local context rather than by sex.

According to Kirkpatrick (1974), differences among legislators were so deep as to void any expectation that elite women formed a unified category.

Many scholars after Kirkpatrick used the concept of substantive representation to frame the question of whether legislators "act for" other women by carrying forward a feminist policy agenda (see, e.g., Swers 2002; Thomas 1994). Although initial studies reported a positive association between numbers of female politicians, on one side, and attention to women's issues and pro-feminist policy outcomes, on the other, later accounts reveal a far less automatic translation (compare, e.g., Saint-Germain 1989; Thomas 1994; with Cowell-Meyers and Langbein 2009; Osborn 2014).

Research on substantive representation tends to identify party and political ideology as more significant than gender. Berkman and O'Connor (1993) report that Democratic state lawmakers were considerably more likely to challenge restrictive abortion policies than Republicans. Swers (2002, 263) finds that "[p]arty affiliation is one of the most reliable predictors of legislative behavior" in the House of Representatives. Carroll (2002) shows a growing ideological gulf between right-wing Republicans and liberal Democrats in state legislatures. According to Bratton (2002) and Osborn (2012), Democratic women in US state houses were more active pro-equality advocates than their Republican counterparts. Bratton (2002, 138) concludes her assessment of gender and race in state-level politics as follows: "the main point of this article is to emphasize the diversity that exists within groups, and thus it is important to recognize that among all groups there is disagreement over what is in a group's interests."

The impact of political ideology is also discernible in the track records of political executives. Before becoming secretary of labor in the George H. W. Bush administration, Lynn Martin was a Republican member of the House of Representatives who refused to pay her full dues to the Congresswomen's Caucus. Martin explained that she "'believes in working from the inside' and 'has always been one of the boys.' She 'hates the term women's issues and wants to focus on people's issues'" (Martin, as quoted in Bashevkin 1998, 183). As UK prime minister, Margaret Thatcher rejected "the strident tones we hear from some Women's Libbers" and grew tired of having "to push my way through protesting feminists chanting, 'We want women's rights not a right-wing woman'" (Thatcher, as quoted in Bashevkin 1998, 173).

In short, like characterizations of all females as averse to the use of force, depictions of the group as consistently attached to left, pro-equality positions are not sustainable. This last point is especially important in research on the United States, where organized anti-feminism has exerted measurable political influence since the 1970s. As argued in the next section, these empirical problems with the conventional treatment of women, war, and feminism exist alongside major theoretical limits.

RETURNING TO THE CONCEPTUAL LEVEL

Studies of substantive representation tend to compare the actions of political elites with respect to conflict and gender equality, on one side, with public attitudes toward those issues, on the other. Our discussion to this point has introduced a broad range of empirical materials that illustrate diverse, often deeply divergent views toward war and feminism among women. These data suggest that useful propositions about the actions of female leaders are unlikely to follow from attempts to generalize about the extremely varied half of humanity which they are presumed to represent.

Moreover, there exist multiple theoretical reasons for doubting prevailing interpretations of women, war, and feminism. First, logic cautions against seeing large societal patterns as valid or reliable bases for predicting individual action. At the heart of any leap from the general to the specific is the potential for ecological fallacies that generate false or misleading expectations (see Idrovo 2011; Robinson 1950). For instance, the tendency for females as a group in most Western democracies to oppose the use of military force offers no guarantee that each individual woman, let alone a specific foreign policy leader, will hold that opinion or act in accordance with it. Similarly, the fact that women in the United States and some other democratic systems are on average more left in their partisan preferences than men, and that some women have deeply engaged in feminist activism, provides no basis for assuming that female members of a political executive will be either progressive or feminist.

Second, political philosophers including Pitkin (1967, 63) warn against mirror or "proportionalist" assumptions that decision-makers with particular demographic features will act for a larger group with whom they share such characteristics. According to Pitkin, the link between descriptive and substantive representation is suspect based on studies of legislatures. In her words, "We tend to assume that people's characteristics are a guide to the actions they will take and we are concerned with the characteristics of our legislators for just this reason. But it is no simple correlation; the best descriptive representative is not necessarily the best representative for activity or government" (Pitkin 1967, 89).

Elite theorists offer a third basis for questioning whether group background is a useful predictor of political action. As Robert Michels (2001) argues in *Political Parties*, first published in 1911, the German Social

Democratic party effectively socialized younger members into existing norms. His "iron law of oligarchy" posits that the longer new recruits are involved in a well-established organization, the more likely they are to resemble their predecessors and uphold that structure. Quoting Michels (2001, 127, 131), "The permanent exercise of leadership exerts upon the moral character of leaders an influence which is essentially pernicious. . . . As the led becomes a subordinate leader, and from that a leader of the first rank, he himself undergoes a mental evolution, which often effects a complete transformation of his personality." Michels rejects the tenets of mirror theory, in Putnam's (1976, 142) words, because "demographic representativeness is neither necessary nor sufficient for responsiveness."

Feminist institutionalism offers additional reasons to doubt the substantive tie between elites and mass publics. Scholarship suggests that when more women are elected to a deliberative body with overwhelmingly male members, new legislators do not easily transform either the policy priorities of the institution or its "rules of the game," including hours of work, seniority practices, styles of debate, and norms of socializing that men have built up over successive generations (see, e.g., Mackay 2008; Poggione 2011). As Kathlene (1998, 197) observes with respect to US state houses, "gender affects more than just the individuals who occupy the legislature. The institution itself is gendered through the rules, norms, and expectations of how business should proceed. In our society, this gendering is also inextricably linked to power" such that those voicing disparate perspectives inside gendered institutions are frequently marginalized. By viewing female decision-makers as structurally constrained in their ability to carry forward or represent, institutional theories conceive of citizen beliefs as tangential to the actions of elites.

A final intellectual stream, postmodernist philosophy, interrogates an even more basic point: that is, the utility of fixed, dichotomous gender categories. According to Judith Butler (1990, 139, 140), gender identity is best defined as "a corporeal style, an act, as it were, which is both intentional and performative, where 'performative' suggests a dramatic and contingent construction of meaning . . . a stylized repetition of acts." Poststructuralists view gender as malleable rather than rigid, since it is constructed within the context of particular times and cultures. Conventional approaches are thus problematic because they adopt singular, universal ideas of masculinity and femininity that occlude within-gender differences by assuming all members of the category "women" perform gender in the same ways and share similar experiences—in defiance of significant sources of variation. Since poststructuralists reject arguments grounded in fixed, unchanging, and ahistorical binaries, they examine gender identity in ways that resist conceptual as well as methodological determinism.

In particular, poststructuralists reject a homogenizing essentialism that lumps together holders of a single identity category. Defined in this context as the assumption that all women share a universal, "irreducible, unchanging" identity (Fuss 1989, 2), essentialism rests at the heart of constructions of pacific woman (as contrasted with fighting man) or, alternatively, left feminist woman (versus conservative anti-feminist man). Butler (1990) draws particular attention to social class and race as important lines of distinction within gender categories that deserve careful attention.

Taken together, these conceptual streams underline the importance of considering women, war, and feminism in ways that break with traditional theorizing. In particular, they suggest that empirical findings concerning a diversity of women are best complemented by a conceptualization of ideas and actions along a wide spectrum that captures the varied possibilities of "acting for" representation. With reference to the political conflict behavior of cabinet ministers, this continuum could potentially stretch in the contemporary United States from committed pacifism and anti-militarism at one polarity to extreme bellicosity and pro-armed interventionism at the other. On matters of gender equality, we can conceive of a possible distribution of perspectives from strongly pro-feminist and progressive at one end to committed anti-feminist and conservative at the other.

Our review of the extent of variation among American women, in particular since the 1970s on matters of gender equality, demonstrates the potential range of a normatively good repertoire for political elites; that is, women leaders can be seen to carry forward the disparate views of members of the general public that are arrayed along both spectrums. As long as those "acting for" behaviors resemble in approximate terms the views of citizens who brought a given political executive to office, they constitute normatively good representational repertoires in democratic theory terms.

Our discussion now turns to the foreign policy contributions of four US leaders. We return to considerations of normative political theory in Chapter 7.

CHAPTER 3

Hawk in the Cold War Twilight

J eane Jordan Kirkpatrick, the first woman in US history to hold a foreign policy seat at the cabinet table, joined the Reagan administration in 1981 as ambassador to the United Nations. Her appointment signaled not just the willingness of Republican leaders to respond to concerns that few women had reached senior positions in the political executive, but also the limits of an assumption that female nominees would necessarily pursue feminist priorities (see Borrelli 2002, 68–70).

As detailed in this chapter, policy decisions during the Reagan era were far from consistent with the issue agenda of progressive women's movements or left interests more generally. America's posture on the international stage, typified above all by Kirkpatrick's interventions at the United Nations, was far more aggressive, belligerent, and conservative than had been the case during the term of Democratic president Jimmy Carter in the late 1970s (see Gaddis 2005, 343). The Reagan administration not only rolled back the clock on gender equality policies inside the United States, but also extended a domestic campaign against reproductive choice to the foreign policy arena (see Bashevkin 1998, 41–44, 68–74).

What role did Kirkpatrick play in designing and executing the international relations agenda of Reagan's first term? Did she create measurable change in US foreign policy? More specifically, how did Kirkpatrick operate with respect to matters of military intervention and women's rights? Did she alter her views in order to conform to masculine stereotypes in cabinet-level office or, instead, were her perspectives well formed at the point of executive appointment?

This chapter introduces materials on the public record, including memoirs, biographies, diaries, and Kirkpatrick's own writings, to address each point. I argue that Jeane Kirkpatrick was a highly influential member of the inner circle that envisaged, articulated, and implemented the international relations doctrine of the first Reagan mandate. A crucial article Kirkpatrick published prior to the 1980 presidential election outlined what became the broad parameters of that approach, and raised her public profile to the point that she was invited to meet candidate Reagan. This interpretation is consistent with the conclusions of a *New York Times* obituary published following Kirkpatrick's death in 2006; it deems her impact to have been unprecedented in that "no woman had ever been so close to the center of presidential power without actually residing in the White House" (Weiner 2006).

Consistent with the findings of feminist diplomatic historiography, however, not all accounts acknowledge the centrality of Kirkpatrick's ideas to Reagan-era foreign policy. A leading academic study of the period ignores her entirely, even though it treats the positions she championed as substantively influential during the early 1980s (see Gaddis 2005). The memoirs of two administration colleagues, Defense Secretary Caspar Weinberger (1990) and Secretary of State Alexander Haig (1992), make no mention of her. The secretary of state who succeeded Haig, George Shultz (1993, 320), acknowledges Kirkpatrick's presence, but treats her as underpowered for diplomatic work. He describes her as "passionate" and hence unsuited to promotion from UN ambassador to national security advisor. Shultz's portrayal recalls older tropes concerning women diplomats, which present them as so emotional that they lack the judicious and rational qualities needed for effective statecraft.

The foreign policy doctrine conceived by Kirkpatrick was decidedly assertive and hawkish. It contained virtually no pacific or "beautiful souls" content that might have evoked images of the UN ambassador as a heavenly seraph floating above the terrain of East-West conflict (see Elshtain 1995). As demonstrated in this chapter, Kirkpatrick not only fits the profile of a transforming public leader, but also stands out as a diplomat who was not afraid to pursue contentious positions in world politics.

As reflected in the following quotation, Kirkpatrick rejected what she saw as radical campaigns in the name of women as a group to overhaul American politics and society: "Some women, speaking in the name of other women, persuaded the men who made up the Democrats' Commission on Party Structure and Delegate Selection of the validity of women's grievances and the reality of their potential power" (Kirkpatrick 1976, 380). She was a moderate liberal feminist who endorsed the ERA, opposed a constitutional ban on abortion, and wanted to be taken seriously in her professional work (see Collier 2012, 173). Like many of the state lawmakers she studied during the 1970s, Kirkpatrick was a committed wife and mother who identified more closely with her immediate family than with women's movements (see Collier 2012, 176). Moreover, as an academic analyst, she rejected the proposition that gender constitutes a primary political anchor. In scholarly publications released before she became UN ambassador, Kirkpatrick (1974, 166–167) maintains that party ideology and geographic background matter far more for female decision-makers, and often serve as sources of significant difference among them.

Kirkpatrick's worldview was dominated by intense streaks of frontier individualism, patriotism, and anti-communism. Like Reagan, her political roots rested in the Democratic Party. Yet the sway exerted by New Left and women's movement interests in that part of the political spectrum led her to become a leading neoconservative critic of the Democrats and, by 1985, to join the Republican Party (see Collier 2012, 167). Like others in the same stream, Kirkpatrick aimed to restore the United States to a position of primacy on the global stage; she projected far greater support for that priority than for any goal related to feminist or left politics. To wit, although Kirkpatrick was not central to Reagan administration efforts to block foreign aid funding for contraception and abortion, neither did she vigorously oppose those directions (see Fornos 1988; Gupte 1984).

Kirkpatrick's repertoire in cabinet office closely resembled her patterns of behavior prior to that point. From the time she was a young adult, Kirkpatrick resisted organizational conformity—including pressures emanating from women's groups and a Democratic Party that seemed increasingly distant from her own moorings. On questions of war and peace, little evidence suggests that she held stereotypically feminine "soft" or consensus-seeking approaches that were set aside in order to conform to the masculine expectations of executive office. Rather, the historical record points toward the exact opposite: Kirkpatrick was recruited to cabinet precisely because her forceful, outspoken rejection of American foreign policy weakness during the late 1970s brought her to the attention of members of the Reagan campaign team.

Kirkpatrick's strengths also imposed measurable costs. Her incisive approach to problems left little room for the flexibility and patience required to understand, let alone accommodate, competing perspectives (see Kirkpatrick 1974). Amidst the constant jockeying for position that occurs in the executive branch, the ambitions of the lone woman cabinet member with an international affairs portfolio were frustrated by her strong commitment to intellectual rigor, personal candor, and principled decision-making, and by the ability of other players to portray those characteristics in the most negative light possible. Competitors could conveniently cite Kirkpatrick's controversial stance on matters ranging from the Falkland Islands crisis to the Iran/Contra deal as evidence that the ambassador lacked the balanced judgment crucial for promotion (see, for example, Shultz 1993, 320).

As detailed in the following sections, Kirkpatrick failed to secure a promotion within the Reagan administration in part because she spoke her mind, resisted compromise, and was so close with the president that others envied her access and influence. Some of these characteristics reflected the very attributes that brought her into Reagan's orbit, notably the traits of being outspoken, fiercely committed to thwarting Soviet and expanding American influence, and unwilling to comply with group norms—notably inside the Democratic Party. This background suggests that, contrary to propositions in the literature on women elites, Kirkpatrick defended an assertive, forceful, and, in that sense, masculine approach to foreign policy decision-making both prior to and in executive office.

This discussion opens with an assessment of the main international accomplishments of the first Reagan administration and, in particular, Kirkpatrick's status as a transforming leader. It then turns to the background she brought to cabinet-level office in order to situate an examination of her term as UN ambassador.

CONCEIVING THE REAGAN DOCTRINE

In his account of postwar foreign policy, John Lewis Gaddis (2005, 353–354) defines the key contribution of the first Reagan administration as the unambiguous containment of Soviet expansionism. This strategy broke decisively with the directions of the Carter years. After the 1980 election, US decision-makers sought in purposeful ways to stymie the growth of communist influence—both where Moscow's sway was already well established and where nascent pro-Soviet regimes existed, such as Afghanistan and Central America (see Arquilla 2006, 43; Diebel 1989, 45; Pee 2015, 50–51, 65). In the Middle East, policies instituted in 1981 and following reversed Carter's emphasis on brokering a peace agreement and finding common ground with the new regime in Iran. Instead, the Reagan team elevated the importance of strategic cooperation with Israel above other considerations (Diebel 1989, 43).

Even though Gaddis (2005), Haig (1992), and Weinberger (1990) ignore her, it is hard to identify a more central player to the conception and execution of this approach than Jeane Kirkpatrick. Most of the scaffolding for what became known as the Reagan doctrine appeared in print for the first time in her article titled "Dictatorships and Double Standards," published in the November 1979 issue of *Commentary* magazine. The text offers a detailed and lengthy dissection of Carter administration actions on the world stage, as well as a new path forward.

Kirkpatrick insists that she wrote the piece for her own purposes; she wanted to understand the evolution of America's relations with the world, and only sent it to the editor of *Commentary* because her husband pressed her to do so (see Collier 2012, 104; Kirkpatrick interview in McGlen and Sarkees 1993, 55). Once released, the stark Cold War slant of Kirkpatrick's prose catapulted her to the status of "warrior queen of neoconservatism" and brought her to the attention of presidential candidate Reagan (Blumenthal 2006, 1).

The essay's lead sentence posits a jarring premise: "The failure of the Carter administration's foreign policy is now clear to everyone except its architects, and even they must entertain private doubts" (Kirkpatrick 1979, 34). Kirkpatrick (1979, 34) portrays the president and his advisors as deeply misguided in their willingness to let the Soviets leap ahead militarily and diplomatically across multiple regions:

> In the thirty-odd months since the inauguration of Jimmy Carter as President there has occurred a dramatic Soviet military build-up, matched by the stagnation of American armed forces, and a dramatic extension of Soviet influence in the Horn of Africa, Afghanistan, Southern Africa, and the Caribbean, matched by a declining American position in all these areas. The U.S. has never tried so hard and failed so utterly to make and keep friends in the Third World.

According to Kirkpatrick (1979), Carter bungled an opportunity to defend the Shah of Iran, choosing instead to embrace the fundamentalist Islamic cleric who succeeded him. Decision-makers in Washington permitted the fall of Anastasio Somoza in Nicaragua, naïvely believing the democratic rhetoric of the Sandinista rebels who removed him from office. In the latter case, she maintains, members of the Democratic administration ignored two key facts: first, Somoza's regime was a reliable US ally; and second, his opponents enjoyed close ties with Cuba.

Kirkpatrick (1979) draws on her own academic research on a variety of nondemocratic governments, including Perón's Argentina. She argues that the United States could and should have maintained relations with both the Shah and President Somoza. Instead of pursuing a practical approach to keeping those leaders in power, however, the Carter administration "actively collaborated in the replacement of moderate autocrats friendly to American interests with less friendly autocrats of extremist persuasion"

(Kirkpatrick 1979, 34). The essay lays out each misstep in what she views as a dangerous process of abandoning allies at their moment of greatest need.

Why did the Carter administration commit these errors? According to Kirkpatrick (1979, 37), American liberals share a woolly-headed belief that democratization can unfold virtually anywhere, even though history shows otherwise. Western liberal systems rely on both citizens and leaders to abide by shared legal norms, to debate each other peacefully, and to trust across social groups. Centuries spent building vibrant political parties, legislatures, and local community organizations reinforce each core value. In Kirkpatrick's (1979) view, no magic potion exists for American leaders to sprinkle across the globe in order to create instant democracies.

"Dictatorships and Double Standards" claims that unlike socialist and communist states, autocracies can in some cases be converted into democracies. This outcome remains unlikely, she argues, if entrenched leaders like the Shah or Somoza are suddenly removed from office such that valuable sources of social order (resting in the military, police, or bureaucracy) collapse after they depart. Without the critical cultural and institutional prerequisites for liberal democracy present in North America or Western Europe, Kirkpatrick (1979, 38) maintains, fallen friendly dictatorships in places like Iran or Nicaragua are likely to give way to sturdy pro-Soviet regimes.

Kirkpatrick reserves her deepest frustration for the conceptual underpinnings of Carter-era foreign policy. She traces them to the work of Zbigniew Brzezinski, a Columbia University academic who served as the president's national security advisor beginning in 1977. Unlike the Nixon-era framework known as détente, championed by Henry Kissinger, Carter's approach began with a view that the Cold War was over. In this rendering, the United States needed to set aside superpower rivalries and employ what Brzezinski (1970, 272) terms a "rational humanist" strategy for aiding developing countries.

Kirkpatrick (1979, 40–41) vigorously rejects the Brzezinski outlook. She sees the defense of American national interests, rather than an abstract concept like rational humanism, as the appropriate *raison-d'être* of foreign policy. In her view, the Brzezinski approach is dangerous because it sees inexorable forces of history unfolding across the globe. This perspective creates a passive mindset in which the United States can do little more than stand by as communist influence spreads.

The double standard of the article's title refers to the willingness of the Carter administration to ignore the lack of individual freedom in China, much of Southeast Asia, and the Soviet bloc at the same time as it condemns the human rights failings of friendly autocracies in such places as Latin America. How could condoning circumstances in one group of states be reconciled with support for change elsewhere? According to Kirkpatrick (1979), this hypocrisy originates in the shared Enlightenment origins of liberalism and Marxism, both of which champion freedom alongside fairness. In Carter-era foreign policy, dominated by an excess of "good intentions" and an absence of hard-headed thinking, these disparate ideologies become so intertwined that the revolutionary ayatollahs of Iran and the Sandinistas of Nicaragua seem preferable to the traditional dictators they depose (Kirkpatrick 1979, 44).

The essay concludes by calling for US foreign policy to be crafted along entirely different lines. Kirkpatrick (1979) says that presidents deserve to be advised not by naïve dreamers, but instead by pragmatists who comprehend and are prepared to defend national interests—using military force if required. Decision-makers need to grasp the difference between friends and enemies, and to act accordingly. America will again stand tall in the world once its relations with the Third World cease to be conducted on bended knee. Wishful thinking about human rights will be replaced by a practical understanding of the cultural and institutional foundations of democracy. "Dictatorships and Double Standards" is in this respect both an exposé of blunders and a blueprint for future political executives to undo the damage they inflicted.

Kirkpatrick's (1979) essay circulated well beyond *Commentary's* usual subscription list. Multiple think tanks in Washington, including the American Enterprise Institute where she had been affiliated since 1977, printed thousands of copies for distribution around the United States (see Collier 2012, 105). Far beyond the capital, two crucial events unfolded within weeks of the article's release. First, hundreds of Iranian students forced their way into the US embassy in Tehran, taking fifty-two diplomats as hostages for more than a year. American news reports provided daily reminders of the imprisonment of dozens of the country's citizens by Islamic fundamentalists. Second, waves of Soviet tanks rolled into Afghanistan under orders from Leonid Brezhnev, whose long tenure at the helm of the Soviet Union was surpassed only by that of Joseph Stalin.

If the time was ripe for a reset of American foreign policy, then who would lead the charge? Aware of attacks from within his own party, President Carter invited a group of disgruntled Democrats, including Kirkpatrick and *Commentary* editor Norman Podhoretz, to the White House in January 1980. From Kirkpatrick's perspective, the effort was fruitless. Carter argued throughout the meeting that Soviet actions in Afghanistan would not alter either his beliefs or his administration's policies. Leaving the White House,

Kirkpatrick told Podhoretz's wife Midge Decter, "I am not going to support *that man*" (Kirkpatrick, as quoted in Collier 2012, 107; italics in original).

As one door closed for Kirkpatrick, another opened. In April 1980, she met for the first time with Republican presidential hopeful Ronald Reagan. Their initial conversation at the Madison Hotel in Washington provided Kirkpatrick with an opportunity to meet not just the candidate but also Richard Allen, who had worked on national security in the Nixon years. Allen had given Reagan a copy of the *Commentary* article when it first came out, and received an enthusiastic response. Reagan then sent Kirkpatrick a note complimenting her "keen insight" and acknowledging the essay's "great impact" on his thinking (Reagan letter to Kirkpatrick, as quoted in Collier 2012, 105).

As a scholar of comparative and American politics with deep ties to the Democratic Party, Kirkpatrick was initially skeptical. Reagan was a former governor of California, known neither for his intellectualism nor his knowledge of international affairs. Yet these two seemingly disparate individuals shared crucial commonalities. Both came from modest families that struggled through the Great Depression. They were direct, plain-talking people with deep roots in America's Midwestern interior and Western frontier. Both held close the values of freedom, liberty, and commitment to country. Each had been a fervent New Deal Democrat vigorously opposed to communism—whether in the guise of leftist infiltration inside their political party or, in the case of Reagan, inside the actors' union in Hollywood (see Cannon 1991; Collier 2012; Reagan 1990).

Between 1981 and 1985, Reagan and Kirkpatrick built on these commonalities to forge a dynamic working relationship that reshaped US foreign policy. The two met frequently for friendly, animated discussions—as revealed in the photograph in Figure 3.1. The main principles of their doctrine were presented to a public audience in Kirkpatrick's *Commentary* article, but their groundwork rested in shared personal experiences beginning in childhood. Coming from America's small-town interior, Kirkpatrick (like Reagan) insisted on defending friends and defeating enemies. She was long known as a tenacious hawk, notably in the postwar Democratic Party, where she gained a reputation as an unwavering hardliner who resisted compromise when core values were at stake. For these reasons, the tough, no-nonsense approach she demonstrated in the *Commentary* article and, later, in the Reagan cabinet hardly represented a sudden change of direction.

The next sections offer a detailed look at the background Kirkpatrick brought to her work as a diplomat.

Figure 3.1. President Ronald Reagan meets UN Ambassador Jeane Kirkpatrick in the Oval Office, 1982.
Courtesy Ronald Reagan Library.

FRONTIER ORIGINS

When Jeane Kirkpatrick welcomed her biographer, Peter Collier, to her Washington office, she pointed toward a small bronze statue on the windowsill. The piece was placed strategically to offer guidance and inspiration while she wrote or spoke on the telephone. The figurine depicted Will Rogers, the quintessential American cowboy from the same region that Kirkpatrick called home. A gift from the State of Oklahoma in recognition of her "favorite daughter" status, the statue evoked "a sense of place and belonging," a feeling of being rooted in the Southwestern frontier, where rugged individuals could conquer whatever challenges awaited them (Kirkpatrick 2007a, 1). As depicted, Rogers struck a decisive pose with "feet anchored firmly in the ground, hips thrust forward" (Kirkpatrick 2007a, 1). Kirkpatrick explained that the sculpture imparted a confident strength upon which she depended. In her words, it was a constant reminder of "how lucky I am to have been born an American, in the heartland of this country, at a time when we had no doubts about our national greatness or our mission" (Kirkpatrick 2007a, 1).

Like many of the state lawmakers she studied as a political scientist, Kirkpatrick came from a hard-working, politically engaged family. She was imbued since early childhood with the values of personal self-reliance and small-town community spirit (see Kirkpatrick 1974, Chapter 2). Her father's kin, the Jordans, were Texas farmers whose hospitality in the midst of the Great Depression loomed large in her memories:

> There was always crusty hot bread freshly baked in a big wood stove in the kitchen, sweet butter that had just been churned, fried chicken, tart plum jelly my grandmother had put up the previous summer, and homemade ice cream she turned on the back porch. There was a quilting frame where she worked like Penelope every night. There was sometimes a horse my grandfather let me ride. (Kirkpatrick 2007a, 2)

Reading this passage in light of the career she built as a public intellectual and diplomat evokes an image of the young Jeane as a budding Boudica— a feisty, independent girl exploring the Texas countryside on horseback, even if she lacked the chariot made famous in the Celtic warrior's fight against the Romans.

Her mother's family left Indiana to settle in the Fort Worth region. When Kirkpatrick's maternal grandfather passed away, her "tall, straight, strong-bodied" grandmother "carried on with the fortitude expected of a young widow in those days" (Kirkpatrick 2007a, 2). That inner strength was tested further when Kirkpatrick's aunt died, leaving five young children in the care of a widowed grandmother. Later on, when Jeane's mother Leona became ill, the same grandmother arrived at the family home in Duncan, Oklahoma, to take her daughter and two grandchildren to Mineral Wells, Texas, so Leona "could 'take the baths'" (Kirkpatrick 2007a, 2).

Kirkpatrick reminisced with great fondness about the "big country of rangeland and prairie" where she was born in 1926 (2007a, 2). In her memories, it had only recently changed from a wild place to a town inside the boundaries of civilization, where social order largely emanated from Christian tradition and Roosevelt's New Deal. In Kirkpatrick's (2007a, 2) words,

> My grandparents on both sides were sincere Protestants who read the Bible for information on how to conduct their daily lives and did not drink alcoholic beverages, smoke, or play cards. . . . They were all Democrats, of course. Not just Democrats, but southern Democrats of the yellow dog variety. . . . FDR cemented the allegiance of everyone in my family to the Democrats. As the Depression unleashed economic forces beyond their control, they came to regard programs like the Rural Electrification Program, the CCC [Civilian Conservation Corps],

Social Security, and the TVA [Tennessee Valley Authority] as godsends and Roosevelt himself as the savior.

The idea that local community involvement mattered, whether through the vehicle of the Texas Christian Church or the school board or the Democratic Party, was thus embedded early on in her worldview.

Despite a strong interest in books and a range of other aptitudes, Kirkpatrick realized her younger brother "would have more opportunities than I and that my mother and father had more respect for male attributes" (Kirkpatrick, as quoted in Collier 2012, 7). Keen awareness that society tended to value typically masculine characteristics and devalue feminine ones meant that she embraced with enthusiasm the company of boys. Consistent with Fraser's (1988, 12) account of the early lives of warrior queens, Kirkpatrick became a proud tomboy. As she explains, "There were many more boys than girls in the neighborhood where we lived. They were my friends. I climbed trees with them, played softball and touch football. Such activities were frowned upon in Duncan for girls. Even as a child, I suppose, I was already engaged in unconventional role behavior" (Kirkpatrick 2007a, 4). Together with experiences atop her grandfather's horse, this tomboy athleticism reveals Kirkpatrick's ability to engage in rough and tumble exploits and thus "fit in" among boys and men, no matter what the strictures of the time said about the proper place of little girls.

Kirkpatrick pursued an array of other activities that also served her well. From the age of four, she took what were called "expression" lessons, where she "memorized poems and performed at local affairs" (Kirkpatrick 2007a, 3). At age seven, she began piano training that led to solo recitals and participation in a music club. While tomboy experience was uncommon for girls of her time, even more unusual was the ability to combine that background with the skills needed to ascend the community stage as a speaker and performer. Kirkpatrick's upbringing in this sense offered invaluable assets for academic as well as diplomatic life: a strong physical presence, the ability to communicate well, and, in particular, a capacity to command with confidence the podium spotlight.

Kirkpatrick's account presents Duncan as a homogeneous place where white, Christian insiders worried little about the gap between their understanding of America's core values and the experiences of minorities living in their midst. She describes indigenous people residing on a nearby reservation as follows: "They were exotic and seemed romantic—symbols of the Vanishing America, which has vanished even more in the years since I was a child" (Kirkpatrick 2007a, 4). Her account ends without asking how or why aboriginal peoples dropped from sight. She notes that even fewer Jews lived in the area, with a total of two Jewish families in a town of more than three thousand (Collier 2012, 4; Kirkpatrick 2007a, 4).

On matters of race, Kirkpatrick (2007a, 5) refers to the Oklahoma of her youth as "the most segregated state in the union"—a place where black servants lived inside the homes of their white employers. She presents the situation as follows:

> The culture that was otherwise democratic, egalitarian, and libertarian was saturated with prejudice against blacks. Words like "nigger-shooter" (for sling-shot) and "nigger toes" (for Brazil nuts) were considered perfectly ordinary, conventional language, like all the other names of things. I was a child, not a social scientist. I was part of a system of race discrimination without being aware of it. But once I began to see the nature of this system, I understood immediately that it was unfair. (Kirkpatrick 2007a, 4)

In the next section of her memoir, Kirkpatrick (2007a, 4) champions the richness of "southern culture," notably "a warmth and grace that are absent in the North." She equates "the strengths of the frontier" with "the strengths of America itself," defined as the qualities of being "open," "inclusive," and "democratic" (Kirkpatrick 2007a, 4).

A more critical reading suggests that small-town Oklahoma in the early decades of the twentieth century was far from welcoming toward the minorities in its midst—whether they were aboriginal, black, or Jewish. What Kirkpatrick demonstrates in this account is a characteristic that stands out in her adult life: a single-minded belief in the greatness of the United States. Carrying a rugged frontier outlook that stressed the importance of individual, family, and community, she became a public intellectual and decision-maker who consistently elevated national prowess above international pressures, and personal agency above collectivist conformity or group-think.

AUTONOMOUS ACTOR

At the age of twelve, Jeane moved with her family to southern Illinois. There she gained an opportunity to live in larger places, borrow books from better stocked public libraries, and learn how different people could see the same events in divergent ways. Kirkpatrick (2007a, 5) notes in her memoir the unsettling experience of hearing the story of the American Civil War recounted from the Union side. After graduating from high school, she studied philosophy at Stephens College in Missouri. Jeane Jordan then took the train to New York City to enroll at Barnard College, the women's division of Columbia University.

Her journey signaled the start of an independent life, and represented a major break from paternal views that two years of study after high school were sufficient for his middle-class daughter (see Collier 2012, 17). Jeane embraced the vitality of the East Coast metropolis, attending lectures by a variety of émigré scholars, including Hannah Arendt and Herbert Marcuse. She went on to do an MA in political science at Columbia and, for her thesis, studied Oswald Mosley, leader of the British Union of Fascists. She decided to apply for a doctorate, and interviewed for a position editing documents at the State Department in order to earn her tuition (see Collier 2012, 23–25).

The man who hired her at Foggy Bottom in 1951 was Evron or "Kirk" Kirkpatrick, a well-connected veteran of US intelligence operations in World War II. Nearly a generation older than his new recruit, Kirk held a PhD from Yale. Immersed as they were in efforts to prevent leftist organizations from infiltrating both the Democratic Party and the federal government, members of Kirk's political and professional circles were known for their visceral and, in some cases, rabid anti-communism (see Collier 2012, 58–59).

Jeane's job entailed reviewing materials the State Department had collected on daily life in Stalinist Russia. The stories of mass starvation as well as internal Communist Party executions and purges became firmly imprinted in her mind. Taken as a group, the documents demonstrated how a repressive state could spread fear across a mass population. They recalled dossiers she had read at Columbia under the direction of Franz Neumann, who emphasized the capacity of the Nazi leadership to dominate local and national governments in Germany, and ultimately engineer mass genocide across most of continental Europe. The subject of fascism and, in particular, National Socialism both convulsed and repelled her. In her words, "I had led a pretty sheltered life up until then. I had little idea of the human capacity for evil. It was a deeply disturbing view that I acquired from these documents and from the sense I was getting of the magnitude of the Holocaust. It changed me forever" (Kirkpatrick, as quoted in Collier 2012, 24–25).

The loss of individual freedom that was inherent in totalitarian regimes, both Nazi and Stalinist, became Jeane's intellectual pivot and political passion—one she shared on a professional and increasingly personal level with Kirk. The couple wed in 1955; it was Jeane's first and only marriage, and Kirk's third, which lasted until his death forty years later. Between 1954 and his retirement in 1981, Kirk directed the Washington-based American Political Science Association.

The birth of three sons in quick succession might have deterred a less determined woman from ever returning to graduate school. Strong encouragement from Kirk, however, combined with her own interest in leaders and mass movements, led Jeane back to doctoral studies at Columbia beginning in 1963. She chose to study Argentina after a 1955 coup d'état deposed the country's autocratic president, Juan Perón. Although Argentina was clearly different from Stalinist Russia and Nazi Germany, the country's evolution provoked similar research questions: How did leaders of populist organizations come to dominate modern nation-states? Would the movement behind the charismatic leader survive his removal from power?

Results of surveys she conducted among both the Argentine public and committed Peronists pointed toward a confluence between the movement's central concerns and those of the larger society. Unlike the Nazi party's focus on destroying what it viewed as the decadence of Weimar Germany or the Russian revolutionary emphasis on eliminating czarist influences, mass mobilization in Argentina did not seek to overturn the traditional order. In this respect, Kirkpatrick's (1971) research demonstrated important variations among twentieth-century political movements, in effect contradicting US suspicions that Perón was either a communist or an admirer of European fascism. Based on her study, the political science department at Georgetown University offered Jeane a tenure-track faculty position.

Kirkpatrick completed her PhD in the spring of 1968 amidst heated, sometimes violent, campus protests against the Vietnam War. She and Kirk were at the time traditional Democrats who rejected New Left politics, including the actions of conscientious objectors and hippie pacifists. As Jeane told her biographer, "I deeply opposed attacks on the integrity of our government and culture. I always believed in the importance of truth, law and authority. Military kids grow up with such values. So do Oklahoma kids" (Kirkpatrick, as quoted in Collier 2012, 64). She later used an image from Mao's China to depict antiwar demonstrators as "American Red Guards" who adopted "objectively fascist behavior" (Kirkpatrick, as quoted in Collier 2012, 65, 70).

These perspectives set both Jeane and Kirk on a collision course with the directions of the Democratic Party. Their friend Hubert Humphrey won the 1968 presidential nomination but lost the fall election to Richard Nixon. In response to the antiwar, civil rights, and women's rights ferment of the times, Democrats agreed to create an internal commission on party structure and delegate selection known as the McGovern-Fraser Commission. Its task was to recommend significant changes to increase the involvement of youths, blacks, and women.

Jeane Kirkpatrick was drawn to the research opportunities presented by this turn of events. In 1972, she attended a conference of fifty women state legislators in order to study their backgrounds and contributions to public life. Kirkpatrick (1974, 219) describes the legislators she met as "women who accept and embody the traditional role definitions. . . . Almost all are wives and mothers and, in addition, most concur in the traditional view that these roles have priority at various times over other commitments. Well-groomed, well-mannered, decorous in speech and action, these are 'feminine' women in the traditional sex-stereotyped sense of that word."

About 60 percent of the politicians at the conference opposed what Kirkpatrick (1974, 164) terms the "women's liberation movement." They rejected claims that women constituted an exploited social group and instead saw the movement as anti-marriage and anti-family. In a passage that parallels views she expressed in essays during the same period, Kirkpatrick (1974, 165) summarizes the lawmakers' view that "women's liberation is a branch of radical politics—and so is regarded with the same distaste as they regard the counter culture, the 'new' politics, student riots, dropouts and flag burners. The belief that women's liberation is anti-system, an impression created by its most radical spokeswomen, does not enhance its attraction for women with a generally good opinion of the society and government."

Kirkpatrick also surveyed thousands of delegates to the 1972 Democratic and Republican Party conventions. They included the mass of new recruits who entered the Democratic organization due to the McGovern-Fraser Commission recommendations. In a more than 600-page study titled *The New Presidential Elite*, Kirkpatrick (1976, 41–43) makes clear her opposition to internal party reforms. In her view, changes introduced after 1968 responded primarily to the anti–Vietnam War agenda of Democrats who opposed Humphrey's candidacy, rather than to a more defensible set of priorities concerning the representation of citizens.

Kirkpatrick (1976, 380) focuses on the feminist dimension of the story: she maintains that members of the party commission caved in to such groups as the National Women's Political Caucus that were "speaking in the name of other women." She identifies Bella Abzug and Gloria Steinem by name, maintaining that they and other Caucus activists supported antiwar presidential candidate George McGovern in 1972 (Kirkpatrick 1976, 448). As revealed in passages like the one quoted in the introduction to this chapter, her book condemns efforts to replace experienced Democratic partisans who were grounded in their local communities and knew how to win elections, with a "new elite" that had both weak party roots and strong allegiance to multiple causes outside the organization.

Kirkpatrick's decision to vote for Nixon in the 1972 presidential election revealed the depths of her estrangement from the Democratic Party (see Collier 2012, 84). She joined early neoconservative networks, including the Coalition for a Democratic Majority and the Committee on the Present Danger, composed of disgruntled Democrats and ex-Democrats who believed their party with its roots in Roosevelt's New Deal was being hijacked by countercultural interests from outside the social mainstream (see Collier 2012, 84–90).

During the 1970s, *Commentary* magazine served as the leading voice of liberals fleeing the Democratic Party. The outlet published a steady stream of writing on the threats posed by New Left influences—whether to higher education, America's cities, or capitalism writ large. Neoconservative prose was tenacious and spirited, as befits the zeal of authors newly converted to the cause of preserving tradition (see Dorrien 1993; Ehrman 1996; Himmelstein 1990).

Jeane Kirkpatrick published her first *Commentary* essay in February 1973. Titled "The Revolt of the Masses," the article presents a shorter, more popular version of the thesis she later developed in *The New Presidential Elite*. It helped to raise her profile from that of a respected Georgetown academic with experience in the Humphrey campaign toward the ranks of the neoconservative elite, arguably the most influential group at the time among American public intellectuals.

Using trenchant, hard-hitting prose, Kirkpatrick (1973) lashes out against the McGovern faction's abandonment of the Democratic majority in the US electorate. The article focuses on McGovern's decision to run an outsider campaign, one he said was "built around the poor and the minorities and the young people and the anti-war movement" (McGovern, as quoted in Kirkpatrick 1973, 59). According to Kirkpatrick (1973), pursuing a "new politics" approach embedded in anti-establishment values alienated large masses of voters because it severed links between the Democratic Party, on one side, and its traditional base among white, blue-collar patriots who saw McGovern as rejecting their values, on the other.

In contrasting old versus new politics, Kirkpatrick (1973) explains her specific objections to women's movement activism of the time. "The Revolt of the Masses" celebrates the pragmatic, compromising ways of Texas Democrat Lyndon Johnson, while dismissing the rigid and immoderate approach of New York Congresswoman Bella Abzug. As a civil rights activist who opposed the Vietnam War, endorsed gay rights, and helped to found the National Women's Political Caucus, Abzug bore the brunt of Kirkpatrick's (1973, 61) critique: "Bella Abzug, with her noisy distrust of leadership, her energetic confrontations, and her adversary demeanor, is almost a caricature of the style of the [New Politics]." Abzug's approach made her a polar opposite of both Kirkpatrick and the more traditional state lawmakers she surveyed.

Kirkpatrick's (1973) main explanation for the Nixon victory in 1972 was as follows: Americans who disapproved of street riots outside the 1968 Democratic convention in Chicago were unnerved by the presence of antiwar demonstrators and their supporters inside the party gathering four years later in Miami. She portrays McGovern as a poor presidential candidate given his "very real weaknesses in organizational and leadership skills" (Kirkpatrick 1973, 58). Above all, Kirkpatrick (1973, 59–60) writes, "McGovern came to be perceived by millions of Americans as a man who had gone over to the enemy"—that is, forces she saw as threatening US interests in Southeast Asia and elsewhere.

Kirkpatrick served as a policy advisor in 1976 to Henry "Scoop" Jackson, a Democrat who shared her hawkish and pro-Israel views (see Collier 2012, 90–91). Once Jackson lost the Democratic presidential nomination to Carter, Kirkpatrick and other neoconservatives effectively became free agents. The party that had shaped their political experiences won the White House, but rested in the hands of decision-makers with an entirely different worldview. At the same time, advisors to a leading Republican candidate began to make their own overtures.

ENTERING THE INNER CIRCLE

Following the publication in 1979 of "Dictatorships and Double Standards," Jeane Kirkpatrick held a series of meetings with Ronald Reagan and decided to endorse him. She provided valuable advice in the run-up to the sole televised debate between Reagan and Carter, held a week before the 1980 presidential election. Thanks to Kirkpatrick and other members of his foreign policy team, Reagan was well prepared (see Collier 2012, 110). He remained calm and upbeat, despite Carter's effort to portray him as a virulent, dangerous hawk.

In closing, Reagan presented a set of unsettling questions. He asked Americans: "Are you better off now than you were four years ago? . . . Is America as respected throughout the world as it was? Do you feel that our security is as safe, that we're as strong as we were four years ago?" (Commission on Presidential Debates 1980). Reagan's implicit response was clear: Carter had sent the economy into a tailspin at the same time as he'd frittered away America's postwar military advantage. Above all, the holding of US diplomats as hostages in Tehran reflected an abject security failure.

Reagan's debate performance effectively translated to a general audience the foreign policy ideas outlined in "Dictatorships and Double Standards." Millions of voters who had deserted the Democratic Party in 1972—the masses whose revolt Kirkpatrick (1973) plumbed in the pages of *Commentary*—were captivated by his message. On election night, the Reagan team turned a tight contest into a rout, sweeping forty-four states and more than half the popular vote.

One month later, while she attended an event sponsored by the American Friends of Hebrew University, Kirkpatrick received a message asking her to telephone the president-elect. Reagan invited her to serve as his UN ambassador. She accepted the offer after posing a disarming question, "Are you sure you think I can do the job?" (Kirkpatrick, as quoted in Collier 2012, 114). With Reagan's firm reassurance in hand, the ambassador designate set out to bolster her position within the new administration. She would hold cabinet status—becoming the only woman of that rank in the first Reagan administration—as well as seats on the White House National Security Council (NSC) and the National Security Planning Group.

Since Jeane planned to engage fully in the work of the United Nations as well as meetings in Washington, she and Kirk decided she would shuttle back and forth from the capital to New York. Their three sons were all in their twenties, but one of them had problems that would long prove troubling. Douglas Jordan Kirkpatrick, the eldest, first showed signs of alcohol abuse in high school (Collier 2012, 82). His difficulties strained family relations to the point that Jeane confessed to a friend during his undergraduate years that she would "trade it all, this and everything else, if only Douglas could be normal" (Kirkpatrick statement to Margaret Lefever, as quoted in Collier 2012, 82). On one occasion after she became UN ambassador, Douglas demanded to see his mother at the US mission in New York, was refused, and began a "drunken scuffle" with guards at the building (Collier 2012, 119). Douglas married three times, threatened a woman he met at a private rehabilitation facility with a knife, and lived temporarily with Jeane's brother in Ohio while she served as ambassador (see Collier 2012, 195–196; Cox News 1989).

Despite these challenges, Kirkpatrick built a cohesive team at the US mission in New York. She named Charles Lichenstein, a veteran of the Nixon White House, as deputy ambassador. José Sorzano, a Cuban refugee and former graduate student, became first representative on the Economic and Social Council. Carl Gershman, a fierce anti-communist she knew from Democratic Party circles, served as chief counselor while Allan Gerson, a former Justice Department prosecutor of Nazi war crimes, was legal advisor (see Gerson 1991).

The ambassador designate described their workplace as "the glass house where everyone throws stones" (Kirkpatrick, as quoted in Collier 2012, 125). In presenting her credentials to the Senate Foreign Relations Committee, Kirkpatrick (1981) outlined how she would assertively defend US interests in that environment: "I think the United Nations Ambassador should seek neither confrontation with other delegates, nor shirk from confrontation when that is necessary to defend American values or national integrity. I assure you that I will engage neither in bluster and bragging, nor in self-abasement in my dealings public or private with delegates from the United Nations' other 152 members." Kirkpatrick (1981) argued that while the organization in some instances contributed constructively to world affairs, at times "the United Nations has been little more than an international forum, whose only official language is doublespeak." She promised that if her nomination were approved, she would communicate precisely and directly with all UN members and agencies.

The ambassador designate then demonstrated her ability to speak with clarity and candor. She informed senators that as the largest single donor to the United Nations, the United States contributed nearly a quarter of the organization's total budget. Kirkpatrick (1981) cited a 1979 report by the US General Accounting Office, which concluded that the return on American investment was "uncertain, in part because of our lack of clear objectives."

Kirkpatrick promised to rectify that problem. After reviewing her academic qualifications and record of sustained public involvement, including as a Democrat, she said the United Nations' core mandate was to look after refugees, children's health, and disaster relief. She would not only press the organization to uphold its purpose, but also firmly discourage "agencies which engage in mischievous ideological struggle against the fundamental principles and interests of the United States and its friends" (Kirkpatrick 1981). In her view, the aims of the incoming presidential team were "both less utopian and more modest than those of some previous administrations. This should, I believe, make them in the end more realistic and achievable goals, and provide us with more workable guides" (Kirkpatrick 1981). Senators on the committee unanimously approved her nomination.

FEISTY DIPLOMAT

Ronald Reagan's diary entry for July 28, 1981, barely six months into his first term, records the following impression conveyed by Kirkpatrick at a private meeting: "She says the U.N. is a worse can of worms than even she had anticipated" (Reagan 2007, 33). Kirkpatrick reported to Reagan in November 1982 that the United Nations was "a miserable place" (Reagan 2007, 110). By that point, Reagan sensed, she was ready to quit (see Reagan 2007, 110). Kirkpatrick remained in the position until 1985, however, and measurably redirected American foreign policy away from the legacy of the Carter years.

In early 1981, Kirkpatrick used her training as a political scientist to understand her new surroundings. She analyzed voting patterns in the UN General Assembly, and found that coalitions of Arab, African, Soviet-aligned, and ostensibly nonaligned countries formed blocs whose members were unwilling to criticize each other. Since European countries failed to rebut charges of neocolonialism, delegates from that continent, in her words, "have long since accepted their prescribed role, grown accustomed to being 'it' in a global game of dunk-the-clown, and have opted to 'understand' the point of view of their Third World accusers" (Kirkpatrick, as quoted in Collier 2012, 125). According to Kirkpatrick, only the United States and Israel lacked bloc support. Both countries were routinely singled out for condemnation and, during the Carter years, American ambassadors failed to assist Israel.

America's new emissary made clear her intention to confront what she viewed as not just a dysfunctional UN system, but also a less than optimal US mission. Kirkpatrick ordered posters for the New York office featuring the face of long-time Chicago mayor Richard J. Daley. She selected that image to remind staffers that they represented the United States inside the United Nations, rather than vice versa (Kirkpatrick conversation with Gerson, July 1981, as reported in Gerson 1991, 24). Kirkpatrick (as quoted in Collier 2012, 127) believed Daley's presence would recall a crucial political lesson, since "he knew the difference between winning and losing and [understood] that winning was better."

As UN ambassador, Kirkpatrick focused on three main goals that followed directly from her 1979 text. First, she sought to weaken Soviet influence; second, she would support individual rights around the world, including in the Middle East, where Kirkpatrick saw democratic Israel as besieged by enemies committed to the destruction of the Jewish state; and third, she wanted to reform the United Nations and, in particular, to curtail the organization's spendthrift ways. She pursued each aim through a series of calculated steps that moved the goalposts forward, often in interrelated ways.

On the first point, Kirkpatrick worked to prevent the election of pro-Soviet states to the UN Security Council. Although she failed in 1981 and

1982 to block Guyana and Nicaragua from gaining seats, her 1984 effort to stop Mongolia was successful. Moreover, during the Soviet occupation of Afghanistan, the United States won support for multiple resolutions calling for a withdrawal of foreign troops from that country (see Finger 1988, Chapter 9).

After meeting in Havana in the fall of 1981, a group of nonaligned UN members released a communiqué critical of American actions. Kirkpatrick (as quoted in Finger 1988, 295) sent an acerbic response to what she termed "a document composed of such base lies and malicious attacks upon the good name of the United States." She reminded all the signatories that if they wanted their nations to be considered "friendly" to the United States, they needed to dissociate themselves from "such charges" (Kirkpatrick, as quoted in Gerson 1991, 79). Kirkpatrick's missive was so undiplomatic that *Time* magazine (1981, 24) described it as a "letter bomb." Kirkpatrick's own legal advisor recalls that many ambassadors who received her letter were apologetic, and indeed were surprised that the new US emissary had even read their statement. In his words, "Those who received the letter realized that as she was taking their words seriously, she demanded the same of them. Her detractors deemed this attitude 'combative.' For better or worse it was a reputation that would stick to her, and the members of her team, until the end" (Gerson 1991, 79–80).

Among the most tense moments of the Cold War twilight occurred two years later, when a Soviet missile shot down an unarmed civilian jet over the Sea of Japan. The Korean Air Lines plane was en route from New York to Seoul via Alaska. All 269 passengers and crew members died. Secretary of State George Schultz, as well as President Reagan, harshly condemned the action, but Soviet spokesmen refused to take responsibility.

The Soviet approach changed once Jeane Kirkpatrick rose in the Security Council to offer audiovisual evidence of how the event unfolded. She played a recording of the Soviet fighter pilots' radio communications, and showed, using a flight map, how the air-to-air missiles they fired caused the jet to fall into the sea. The official Soviet news agency then admitted the plane had been shot down, but claimed the Korean pilot had ignored warnings to leave prohibited airspace (see Collier 2012, 143).

On a Security Council vote condemning the Soviet Union, Zimbabwe abstained. Kirkpatrick used that decision to demonstrate the cost of failing to support US positions. She succeeded in imposing sanctions, despite attempts by the African Affairs desk at the State Department as well as the Congressional Black Caucus to prevent them (see Finger 1988, 296).

As of December 1983, US aid to Zimbabwe was nearly halved from $75 to $40 million (see *New York Times* 1983b).

Holding the Soviets and their allies to account dovetailed closely with Kirkpatrick's second priority: defending American values and the legitimacy of countries that uphold democratic rights. Nowhere was this goal more rigorously pursued than in actions related to the Middle East. As Finger (1988, 363) argues in his survey of twelve postwar diplomats, "No US representative to the UN has been a firmer friend of Israel than Jeane Kirkpatrick." The list of ambassadors to whom Finger (1988) compares her includes former Supreme Court justice Arthur Goldberg, the first Jew to serve as US ambassador to the United Nations.

In a 1981 memo to Secretary of State Al Haig, Kirkpatrick explains why the US should defend Israel at every turn. Resolutions attacking Israel, she writes, "are part of the ongoing campaign at the UN to equate Zionism with racism and Israeli practices in the occupied territories with Nazi atrocities" (Kirkpatrick, as quoted in Gerson 1991, 60). She argues that efforts to isolate Israel should be resisted by a new administration committed to reliability and consistency in foreign policy. As the memo concludes, "There is the matter of the integrity of what we say and do at the UN" (Kirkpatrick, as quoted in Gerson 1991, 60).

In Kirkpatrick's view, previous UN ambassadors—with the support of both the State Department and members of the diplomatic team in New York—mistakenly supported or tolerated anti-Israel initiatives. According to Gerson (1991, 65), Kirkpatrick chafed under instructions from Washington, and specifically the State Department hierarchy she referred to as "the Building." Those pressures caused her to vote in 1981 to censure Israel for attacking a nuclear reactor under construction in Iraq. Without her forceful intervention, Kirkpatrick told Gerson (1991, 14), directions from Washington would have seen the United States endorse a UN resolution condemning Israeli "aggression" against Iraq. To the new head of the mission in New York, Israel's decision to bomb the reactor constituted a necessary act of self-preservation.

Kirkpatrick (as quoted in Gerson 1991, 23) informed her legal advisor that she was unnerved by the willingness of European allies to see "Israel as a terrible embarrassment and nuisance." At the same time, Arab countries saw Israel "as a 'Crusader remnant'" of brief duration (Kirkpatrick, as quoted in Gerson 1991, 23). Gerson's first assignment was to find a way to limit any further erosion of Israel's status, by developing a rationale to stop the Palestine Liberation Organization (PLO) from doubling the size of its UN observer mission from two to four members. Both Kirkpatrick and Gerson rejected ideas that the PLO was working toward greater self-determination for oppressed Palestinians, and instead saw the group as a thinly disguised terrorist organization. Even though Gerson developed a compelling argument against more observers, Kirkpatrick's memo on the subject ended up buried in the State Department bureaucracy and never reached Haig's desk. The secretary of state approved the PLO request (see Gerson 1991, 43).

This turn of events reinforced the ambassador's commitment to supporting Israel and using financial penalties to backstop her position. As a 1981 conference on African refugees became bogged down in debates over the admission of Israel's delegate, Kirkpatrick offered an ultimatum to Arab states: unless the Israeli representative was seated, the United States would leave and take with it a $285 million pledge toward addressing the refugee problem. In the choice between what the US chief of mission called "vile rhetoric" and funding, her opponents took the money (Kirkpatrick, as quoted in Collier 2012, 131).

In spring 1982, a Jewish man from Baltimore opened fire at the Dome of the Rock mosque in Jerusalem. Two Arabs praying at the holy site were killed and about forty injured. The American was charged with murder, and Israel's UN ambassador deplored what he termed "a despicable act of sacrilege" by one person (Ambassador Yehuda Blum, as quoted in Gerson 1991, 102). Once the Arab bloc took the matter to the Security Council, Kirkpatrick faced threats that she would endanger US citizens around the world if she stopped a resolution that made Israel responsible for the crime and referred to Jerusalem as occupied Arab land. Kirkpatrick vetoed the proposal—one of fourteen resolutions she blocked in her first three years as ambassador. Her predecessor in the Carter administration, Andrew Young, vetoed a total of three resolutions during his initial three years (see Finger 1988, 313).

Kirkpatrick's last goal of organizational reform attracted support from an unexpected quarter. The Soviet Union had for more than twenty years refused to contribute toward what it viewed as excessive spending on UN peacekeeping. Together with the British and Soviet ambassadors, Kirkpatrick appealed in the fall of 1982 to the secretary-general to contain spiraling costs. She also appended a clause to each General Assembly resolution that increased spending. It stated that in no case would UN obligations exceed the organization's approved budget (see Finger 1988, 311–312). Taken together, these actions signaled to UN leaders that the United States was no longer writing blank checks or turning a blind eye to the actions of other member states.

Kirkpatrick's clear policy agenda and her frustrations with the State Department hierarchy help to explain why she sought to rise above the rank of UN ambassador. Yet her ambitions came to naught, in large part because of events surrounding a group of windy, barren, largely forgotten islands in the South Atlantic, ruled by Britain since the 1830s and counter-claimed by Argentina to this day. The Falklands crisis embroiled Kirkpatrick in a public dispute that revealed conflicts between her deepest philosophical beliefs, on one side, and those of other members of the cabinet and of Reagan's key ally in the United Kingdom, on the other.

When war broke out between Britain and Argentina in the spring of 1982, Margaret Thatcher had led Britain's Conservative Party for seven years and a majority government for three. She had learned how to manage the egos of the men in her cabinet—and, with one brief exception, they were entirely men (see Bashevkin 1998, 24–25). Her speaking abilities were exceptional, whether she addressed a small group in person or millions on television. Thatcher commanded admiration at the highest levels of global politics, reaching inside Republican circles to cultivate a warm, collegial relationship with Ronald Reagan (see Campbell 2008).

Within this larger scenario, Jeane Kirkpatrick stood as an academic and public intellectual turned diplomat who was ideologically close with Reagan and met regularly with him. Yet her political support base did not extend far beyond the neoconservative network. In fact, Kirkpatrick's legal advisor at the UN describes her as an outsider with "next to no acquaintance with how the U.S. Government actually ran" (Gerson 1991, 39). Her relations with other members of the cabinet, such as Secretary of State Al Haig, were known to be strained. As Reagan (2007, 87; punctuation as in original text) observes in a diary entry dated spring 1982, "She and Al H. have been at each others throats."

Haig arrived in his position after a military career that included five years as Supreme Allied Commander in Europe. Kirkpatrick, by contrast, came from the less stratified realm of universities and think tanks. At her confirmation hearing, she told members of the Senate Foreign Relations Committee that she expected the secretary of state "to serve as the general manager of American diplomacy" who was open to input from individual players on the team:

> I also believe the United Nations Ambassador should not be merely a passive reflector, a ventriloquist dummy, if you will, for policies in which she has no role

in formulating. As a member of the Cabinet of this administration, if confirmed, I expect to make a regular and meaningful contribution to the development of foreign policy of the Reagan administration, which at the UN, it will then be my job to articulate, explain and defend. (Kirkpatrick 1981)

Haig's command-and-control style, alongside Kirkpatrick's insistence on applying her own knowledge and insight, created a combustible combination.

Kirkpatrick (1979) maintains that autocratic leaders in Latin America deserved a far more sympathetic hearing in Washington than they generally received. Her endorsement of cordial relations with Argentina, the site of her doctoral research, did not go unnoticed. One evening in early April 1982, Kirkpatrick was the guest of honor at a gala dinner hosted by Argentina's ambassador to the United States. Thatcher (1993, 180) bitterly recalls this turn of events in her memoir, writing, "As our ambassador later asked [Kirkpatrick]: how would Americans have felt if he had dined at the Iranian Embassy the night that the American hostages were seized in Tehran?"

Hundreds of Argentine troops landed the next day on what they called the Islas Malvinas. Despite Haig's claim that Kirkpatrick had prior knowledge of the invasion, she insists she was caught off guard both by Argentina's decision to send forces and Britain's determination to dispatch its own military (see Collier 2012, 135). In her words, "I thought it inconceivable that . . . a European power would send a ragtag armada 8,000 miles to fight for a place inhabited by 1,000 sheepherders" (Kirkpatrick, as quoted in Collier 2012, 135).

Kirkpatrick met regularly during the Falklands crisis with her Argentine contacts, including the foreign minister. She tried to convince them to agree to Britain's conditions for calling off a military response. These discussions were, according to some accounts, approved in advance by Reagan's national security advisor (see Collier 2012, 136; Gerson 1991, 118). Reagan telephoned Thatcher in the spring of 1982, asking her to agree to a ceasefire, apparently after Kirkpatrick exerted pressure on him (see Campbell 2008, 152).

Haig sought to broker a diplomatic solution, traveling tens of thousands of miles to meet both sides (see Hopkins 2008, 232). Defense Secretary Caspar Weinberger (1990, 213) offered assistance to the British forces, in his words, "to help with everything short of actual participation in the military action itself." British planes were allowed, for example, to refuel at an American-operated airfield on Ascension Island. Weinberger (1990, 212) recalls that given the long distance to the South Atlantic, military advisors in both the United States and United Kingdom believed "the British decision to retake the Falklands was a futile and impossible effort."

As the conflict escalated, debates inside the administration pitted Kirkpatrick's support for neutrality against her colleagues' endorsement of Britain. The UN emissary claimed that Argentina was a solid and nearby ally, including in efforts to weaken the Sandinista government in Nicaragua. She believed any position other than neutrality would damage relations with a valued friend and with Latin America generally. In NSC meetings, the secretary of defense opposed that view. Weinberger (1990, 207) maintains in his memoirs that

> the rest of Latin American had no interest in helping an invasion perpetrated by the Argentine military dictators; that there would be no support by other South American countries for Argentina; that there would be no adverse reactions by any of those countries if we helped Britain. On the other hand, there would be fury in the British Isles, and serious loss of confidence in America as a friend among our NATO and our Pacific allies—and among Latin American nations too—if we supinely accepted aggression, and stood by wringing our hands as we talked "negotiations" and "settlements."

Reagan chose at the end of April to endorse Britain's position, which called for immediate Argentine withdrawal from the islands. Haig instructed Kirkpatrick to support the United Kingdom at the Security Council by vetoing a ceasefire resolution (see Collier 2012, 138).

Kirkpatrick appealed to Haig to reconsider once the military balance tipped heavily in Britain's favor (see Collier 2012, 138). When the Security Council met on June 4, he was away at an international summit in France with Reagan, Thatcher, and others.[1] The ambassador voted as directed, only to receive a message moments later instructing her to abstain. The drama reached a crescendo as Kirkpatrick, suspicious as to why Haig was suddenly on her side, told chief counselor Carl Gershman to explain by telephone that she had already voted and that votes could not be reversed. Haig relayed instructions back to the ambassador to announce that her directions were to abstain. Kirkpatrick asked Gershman to tell Haig that she was not prepared to make the US delegation look weak and chaotic. Gershman returned with the secretary of state's ultimatum: "You are instructed to announce publicly that you were supposed to vote for an abstention" (Haig instructions, as quoted in Gerson 1991, 129).

Kirkpatrick followed those directions, but in a strikingly independent way. Her address to the Security Council lamented the United Nations' inability to broker peace in a centuries-old conflict. This was a confusing statement, since it came from a delegate who had just vetoed a cease-fire resolution. Kirkpatrick then read a poem by Argentine writer Jorge Luis Borges that deplored the loss of life in conflict. She expressed a personal hope "that Argentina will have few such offerings from this war" (Kirkpatrick, as quoted in Gerson 1991, 130). No mention was made of British casualties.

Kirkpatrick then announced the following: "My government has been rent by a clash of values, loyalties and friends. That clash continued even to the registration of the vote on this issue. I am told it is impossible for a government to change a vote once cast, but I have been requested by my government to record the fact that were it possible to change our vote we should like to change it from a veto—a 'No,' that is—to an abstention" (Kirkpatrick, as quoted in Collier 2012, 138–139). In a speech a few days later to the Heritage Foundation, she suggested that the United States risked being viewed as "amateurish" unless it learned to operate more effectively in international forums (Kirkpatrick, as quoted in Collier 2012, 139).[2]

Unlike her previous status as a scholar and public intellectual, Kirkpatrick in 1982 held a senior position in the political executive. As such, her remarks to the Heritage Foundation were seen as inappropriate criticisms of a fellow cabinet member, the secretary of state. Influential editorials and columns poured forth, including in the *New York Times*. They portrayed the UN ambassador as biased in favor of Argentina, less than professionally capable, and better suited to academic than diplomatic work (see Collier 2012, 139).

Once reporters asked why he had not communicated directly with Kirkpatrick about how to vote, Haig said, "You don't talk to a company commander when you have a corps in between" (Haig, as quoted in *New York Times* 1982). Kirkpatrick offered her response on a major current affairs program: "To tell you the truth, I don't even know anything about company commanders. I don't know really much about military rank and military titles, and I don't even care much about military rank and military titles" (Kirkpatrick statement on *Meet the Press*, as quoted in *New York Times* 1982). She confessed that such terms may be "more meaningful to Secretary Haig, who is, after all a general, than they are to me, a professor in my ordinary life" (Kirkpatrick statement on *Meet the Press*, as quoted in *New York Times* 1982). As an outsider "maverick," in the words of one of her closest advisors, Kirkpatrick was not prepared to let a consummate insider ease her out the door (Gerson 1991, 25).

Haig sent Reagan a letter of resignation in late June, believing it would be rejected (see Collier 2012, 140). Instead, the president accepted Haig's offer and appointed George Shultz as his successor. At the time, Kirkpatrick was away on a visit to Togo. Her Soviet counterpart at the United Nations remarked that she was the only hunter who had felled her prey in Washington while off on safari in Africa (see Finger 1988, 298).

At least initially, Kirkpatrick and her staff welcomed the prospect of working with Shultz. Not only was his interpersonal style more polished and civil than that of Haig, but also Shultz and Kirkpatrick held similar positions on many substantive issues. For example, they agreed on threatening to withdraw from the General Assembly and curtailing payments to the United Nations if Israel were thrown out (see Gerson 1991, 176).[3] Yet the 1982 Lebanon crisis imperilled their relationship. Kirkpatrick worked with Israeli, Arab, and European delegations in New York while her colleagues tried in Lebanon and elsewhere to secure the transfer of PLO fighters from Beirut, ultimately to Tunis. Kirkpatrick resented that she remained outside the main channels of discussion within the administration, even under a new secretary of state (see Gerson 1991, 171).

Diplomatic turf wars seemed to wear her down. As Gerson (1991, 139) asks, "Had battle fatigue set in? It is not easy to say repeatedly 'No' when everyone else is urging you to say 'Yes.' Endless negotiation and the strain of petty squabbling, a way of life for others, was not her métier. She didn't relish the fight. Public reputation aside, the 'conflictual' element of her personality was not, as we knew, as dominant as others might think." Gerson (1991) observes that even though Kirkpatrick enjoyed intellectual give-and-take, she resented the constant need to cultivate influence and ward off competitors inside a presidential administration.

Aware of her frustration, Reagan asked Kirkpatrick to travel to Central America in early 1983 and report her findings directly to him. She visited Costa Rica, El Salvador, Honduras, and Panama. Her impressions coincided closely with views expressed years before (see Kirkpatrick 1979). Stated simply, the fall of the Somoza dictatorship in Nicaragua had permitted the rise of a Soviet- and Cuban-backed Sandinista regime that was exporting revolution to the rest of the region. The pro-American government in El Salvador was at risk of imploding as a result (see Collier 2012, 151).

Kirkpatrick saw the State Department as largely complicit in each of these developments. Much like members of the liberal intelligentsia who ignored Soviet intentions in the Western hemisphere, some US diplomats believed that Marxist guerrillas were liberating the people of El Salvador. Kirkpatrick reported that the idea of compromising with Cuban-inspired revolutionaries had spread as far as Deane Hinton, Reagan's appointee as ambassador to El Salvador. The president's diary entry for February 17, 1983 records his response to the impressions Kirkpatrick conveyed. In his words, the UN envoy recounted "[a] grim story. Our Ambas. Hinton under the direction of the same kind of St. Dept. Bureaucrats who made Castro possible are screwing up the situation in El Salvador. I'm now really mad" (Reagan 2007, 132). He writes that CIA director Bill Casey will update Secretary of State Shultz, following which "I'm determined heads will roll, beginning with Ambas. Hinton" (Reagan 2007, 132). Within months, Reagan fired not only Hinton but also the assistant secretary of state for Latin America (see *New York Times* 1983a).

Kirkpatrick's ability to shape these decisions reflected her ideological closeness with Reagan, as well as their personal rapport (see Collier 2012, xiii). Moreover, it revealed the unusual status of every American ambassador to the United Nations. Under the terms of legislation passed by Congress in 1945, appointees hold a direct reporting relationship to the president and, for that reason, potentially wield more clout than diplomats who work strictly for the secretary of state (see Gerson 1991, 28).

Kirkpatrick's role in Central America, however, unleashed the same kinds of attacks she had experienced during the Falklands crisis. Critics seized on Reagan's actions as evidence that he was being pressed toward extreme positions by advisors including Kirkpatrick, Casey, Weinberger, and national security advisor Bill Clark. Moderates such as Shultz, White House chief of staff James Baker, and Baker's deputy Mike Deaver were seen as increasingly marginalized by the hardliners. Some accounts maintain that Shultz only offered to remove his assistant for Latin America after Reagan agreed to cede full control over policy in that region to the State Department (see Gwertzman 1983; LeoGrande 1998, 221).

Kirkpatrick lashed out at her critics, this time in an essay published in the *Washington Post*. Under the title "Pardon me, but am I that hardliner the anonymous sources are talking about," she argued that the United States needed to counteract a growing leftist insurgency in El Salvador. She recommended American military assistance, rather than direct intervention, as the best route toward that goal (see Collier 2012, 151–152).

In his memoirs, Shultz (1993, 310) contends that he was not briefed in advance about large-scale US military exercises in Central America during the summer of 1983. He worried that Weinberger, Clark, and Kirkpatrick had Reagan's ear, possibly to the point of convincing the president to blockade Nicaragua. As Shultz (1993, 312) observes, "I was totally out of the decision loop . . . I could not trust the answers I got from the White House staff. The functions of the secretary of state were being usurped by the NSC staff." When called to testify before the Senate Foreign Relations Committee in early August, Shultz said he regretted not having consulted with legislators prior to the military exercises (see Deseret News 1983).

In the same period, Shultz learned that Clark's deputy, Bud McFarlane, had visited six Middle East countries. Outraged that the White House and, in particular, the NSC were continuing to erode the authority of the secretary of state, Shultz met Reagan to convey his views. He offered to resign (see Gottlieb 1987; LeoGrande 1998, 221).

Rather than risking the loss of Shultz, Reagan appointed Clark as secretary of the interior. Kirkpatrick made known her interest in the vacant post of national security advisor—an appointment that would situate her entirely in Washington and reunite her family at a time when Kirk was aging and Douglas's alcoholism showed no sign of abating. Above all, the promotion would place her closer to a president with whom she shared many core values. The president knew, in his words, that "Jeanne wants out of the U.N." (Reagan 2007, 187; spelling as in original).

In the fall of 1983, Kirkpatrick's supporters (likely including Casey and Weinberger) lobbied Reagan directly. Shultz (1993, 320), by contrast, argued that he "respected her intelligence, but she was not well suited to the job. Her strength was in her capacity for passionate advocacy. She was not at all the dispassionate broker and faithful representative of divergent positions that the national security advisor needs to be." Aware of that opposition, Reagan (2007, 187) noted the "bad chemistry" that would result from pairing Shultz at State with Kirkpatrick at the NSC.

In mid-October, Reagan appointed McFarlane as national security advisor. At least two accounts suggest that Nancy Reagan exercised the decisive veto against Kirkpatrick's promotion (see Collier 2012, 162; Shultz 1993, 319). The advice of the first lady may have been grounded in a view that peace with the Soviets would enhance Reagan's legacy; therefore, her husband needed to weaken the influence of administration hardliners (see Collier 2012, 161). Moreover, Nancy was said to feel uneasy about Ronald's attraction to Kirkpatrick. According to one close observer, "Jeane and Margaret Thatcher were the only two women who made Nancy nervous. The president had an intellectual spark with both of them" (Richard Allen, as quoted in Collier 2012, xiii).

The day McFarlane's appointment was announced, Kirkpatrick met for an hour with the president. She said she wanted to return to Washington, and made clear her hopes for a promotion within the administration.

Figure 3.2. Ambassador Jeane Kirkpatrick addresses UN Security Council on crisis in Lebanon, 1984.

AP Photo; photo by Joel Landau.

Reagan offered her a position as his international affairs advisor but, as he writes, "I couldn't convince her it was a job where she'd have a real voice in determining policy" (Reagan 2007, 188). They agreed she would consider the invitation, and held conversations about it in the subsequent months. As shown in Figure 3.2, Kirkpatrick maintained a vigorous public presence in her role as UN ambassador.

ASSESSING PUBLIC LEADERSHIP

In the absence of a better offer from the president, Kirkpatrick remained as UN ambassador through early 1985. She continued to craft and defend the main lines of US foreign policy, including the invasion of Grenada in October 1983, which she portrayed as a response to requests by the country's Caribbean neighbors to limit communist influence (see Collier 2012, 156–157). Along with Casey, she endorsed the National Security Planning Group decision in June 1984 to fund the Contras in Nicaragua after Congress cut off support. Shultz (1993, 413, 808) writes that he firmly opposed that choice.

The Iran-Contra scandal followed from efforts to transfer US arms via Israel to reputedly moderate elements of the regime in Tehran, and then funnel the proceeds to anti-Sandinista groups in Central America. Proponents of the deal inside the Reagan administration believed the arrangement would assist the Contras and also encourage Iran's ally in Lebanon, the Hezbollah, to release American hostages. Kirkpatrick's support became public knowledge when McFarlane testified at a congressional hearing that "he should have stood up against the initiative to secretly support the contras. But 'if I'd done that,' he said, 'Bill Casey, Jeane Kirkpatrick and Cap Weinberger would have said I was some kind of commie'" (Weiner 2006).

In Kirkpatrick's view, excessive legislative meddling in US foreign policy rested at the heart of the imbroglio. If Congress had allowed funding for the Contras, then the CIA would not have needed to find a circuitous alternative (see Collier 2012, 172). In a eulogy delivered at Casey's funeral in 1987, Kirkpatrick rejected the officiating bishop's criticism of administration policies in Central America. Reagan's (2007, 495) diary records his delight at her lively defense of aid to the Contras, which elicited applause from the assembled mourners.

By the time Kirkpatrick stepped down as UN ambassador in April 1985, Reagan had secured a strong second mandate—winning forty-nine of fifty states in the 1984 presidential contest. The GOP captured close to 60 percent of the popular vote in a two-way race, despite Geraldine Ferraro's status as the first female vice-presidential candidate in a major party, and despite endorsements the Democrats received from the National Organization for Women, the National Abortion Rights Action League, and the National Women's Political Caucus. Efforts to increase voter registration rates among women in order to maximize support for the Mondale/Ferraro ticket also failed to turn the tide (see Melich 1996, 179–180).

Feminist attempts to defeat Reagan were closely linked to his administration's record on women's rights. Not only did Republican policies limit domestic progress in areas including legal equality, reproductive choice, and employment rights, they also extended a socially conservative agenda to American foreign policy (see Bashevkin 1998). As Finkle and Crane (1985) show, pro-life interests lobbied Reagan and his advisors heavily in the months before the 1984 election in order to block US funding for abortion and family planning services in developing countries. Jeane Kirkpatrick remarked that providing foreign aid without those services was akin to "pouring water into a bucket with a hole in it," which suggests she did not endorse what became known as the Mexico City policy (see Fornos

1988; Gupte 1984). Yet at no point did Kirkpatrick actively use her diplomatic position to carry forward feminist views on reproductive choice.

Reagan's re-election depended in no small part on the contributions of his UN ambassador. Kirkpatrick not only developed a detailed critique of Carter-era foreign policy and worked to articulate and implement an alternative vision that became the Reagan doctrine, but also delivered a riveting public reprise of those experiences at the 1984 Republican Party convention. Speaking from a podium in Dallas, not far from her childhood home, Kirkpatrick described in detail her political origins and her growing disenchantment with the Democrats. She condemned the "blame America first" liberals who refused to see Arab terror and Soviet aggression when both confronted them at close range (Kirkpatrick 1984). She reminded her audience of the Carter administration's willingness to cede Iran to the ayatollahs and Nicaragua to the Sandinistas. She portrayed the re-election of Ronald Reagan in 1984 as crucial in order to reverse a steep decline in America's prestige and confidence on the world stage. As the highest-ranking woman in the administration, Kirkpatrick asked voters to ensure a second Reagan term in order to demonstrate both their pride in the accomplishments of the last four years, and their rejection of the malaise and weakness of the Carter years.

The speech left no doubt as to whether Kirkpatrick had a future outside the Reagan administration. After resigning from the cabinet, she enlisted a top agent for the international speakers' circuit and signed a lucrative book contract for her memoirs. She wrote a syndicated newspaper column whose readers included the US president. Republican allies asked her to seek the 1988 presidential and vice-presidential nominations, but she chose instead to retain her positions at Georgetown University and the American Enterprise Institute. Her annual income soared well beyond a million dollars, permitting the purchase of homes in Maryland and the south of France. The Kirkpatricks also bought a property in central Washington to serve as the headquarters for a foundation Kirk ran after he retired (see Collier 2012, 169–180, 192).

Asked about her impact as a member of the Reagan cabinet, Kirkpatrick highlighted her role in restoring America's stature. In her words, "the United States was in something close to a pariah status at the UN in January 1981. . . . We managed to move into a situation in which American interests were, in fact, given the decent consideration which they hadn't been: a situation in which the United States was no longer the whipping boy of the world" (Kirkpatrick interview in McGlen and Sarkees 1993, 56). As a second key contribution, Kirkpatrick identified her efforts "to get much more serious and much more evenhanded consideration of human rights issues by the UN" in order to improve "the UN Human Rights Commission from what it had become, which was a political playground, run by the Communist Bloc" (Kirkpatrick interview in McGlen and Sarkees 1993, 56–57). Third, she pointed to efforts "to influence the Security Council to cease its obsessive preoccupation with attacks on Israel and to instead devote somewhat more attention to crisis areas in the world as they appeared" (Kirkpatrick interview in McGlen and Sarkees 1993, 57).

Kirkpatrick believed that her foreign policy goals enjoyed strong support from President Reagan as well as the American public. Among the only barriers she faced were biases held by some members of the White House staff who preferred to work with other men. In her words, "I have heard it said that one top White House person, opposing my appointment to a higher-level job at one point, said, 'at the end of the day when people sit around with their feet up, she just isn't one of the boys.' That wasn't said in my presence, obviously, so it's hearsay, but it's hearsay from very close sources" (Kirkpatrick interview in McGlen and Sarkees 1993, 58).

Kirkpatrick (in McGlen and Sarkees 1993, 58) maintains that as a female foreign policy appointee, she was "under continuous scrutiny of a critical nature" and treated as an outsider on issues related to the use of force. She invoked the phrase "Marine factor" to explain her circumstances:

[There were a lot of Marines in the Reagan Administration at the top.] I'm not wholly sure what all I thought was involved in the Marine factor, but it had something to do with macho concerns about not being or seeming less willing to use force than anybody else that was present. I sometimes felt that being a woman just removed me entirely from that particular set of concerns and left me freer to examine or raise questions about the various options and so forth. I'm not sure, however, how much this had to do with male-female differences. (Kirkpatrick interview in McGlen and Sarkees 1993, 58)

In the same interview, Kirkpatrick (in McGlen and Sarkees 1993, 54) admits that only after her appointment as ambassador did she realize she was both the first woman in that position and "the first woman ever to represent any major power" at the United Nations.

Aware of the obstacles in her path, Kirkpatrick sought to make her mark as an unswerving champion of American interests rather than as the representative of any women's movement agenda. She helped to ensure that Reagan's first-term foreign policies diverged in stark terms from those of the Carter presidency. Moreover, she carved out a distinctive, often challenging and independent voice, despite the presence of other actors who sought to pull in competing directions. Kirkpatrick acknowledged the odds against her influence were large, going as far as to portray herself as "a mouse in a man's world" (Kirkpatrick, as quoted in Crapol 1987, 167). Overall, her stature as a lead architect and builder of the Reagan doctrine in international affairs means that Jeane Kirkpatrick was a transforming public leader.

Kirkpatrick's legacy is also worth considering in light of her publications as a political scientist. In her study of state legislators, Kirkpatrick (1974, 174) defines leaders as individuals who seek power and wield it by placing themselves in positions of preeminent authority. As UN envoy, Kirkpatrick secured seats in the cabinet, NSC, and National Security Planning Group. Where she arguably fell short was with respect to the human rather than structural dimension of power. According to the criteria set forth in Kirkpatrick (1974, 174, 175), effective leaders command an "electric" interpersonal style that allows them "to interact with subtlety, sensitivity and flexibility, and 'warmth.'"

In Kirkpatrick's careers as a public intellectual and diplomat, she displayed an approach to human interaction that was more direct and principled than either nuanced or malleable. Since her willingness to adopt strong, often controversial positions was grounded in deeply held values, the patterns of behavior she practiced tended to violate her own equation of effective leadership with personal flexibility. The fact that she and Ronald Reagan held many of the same core beliefs permitted her to establish a close working relationship with him, but did little to endear her to competitors for influence within his administration. In effect, characteristics she shared with candidate Reagan provided Kirkpatrick's initial currency for access to the top. Over time, however, moderates in the cabinet, as well as advisors in the White House (likely including Nancy Reagan), preferred pragmatic problem-solving and a legacy of negotiation with the Soviets to the cerebral purity of a public intellectual turned diplomat.

Rather than becoming a leader who excelled at subtlety and bridge-building, as her own study recommends, Kirkpatrick adopted what she depicts as less effective public repertoires. In the role of UN ambassador, for instance, she frequently served as chief carrier of neoconservative ideas in the administration. Kirkpatrick (1974, 175) calls this the righteous "moralizer" style, typified by the elevation of "abstract ideological goals and moral imperatives" above all else. Since crusaders tend to evaluate other actors based on rigid, right/wrong tests of individual rectitude, they cannot reach across divisions to create workable coalitions or friendships. In Kirkpatrick's (1974, 175) words, the moralizer "is always something of a maverick and an agitator." Wedded to a perspective that pits forces of light against those of darkness, and lacking deep interpersonal ties, she commands limited sway over the broad currents of decision-making.

The fact that Jeane Kirkpatrick held as much influence as she did over the foreign policies of the first Reagan term demonstrates the extent to which her ability to present those views and convince the president of their wisdom trumped the inherent limitations of being, in her words, a moralizer. Where the constraints of that approach became clear were in her inability to secure promotion to a more senior post than that of UN ambassador and, as a result, in her absence from the second Reagan administration. A male advisor who had so significantly shaped the foreign policies of a presidential campaign and of a candidate's first term in office would likely have been rewarded with a higher position in the second mandate. After the 1984 election, however, Reagan's team shifted from hardline to more conciliatory postures toward the Soviet Union (see Dueck 2010, 222–223; Nau 2015, 185). Kirkpatrick's substantive influence dating from 1980 went into marked decline, along with her prospects for upward mobility in the administration.

Using Kirkpatrick's (1974) rubric, her tendency to operate as a moralizer was compounded by two related difficulties. First, she sought to be a "problem-solver" who would implement the substantive agenda that brought her to Reagan's attention (Kirkpatrick 1974, 174). She traveled to Central America, for example, to advance specific policy goals for that region and to deepen her ties with the president. Pursuing special assignments to El Salvador and elsewhere, however, created trouble within the cabinet by signaling to others the extent to which Reagan valued Kirkpatrick's advice. Second, her desire for presidential approval encouraged various "personalizer" behaviors that enabled his ambitions even after he had stymied hers (Kirkpatrick 1974, 174). To wit, Kirkpatrick stayed on as UN ambassador for a full eighteen months after Reagan had promoted McFarlane to the position of national security advisor.

In short, applying Kirkpatrick's (1974) evaluation scheme to her diplomatic career suggests that a scholar who probed the barriers facing women in public life met and reinforced quite a few of them herself. The evidence of moralizing, problem-solving, and personalizing traits, rather than effective and flexible repertoires, stands out in her record. They indicate that Kirkpatrick as a top diplomat was often drawn toward autonomous (rather than team-oriented) and principled (rather than pragmatic) approaches that, in her work as an academic analyst, she depicted as not conducive to authoritative public leadership.

Over time, the profile Kirkpatrick built after her resignation as UN ambassador began to fade as her husband Kirk's health deteriorated and the problems with their son Douglas escalated. Jeane's intellectual, political, and romantic partner of more than forty years, by then in his early eighties, died in 1995. Without Kirk, she was left to cope on her own with Douglas's failed attempts at rehabilitation. Once an effort to place him in charge of the family foundation fell apart, Jeane saw no workable solution for the turmoil in her eldest child's world (see Collier 2012, 202). Douglas collapsed in mid-2006 at the age of fifty. His grieving mother told her surviving children that she wanted to die by year's end (see Collier 2012, 206).

The final goals Kirkpatrick set for herself were to reach her eightieth year and publish a book-length study of US foreign policy. At a small birthday celebration, she seemed weak, frail, and uninterested in eating—presumably to will her quick demise (see Collier 2012, 208). Kirkpatrick's last volume was published shortly after her death in December 2006.

Making War to Keep Peace likely reverberated as its author intended (see Collier 2012, 207). Kirkpatrick (2007b) condemns Democrats in the Clinton administration who ceded American sovereignty to the United Nations, as well as Republicans in the George W. Bush years who forgot that prudence rather than recklessness forms the best basis for foreign policy. The text returns to the arguments that brought Kirkpatrick (1979) to Reagan's attention decades earlier. Kirkpatrick (2007b) insists the United States needs to shepherd its resources carefully on the global stage, ensuring that neither naïveté nor triumphalism interferes with hard-headed thinking about national interests. *Making War to Keep Peace* reminds readers of her fundamental belief that democracies take centuries to develop: they are not packaged goods ready for export from either a military base or a diplomatic mission. Had she gazed down from a hawk's nest high in the sky, Kirkpatrick might have enjoyed the lively debate her ideas continued to generate.

CHAPTER 4

Taking Charge of the New World Disorder

Following four years as UN ambassador, Madeleine Albright became the first woman to serve as America's top diplomat. Her appointment as secretary of state responded directly to the recommendation of First Lady Hillary Rodham Clinton, who urged her husband to promote Albright after his re-election in 1996 (see Albright 2003, 280). Albright's ability to secure a more senior position contrasted with the blocked opportunities faced by her lone female predecessor as emissary to the United Nations. As discussed in Chapter 3, pressure from First Lady Nancy Reagan and others had prevented the promotion of Jeane Kirkpatrick (see Collier 2012, 162; Shultz 1993, 319).

The disparate trajectories of Albright versus Kirkpatrick stand alongside their contrasting personal backgrounds, styles of leadership, and approaches to international relations. Albright was a proud, appreciative immigrant to the United States from her birthplace in Central Europe. More of a congenial networker than cerebral intellectual, she thrived on human interaction and, in many respects, projected the flexible, "electric" orientation toward leadership that Kirkpatrick's (1974, 174) study of state legislators identifies as highly effective. She sought practical ways to solve problems in an era that saw the disappearance of the previous Cold War order (see Albright 2003, Chapter 10; Hannay 2008). Even after the Soviet Union had imploded in the late 1980s and the United States stood as a solo superpower, America still needed to shepherd its influence with care (see Albright 2003, 642; 2006, 50, 289; 2008, 39).

To what extent did Albright shape and implement the foreign policy directions of the Bill Clinton years? Can she be considered a transforming actor in international affairs? How did Albright view matters of military force and women's rights? Were her actions in executive office a response to masculine norms at that level or, instead, did they coincide with a prior track record?

This chapter relies on publicly available sources, including memoirs, biographies, and multiple books that Albright published about her experiences. We argue that she played a central role in conceiving, communicating, and executing significant foreign policies of the Clinton period—especially with respect to Bosnia and Kosovo in the former Yugoslavia. Our discussion concludes that like Kirkpatrick during the 1980s, Albright served as an influential decision-maker in the 1990s.

As outlined in Chapter 1, feminist scholars document the multiple, sometimes contradictory ways in which female leaders are evaluated. Studies of Clinton administration foreign policy level a set of underpowered as well as overpowered allegations against Albright. On one side, observers place Albright in a cabinet where her "emotionalism" (Hyland 1999, 163) and "emotional frustration" (Dumbrell 2009, 151) proved unhelpful. Hyland (1999, 163), for instance, contrasts her approach to the Middle East conflict with the "persistent patience" of Warren Christopher, Clinton's first-term secretary of state.

Many of the same narratives also suggest that Albright was overpowered for diplomatic work. According to Dumbrell (2009, 15, 168), her personality was "extremely assertive and extrovert" to the point that she demonstrated a "tendency towards excessive self-certainty." According to Hyland (1999, 56–57) and Rodman (2009, 219), the decision to undertake aggressive and ultimately ineffective military action in Somalia can be traced to Albright's interventions in administration debates.

No matter how it is portrayed, Albright's willingness to use force to defend humanitarian values helped to define US foreign policy during the Clinton years. As the following quotation indicates, other administration decision-makers challenged her directly in debates over Central Europe: "I'm tired of this. Every time someone talks about using force, they're subject to ad hominem attacks. Five years ago, when I proposed using force in Bosnia, Tony Lake never let me finish my argument. Well, now I'm Secretary of State and I'm going to insist we at least have this discussion" (Albright 2003, 488). Albright won support for two separate military interventions in the Balkans despite opposition from male colleagues. By endorsing a muscular response to crises in the former Yugoslavia, Albright forged an international relations legacy that parallels that of Kirkpatrick in that it is inconsistent with understandings of women as "beautiful souls" who waft as ethereal angels above the field of battle (see Elshtain 1995).

In terms of gender representation, Albright built innovative networks of women diplomats at the United Nations and later as secretary of state. She directed their attention toward such issues as rape as a weapon of war and, in that manner, responded to concerns raised by feminist activists and organizations outside the United States (see True 2003). Albright's emphasis on creating women's networks and listening to perspectives that originated outside traditional foreign policy circles reveals another significant difference between her record and that of Kirkpatrick.

Albright's career offers little support for claims that female decision-makers abruptly conform to masculine stereotypes when they reach cabinet office. Before becoming UN ambassador and America's chief diplomat, Albright (2003, 101) projected an agentic approach to foreign policy that was consistent with the sustained influence of her father, Josef Korbel, whom she describes as her most trusted advisor. Korbel served as a senior member of the Czechoslovakian government in exile in London during World War II, after which he returned to Central Europe to assume a series of diplomatic positions. The family left Europe in the late 1940s for the United States, where Korbel became a professor of international relations.

Albright's track record shows that she was a confident actor prior to joining the cabinet. Like Kirkpatrick, her academic background and ability to impart knowledge in a persuasive way made her highly attractive to a president with limited exposure to the world stage. Willing to stake out clear positions about US national security and, in particular, American interests in regions of the world that she knew well, Albright recognized the importance of timely, direct interventions in foreign policy debate. In particular, her experiences during the 1980s as an advisor to candidates Geraldine Ferraro and Michael Dukakis revealed that boldness and strength were essential assets for US leaders. Albright went about developing an approach to international affairs that was flexible, nuanced, and not doctrinaire— but also forceful when necessary.

Her worldview saw the globe as a large, interconnected puzzle full of oddly shaped pieces carved from centuries of conflict and compromise. Abstract theories were of little use in explaining either how the map came to be, or predicting how it might look in the future. For Albright, whose family had sought political refuge twice by the time she was eleven years old, individuals and the connections among them played a central part in human history. She used her own experiences to inform American legislators and members of the general public about what their country was doing on the international stage, and why.

Albright identified the key to diplomatic success in a post–Cold War world as working when possible with other countries to secure US interests. She termed her approach "assertive multilateralism" (Dobbs 1999, 349; see also Albright 2003, 222). Designed both to enhance America's stature and head off the possibility of triumphalism, this view recognized that the world's dominant power might in some cases need to act on its own. Assertive multilateralism became a pivot for what she anticipated would be constructive international engagement during the Clinton years.

Albright maintained her approach to women's rights upon joining the political executive. Her commitment to feminist causes stood on the public record. She served in the 1980s as the inaugural director of a Georgetown University program that aimed to increase numbers of female diplomats, and was deeply embedded in networks of professional women in Washington (see Albright 2003, 100). The pro-equality efforts she undertook as ambassador and secretary of state were thus consonant with a much older repertoire.

The next section begins with a look at Clinton-era foreign policies as a basis for assessing Albright's role as a transforming leader. The following sections then turn to the experiences that shaped her actions in the political executive.

DECISIVE ACTION IN THE BALKANS

Observers portray the first Clinton administration as preoccupied with domestic matters and hence neglectful or, in some cases, misguided at the international level (see Rodman 2009, 203). Rodman (2009, 220) describes ill-conceived foreign policies that moved slowly from strategy toward execution, thus creating within the team "increased inhibitions and diminished credibility." Hyland (1999, 64) summarizes views of the administration as lacking coherent direction: "Critics believed that Clinton and [first-term Secretary of State Warren] Christopher shared one crucial characteristic: neither displayed strong convictions about what American foreign policy should accomplish except to please voters."

Claims that Clinton's initial years were "indecisive, incoherent, contradictory, confused and lacking vision and purpose" (Boys 2015, 276) are often juxtaposed with an argument that purposeful leadership emerged over time. In this rendering, the decision that was eventually made to intervene in Bosnia reveals "a president gradually leading his government to overcome its inhibitions and internal divisions and marshal the leverage to give effect to its diplomatic aspirations" (Rodman 2009, 220). Rodman

(2009, 225) maintains that the pattern continued: Clinton stood out as capable and clear-headed during the Kosovo crisis of the late 1990s, when he won international support for a military intervention that did not extend beyond the use of American air power.

When Clinton's two terms are considered as a unit, avoiding rigidity stands as a crucial cornerstone of the administration's foreign policy. The end of the Cold War, marked by the fall of the Berlin Wall in 1989, meant that US decision-makers faced a largely unknown global dynamic. East/West polarities that defined the post-1945 era had suddenly disappeared. By adopting "a flexible and pragmatic response to an evolving world order," American leaders could grapple in creative ways with changing circumstances (Boys 2015, 283). This willingness to set aside prevailing doctrines meant that the United States was able to pursue its national interests in highly adaptive ways.

Although analysts tend not to credit her for bringing coherence to what began as a disorderly foreign policy regime, Madeleine Albright was largely responsible for both the focus and openness to new ideas that characterized the Clinton era. Born in Prague, her early life was molded by the tempests that roiled interwar and postwar Europe. That childhood offered no basis for relying on the fixed ideas that shaped Jeane Kirkpatrick's outlook. Instead, Albright's formative experiences showed that complexity and uncertainty were recurring features of international relations. Although the United States shone as a powerful beacon of hope for the Korbel family, their eldest daughter understood that the larger world was a highly interdependent and often precarious place. The end of Soviet communism, she believed, meant that the United States needed to deepen ties with traditional allies and to begin cooperating with other countries. For Albright, effective American diplomacy required close attention to shadings and subtleties, strong powers of persuasion, and a willingness to navigate ever-shifting shoals.

A crucial juncture marking the Clinton administration's transition toward effective action came in debates over the breakup of Yugoslavia. For Albright, the disintegrating federation was a familiar place: her family had lived in Belgrade both before and after World War II. Given his deep knowledge of the region, Josef Korbel had predicted decades earlier that the death of Yugoslav leader Marshal Tito would hold disastrous consequences. Ethnic divisions were never far from the surface in the Balkans, Korbel (1951, 55–56) wrote, and could be exploited by regimes less committed than Tito's to a unified country.

Similar to her father, Albright evaluated international problems through a process of inductive reasoning. Unlike Kirkpatrick's deductive approach, with its emphasis on abstract concepts, Albright usually began with a case she knew well and derived a set of general patterns that logically followed. Personal background, as well as extensive study of Central and Eastern Europe, underpinned Albright's efforts to shape US responses to events in the Balkans. Somalia and Rwanda, which were also sites of crisis during the early 1990s, represented places she had never lived, and had never studied in depth, and hence she depended on others to provide perspective. For Europe's middle, however, Albright was the Clinton administration's experiential as well as academic expert (see Clinton 2005, 737).

The main foreign policy challenge of Albright's term as UN ambassador occurred in Bosnia-Herzegovina. Located in the relatively affluent center of what had been Yugoslavia, Bosnia and its capital city, Sarajevo, were wracked by conflict as Eastern Orthodox Serbs under the leadership of Radovan Karadžić heeded the encouragement of Serbian president Slobodan Milošević to "cleanse" the area of Catholic Croats and, in particular, Muslims—who were known as ethnic Albanians or Bosniaks (see Glenny 2012, Chapter 9; Power 2013, Chapter 9).

In January 1993, Albright told the Senate Foreign Relations Committee considering her cabinet nomination that the conflict was not a new one. The Bosnian War began at least eight months before Bill Clinton's election as president and nearly a year before his swearing in. Bloodshed at Europe's geographic heart was marked by frequent violations of human and particularly women's rights. Serb forces operating in the hills above Sarajevo imposed a nearly four-year siege of the city. Sources reported the systematic rape of women and girls—primarily by Serb militias targeting members of the Bosniak community (see Glenny 2012, Chapter 9; Power 2013, Chapter 9).

Toward the end of the George H. W. Bush years, attempts to resolve the conflict produced few results. Bush's secretary of state, James Baker, had gone as far as to reject American intervention in Bosnia on the grounds that the United States had "no dog in this fight" (Baker, as quoted in Dumbrell 2009, 83). United Nations peacekeepers stationed in Bosnia had only light arms, which made it hard to enforce a ceasefire between sides that were, in the Serb and Croat cases, well stocked militarily. The United Nations was thus unable to protect or provide basic aid to besieged civilians, particularly the Muslims of Bosnia, who constituted the area's largest ethnocultural group (at more than 40 percent of the population) yet enjoyed none of the external supports that benefited Serbs and Croats (see Glenny 2012, Chapter 9; Power 2013, Chapter 9).

Albright's (2003) memoir conveys a growing awareness that neither the secretaries of state nor defense in the first Clinton administration could find a workable solution. As revealed in the quotation in the introduction to this chapter, Albright had a hard time convincing her colleagues to take decisive action. Yet she gradually won the support of Vice President Al Gore and National Security Advisor Anthony Lake (see Dumbrell 2009, 84). The group pressed for a two-pronged "lift and strike" strategy to (a) release the existing weapons embargo, thereby permitting the Bosniaks to arm themselves; and (b) threaten US air strikes in order to dissuade the Serbs from continuing their sectarian attacks. According to Albright (2003, 228), Clinton agreed to this approach but dispatched Secretary of State Warren Christopher, a careful lawyer by inclination, to European capitals in the spring of 1993 (see also Clinton 2005, 512). Albright (2003, 228–229) understood that winning European support for air strikes in Bosnia would require a great deal of diplomatic arm-twisting, which Christopher was reluctant to undertake.

Christopher reported that US allies opposed a change of strategy. Some worried about their own peacekeepers in Sarajevo, while others opposed the idea of ending the arms embargo in order to protect the Muslim population (see Albright 2003, 228; Christopher 2001, 254). According to European decision-makers, peacekeeping was a neutral task that could not assist one ethnocultural community (see Major 1999, 540–541).

Decisive action in Bosnia was further complicated by US efforts to foster friendly relations with Eastern Europe. Any attack against Russia's Serb allies risked pushing those ties in the opposite direction. Moreover, Christopher and others in the administration believed that ethnic tensions in the Balkans were so deep-seated as to be intractable. In the words of Clinton's first secretary of state, Bosnia constituted "a problem from hell" because hatred across groups was "almost terrifying" (Christopher, as quoted in Power 2013, xii).

Albright's willingness to champion the use of force in Bosnia surprised her colleagues. The chairman of the Joint Chiefs of Staff while she was UN ambassador, four-star General Colin Powell (1995, 576), recalls how Albright's assertiveness nearly caused him an aneurism. At the end of one White House briefing, Albright challenged Powell to explain why his presentations always concluded with the same dismal prognosis: US forces could not release the Serb blockade of Sarajevo without extensive, costly troop commitments. Powell (1995, 576) writes that he "patiently explained" to Albright that "we should not commit military forces until we had a clear political objective." Above all, he worried that trying to end the siege could create another Vietnam-style quagmire.

Albright's (2003, 230) loss of patience spilled out as a pointed question: "What are you saving this superb military for, Colin, if we can't use it?" The query revealed Albright's conviction that an array of sanctions combined with limited military force can sometimes accomplish as much or more than overwhelming firepower. It would take years to convince President Clinton of that view, but, in the meantime, Albright's position was reinforced by mounting evidence of a major humanitarian tragedy in Bosnia. The UN refugee division reported in March 1993 on the organized slaughter of Muslim civilians by Serb forces. The following month, at a ceremony marking the opening of Washington's Holocaust Memorial Museum, Clinton and Elie Wiesel spoke about the deteriorating situation. Wiesel (as quoted in Cannon 1999, 883) told reporters that he implored the president to intervene, saying, "I have been in the former Yugoslavia and I cannot sleep for what I have seen."

In the autumn of 1994, Richard Holbrooke became head of the State Department's European Affairs desk and lead US negotiator for the Bosnian crisis. An experienced diplomat, Holbrooke believed the United States needed to act in order to end the conflict. Although he and Albright agreed on that point, they diverged sharply on how to attract Serb leaders to the negotiating table. Albright (2003, 242) disagreed with Holbrooke's recommendation to the president that sanctions against Serbia be released before a deal was in hand. She convinced Clinton not to lift sanctions, and predicted more accurately than Holbrooke how Milošević would react to signals from the West. Holbrooke (1998, 88) later admitted that Albright's advice to "take a hard line on sanctions proved correct; had we not done so, we would have begun the negotiations with almost no bargaining chips."

Heavy Serb shelling of Sarajevo eventually propelled the United States and its allies to intervene. In May 1995, NATO forces with a UN mandate initiated the first ever combat operation in the fifty-year history of the Atlantic alliance. Air strikes by American, British, and French planes enraged the Bosnian Serbs, however, who took hundreds of UN staff as hostages (see Dumbrell 2009, 85). Albright counseled Clinton to adopt a four-pronged strategy that would end UN peacekeeping in Bosnia, arm the Muslims, continue the air war, and press for a negotiated settlement. He agreed with key elements of her position, as did Lake (see Albright 2003, 236; Lake 2000, 132).

In July 1995, Serbs massacred, raped, and forced the removal of thousands of Muslims who had taken refuge in the "safe" city of Srebrenica. Echoing Jeane Kirkpatrick's account a decade earlier of the Soviet downing of a Korean airliner, Madeleine Albright rose in the UN Security Council to present eyewitness and surveillance evidence of events in Bosnia. Hundreds of Muslim men had been taken from Srebrenica, forced to assemble, machine-gunned to death on a soccer field, and hastily buried. Hundreds of teenage boys were sent to another location, then shot in a field. One of them hid among the corpses and later escaped, although he too was wounded (see Albright 2003, 238–239).

Furious that Serbs were killing civilians with impunity, Albright intervened more pointedly in administration discussions. At a meeting of Clinton's foreign policy team, she maintained that since American forces would eventually have to intervene in Bosnia, it was preferable to dispatch them under terms set by the United States. Waiting to act until the Europeans reached a consensus had only served to undermine NATO, the United Nations, and America's standing (see Albright 2003, 239–240). Lake agreed, while Christopher and Defense Secretary Les Aspin expressed concern that military intervention would create another Vietnam (see Albright 2003, 240; Lake 2000, 132).

Clinton endorsed Albright's position. He sent Lake to Europe to inform the allies of US plans to intervene (see Clinton 2005, 667). In late August 1995, Serb mortar attacks against a marketplace in Sarajevo killed or wounded more than a hundred civilians. Two days later, the United States and thirteen NATO allies began an air campaign against the Serbs known as Operation Deliberate Force. Coordinated with Croatian and Bosniak ground troops as well as UN peacekeepers in Bosnia, the operation's purpose was to implement the strategy Albright had advocated since 1993. Operation Deliberate Force ranked as the most significant NATO military action to that point (see Albright 2003, 241).

Within a month, Serb leaders indicated they were ready to sign a ceasefire and negotiate. Delays in launching air strikes, however, had allowed Karadžić's forces to control and ethnically "cleanse" large areas of Bosnia. When the Serbs sought concessions before peace talks began in Dayton, Ohio, in November 1995, Holbrooke advised Clinton to accept their preconditions. Albright (2003, 242) spoke privately with the president, who agreed with her view that Milošević needed to feel unrelenting international pressure. She then "had a most undiplomatic conversation" with Holbrooke, whom she saw as "very aggressive" (Albright 2003, 242, 275).

As a lead international strategist within the administration and consistent supporter of military intervention in Bosnia, Albright demonstrated an ability to focus the often meandering foreign policy debates of the first Clinton term. She raised contentious questions, thought independently, and crafted a coherent road map for multilateral action, despite having to work with such abrasive personalities as Holbrooke (see Dobbs 1999, 406). Most important, Albright maintained the confidence of a president who agreed that violence against civilians in Central Europe warranted more than vacillation by the United States. Albright (2003, 240) recounts, "During my years as UN ambassador, I felt I got more respect from the President than I did from most members of the foreign policy team. Where others were sometimes dismissive, he was uniformly attentive and heard me out."

In formal terms, the Bosnian War ended in late 1995 with the signing of a treaty in Dayton. Like the conflict itself, the provisions ending it were not at all balanced. The deal negotiated by Christopher and Holbrooke rewarded the Serbs by granting them control over a new republic, affiliated through a weak central government to a federation of Croats and Bosniaks. One visitor to Bosnia-Herzegovina more than fifteen years after the Dayton talks described a poor country, deeply divided along ethnic lines, ruled by a "mess of overlapping governments" (Engelhart 2011). Bosnia in 2011 had three presidents, one for each religious community, and more than 150 cabinet ministers (Engelhart 2011).

The fact that multilateral military intervention stopped the shooting war, however, stands as a major legacy of the first Clinton mandate. Madeleine Albright's idea of using limited force inside a NATO alliance became a model for action in Kosovo later in the 1990s. As discussed in Chapter 6, Balkan precedents also shaped Obama administration decisions about Libya.

What factors explain Albright's willingness to use economic and military sanctions, diplomatic pressure, and threats of armed force to protect civilians—and, in particular, women and girls in the Balkans? As demonstrated in the following sections, the approaches Albright employed as UN ambassador and secretary of state built on her own exposure to some of the modern world's most serious crises. Little evidence suggests that her perspectives toward either national security or gender equality shifted when she arrived in the political executive.

DAUGHTER OF CENTRAL EUROPE

Madeleine Albright grew up in the convulsed Europe of the 1930s and following. Fascism and communism directly shaped her life: the Nazi occupation caused the Korbels to flee Czechoslovakia, while the Stalinist tilt of the postwar government led to them to emigrate a second time. Since Albright was displaced twice by early adolescence, she saw vulnerability as a fact of human existence. Knowing firsthand the impact of conflict on civilians, she viewed survival as dependent on personal resilience and on the willingness of others to assist strangers (see Albright 2012).

In her memoir, Albright (2003) looks back fondly on the family's arrival in New York Harbor. She recalls a clear day in the fall of 1948 when she held her sister's hand and first glimpsed the Statue of Liberty (see Albright 2003, 21). Moved by the promise of a calm haven from turmoil across the sea, she felt a wave of gratitude and affection toward her new home.

Albright's family background became a subject of intense debate during the mid-1990s. A *Washington Post* feature article by Michael Dobbs reported that all of Albright's grandparents were Jewish by birth. After her maternal grandfather died of natural causes in the 1930s, the three surviving grandparents perished in the European Holocaust—as did many members of their extended families (see Dobbs 1999, front material containing family tree, 96). Albright said she had no knowledge of this history (see Dobbs 1999, 5).

Much of the public controversy focused on two questions: What had Albright's parents—both of them deceased by this point—told her about their families? How it was possible that a worldly, well-educated woman could be unaware of her Jewish roots until she was nearly sixty years old? Even though Albright (2003, 301–304) insists she was honest and forthright in her statements, Dobbs (1999, 10) maintains "there are simply too many contradictions and inconsistencies in her story for it to be believable."

Little doubt exists that the Körbels fully and unequivocally embraced Czechoslovakian identity. The fall of the Austro-Hungarian Empire in 1918 paved the way for a Czech social democratic government under the leadership of Tomáš Masaryk. Like many others of the same time and place, the Körbels assimilated because they could benefit from the liberal politics and economic prosperity of the interwar years. Rejecting Jewish identity also seemed advantageous because it minimized ties to the often tragic history of Jews in Czech lands (see Dobbs 1999, 22).

Jews began to settle there during the Crusades when local monarchs actively sought the community's diplomatic services and financial support, and relied heavily on tithes collected from its merchants and traders. Hapsburg-era financier Mordechai Meisel attained the status of Court Jew. That rank connoted wealth, access to power, and special privileges usually reserved for members of the nobility (see Kieval 2000, 17–18).

The contributions of Meisel and others, however, failed to inoculate the community against anti-Semitism. Major pogroms occurred in Prague in 1389 and again in 1744. Smaller-scale riots and other acts of violence were common during the mid-fifteenth century and following. Expulsions of Jews from Czech lands took place in the mid-1500s, mid-1600s, and mid-1700s. Fire destroyed the Prague ghetto and many of its synagogues on three occasions beginning in 1516. At the dawn of the twentieth century,

Jewish men in a small Bohemian town were accused of the "ritual murder" of a Catholic woman, based on allegations that the flat bread Jews ate during Passover came from the blood of gentiles. As the investigation and trial unfolded, Jews were attacked in multiple locations, including Prague (see Dobbs 1999, 18–19; Kieval 2000, 167–168).

The broad lines of this story were likely well known to Albright's parents and grandparents. Their response, like that of many Czech Jews, was to integrate as much as possible into the host society. Madeleine's mother's parents, the Spiegels, lived in a Bohemian town, where they may have attended synagogue a couple of times a year but were not known to be observant (see Dobbs 1999, 23–24). Her father's father, Arnošt Körbel, built a successful building supply business and banned family members from attending synagogue (see Dobbs 1999, 18–21).

Arnošt Körbel dispatched his youngest child, Josef, to study in Paris. The Spiegels sent their daughter Anna (known as Mandula) to boarding school in Geneva. Josef and Mandula married in Prague in 1935 after he completed a doctorate in law at Charles University (see Albright 2012, 51; Dobbs 1999, 25).

Committed to the governments of Masaryk and his successor Edvard Beneš, Josef Körbel was in many respects a modern Court Jew. He served in the Czech military and, together with Mandula, worked hard to cultivate social ties with influential people. Josef secured a diplomatic appointment, and in 1937, the year their eldest child was born, he was assigned to Belgrade, Yugoslavia, where he worked as press attaché at the Czech embassy (see Albright 2012, 59; Dobbs 1999, 32).

About 360,000 Jews lived in Czechoslovakia during the interwar years, comprising less than 3 percent of the country's population. Many were assimilated, but few held positions in the Czech foreign service. As one of his contemporaries explained, Josef Körbel rose upward "by not giving any signs of his Jewishness" and by building a network of patrons in the governing party (Avigdor Dagan, as quoted in Dobbs 1999, 28). Körbel indicated on official forms that his religion was "without confession" (Albright 2012, 51; Dobbs 1999, 28).

The rise of National Socialism not only cut off chances that Jews such as Albright's father could deny their identities, but also ended the Czech experiment with social democracy. Under terms largely dictated by Hitler, British and French leaders agreed in the 1938 Munich Agreement to let the Nazis occupy the primarily German-speaking third of Czechoslovakia known as the Sudetenland. At the same time, all three powers guaranteed on paper the safety of the rest of the country (see Dobbs 1999, 34).

For Albright's family, the Munich accord demonstrated how a state could be purposefully dismembered. As Josef Körbel later lamented, Czechoslovakia surrendered its independence "without firing a shot" (Körbel, as quoted in Dobbs 1999, 38). Despite the terms of the agreement, the Nazis not only annexed the Sudetenland, but also split and occupied the rest of what was once Czechoslovakia. The Germans supported far right nationalists in a breakaway Slovak state—which in turn divided and weakened a country that had only come into being about twenty years earlier. Germany then invaded Poland in September 1939, an act that led British Prime Minister Neville Chamberlain and others to realize they had been deceived. By that point, the United Kingdom and France were prepared to declare war (see Albright 2012, Chapters 8–9).

German pressures on a new, more compliant Czech government, as well as the regime in Belgrade, meant that Josef lost his position in the Yugoslav capital. The family returned to Prague in late 1938. Within days of the Gestapo's arrival, Körbel obtained exit visas for himself, his wife, and their daughter. Madeleine's three living grandparents never saw her or her parents again. In 1942, Mandula's mother was sent to Theresienstadt outside Prague and likely died in the gas chambers at the Sobibor death camp in Poland. Her father's mother left Theresienstadt for Auschwitz-Birkenau in 1944. Arnošt Körbel died of typhoid shortly after reaching Theresienstadt in 1942 (see Dobbs 1999, 68, 75, 97).

Mandula Körbel (as quoted in Dobbs 1999, 46) later wrote that the family's ability to return to Belgrade and secure passage from there to Greece and England relied on "some good friends and lots of luck and a little bribery." Josef's connections with Yugoslav newspaper editors offered a chance to flee a region where neither Jews nor people associated with the former Czech government were wanted. The voyage took the Körbels away from Central Europe for the next six years (see Albright 2012).

LIFE IN EXILE

The family arrived in England in May 1939—the same month as Madeleine turned two. Unlike Jeane Jordan, who was born and raised in the United States, Madeleine Körbel had to work hard to "fit in" in the United Kingdom and, later on, the United States. By her own account, she became "a proper little English girl" whose fluency in the local language quickly surpassed that of her mother (Albright 2012, 286). The Körbels worked hard to integrate into the Czech refugee community. Although they celebrated Christmas both in Prague and London, the Körbels were only baptized as

Roman Catholics in 1941 (see Albright 2012, 181, 190; Dobbs 1999, 84). According to Dobbs (1999, 84, 86), both Josef and Mandula saw Jewish identity as a source of danger and a heavy historical burden.

Like Jeane Jordan, Madeleine Körbel demonstrated strong personal confidence at an early age. After her sister Kathy arrived in 1942, Madeleine walked blocks on her own in London, pushing a stroller, to a store where she redeemed the family's ration coupons. Madeleine starred in a short film about Czech refugee children living in England (see Albright 2003, 11; Dobbs 1999, 80).

During the same period, Josef oversaw four radio broadcasts transmitted daily to Central Europe by Czechoslovakia's government-in-exile. The news and commentary prepared under his supervision were communicated using BBC facilities, meaning they had to pass British censors and also retain the confidence of Czech leaders, who ranged from communists on the left to conservative nationalists on the right (see Albright 2012, 258; Dobbs 1999, 83–87). Albright (2003, 13) recalls the long hours her father spent on weekends with his compatriots, trying to build consensus in a fractious group.

Moreover, she experienced as a child the consequences of international conflict. Three years old when the German blitz began, Madeleine grew accustomed to overnight bombing raids. When they lived in central London, the Körbels descended with neighbors to a basement full of water and gas pipes. On one occasion, a German bomb demolished buildings across the street from where Josef was working (see Dobbs 1999, 79). After moving to the suburbs, the family relied on a metal cage with a table top that was known as a Morrison shelter. In Albright's (2012, 291) words, "the heavy rectangular steel object became a center of our lives. We ate on it; the adults had their coffee and drinks while sitting around it; Kathy and I played on top of it; and when the siren sounded, all six of us dived under it." Memories of the blitz sharply distinguish Albright's early recollections from those of Kirkpatrick, who spent her childhood climbing trees and playing baseball on the American frontier.

When Madeleine was eight, the war ended and the Körbels returned to Prague. Her father worked for the new foreign minister, Jan Masaryk, in a multiparty government headed by Edvard Beneš. Josef's status brought with it a residence befiting the modern Court Jew: a spacious apartment high above the Vltava River on Castle Square. The family dropped the accent from their surname, becoming Czech-sounding Korbels, rather than the more Germanic and possibly Jewish Körbels they had been (see Dobbs 1999, 108). In the fall of 1945, at the age of thirty-six, Josef was named Czech ambassador to Yugoslavia and Albania.

Madeleine studied with a governess in Belgrade until her parents sent her to boarding school outside Lausanne, Switzerland. Albright (2012, 374) had little knowledge of French at the point she arrived at her dormitory. Less than six months after his daughter left Belgrade, Josef faced the threat of losing his job as communists took effective control of the Beneš government. He managed to secure a new role as Czech representative to the UN commission on the conflict in Kashmir. Josef, Mandula, Kathy, and John (born in 1947) traveled from Belgrade to England via Switzerland, where Madeleine learned of her father's UN posting. She began school in the fall of 1948 in London, where the family was consigned to a basement flat. Josef traveled to South Asia with the UN commission while he sought American visas for the family (see Albright 2012, 404–407).

Mandula, the three children, and a Yugoslav maid traversed the North Atlantic in late autumn. They spent most of the journey seasick in their cabin. Albright's (2003, 21) memoir recalls high winds, choppy waters, and persistent cold rain for much of the voyage. Her next image is arresting: the weather suddenly improves as the ship nears port. Clear blue skies welcome the family to New York.

Aware at the age of eleven that she had escaped Nazi and then Soviet grips on Czechoslovakia, Madeleine Korbel was a deeply grateful immigrant. She entered grade six on Long Island, near the temporary site of the United Nations, and focused once again on fitting in and succeeding academically. By her own account, "I spoke four languages—Czech, Serbo-Croatian, French, and English—but I didn't yet speak American. As quickly as possible, I got rid of my English accent" (Albright 2003, 22–23).

In the tradition of the Court Jew, Josef Korbel used political intelligence as his currency to gain entry to the United Kingdom and then the United States. He informed Allied contacts about what had transpired in postwar Prague as well as Belgrade, and requested assistance on that basis. In 1949, Josef asked the American ambassador to the United Nations for political asylum. He received it within four months (see Dobbs 1999, 137).

Through contacts in New York, Josef found work as a visiting professor of international relations at the University of Denver. The family lived modestly in Colorado, where father and daughter spent hours together every week on chores that included washing dishes and cleaning the house (see Albright 2003, 35). He spoke at length about the impact of the Munich agreement and the consequences of European anti-Semitism.[1] Madeleine became a committed Democrat, echoing Josef's liberal views. She won a scholarship to begin undergraduate studies in 1955 at Wellesley College (see Albright 2003, 35–36; Dobbs 1999, 147).

The trip to Boston's leafy suburbs marked Madeleine Korbel's emergence as an autonomous person. As she later reflected, however, all the stories her parents had told about war and death in Europe meant that she never experienced childhood (see Albright 2003, 34).

EFFECTIVE NETWORKER

Korbel arrived at Wellesley seeking a career in journalism or diplomacy, and marriage to "the perfect partner" (Albright 2003, 39). She made new friends to ease the integration into yet another setting, an experience that confirmed her need for group interaction (see Albright 2003, 41). Networking skills developed in this period allowed Korbel to refine her skills of persuasion and consensus-building.

Korbel wrote her senior thesis on Soviet influence in postwar Czechoslovakia—a subject suggested by her father (see Albright 2003, 54). It used detailed knowledge of one case to move from the specific toward the general, an inductive process that Josef also followed (see Korbel 1951). This strategy was the reverse of Jeane Kirkpatrick's deductive reasoning that began with grand theories about authoritarianism, for example, to evaluate cases ranging from Britain to Argentina (see Kirkpatrick 1971). Just as Kirkpatrick preferred to work with abstract concepts, Albright built on practical insights grounded in the details of a context she knew well. If Kirkpatrick formed generalizations about the narrow from the broad, then Albright seemed far more comfortable working in the opposite direction.

Wellesley College of the 1950s was a place where finding a husband was at least as significant as earning a degree (see Albright 2003, 39–40). Madeleine met Joseph Albright one summer when they both worked at the *Denver Post*. Joseph's mother was part of the Patterson family whose holdings included that newspaper. Within days of graduating from Wellesley, Miss Korbel became Mrs. Albright (see Albright 2003, 45–59).

Madeleine held a series of newspaper and editorial jobs until 1961, when the couple moved to Long Island for Joseph's work. Twin daughters arrived that year, and Madeleine enrolled in an intensive Russian course. When Joseph was transferred to Washington, Madeleine began graduate work in international relations at Johns Hopkins University. In 1967, the third Albright daughter was born (see Albright 2003, 61–70).

After the family moved back to Long Island, Madeleine enrolled at Columbia University. She took a course on comparative communism with Zbigniew Brzezinski and wrote her MA thesis on the intelligence-gathering role of Soviet diplomats during the 1960s (see Albright 2003, 72–76). Like

Kirkpatrick, Albright was a married mother of three when she confronted antiwar protests on the Columbia campus. Both were mature women whose priority was completing their studies rather than joining demonstrations. Not surprisingly, they reached similar conclusions about Vietnam: even if stopping the spread of communism was a reasonable goal, the cost of the conflict in lives lost and domestic political strife meant that the United States was unlikely to emerge victorious.[2]

Once the family returned to Washington, Madeleine's volunteer work brought her to the attention of a fundraiser for Senator Edmund Muskie (see Albright 2003, 84–87; Dobbs 1999, 232–235). Albright (2003, 88) presents her community and political involvement during the early 1970s as an invaluable source of personal growth, since it created strong social networks and imparted valuable organizational skills. She built a reputation as someone who did not hesitate to move aside the deadwood in an organization and find fresh recruits to take their place (see Dobbs 1999, 236–241).

She directed the same focus and commitment toward doctoral studies. In order to complete her project on the role of Czech journalists in the 1968 Prague Spring uprising, Madeleine awakened at 4:30 each morning (Albright 2003, 89). She did not enjoy the long hours spent reading in archives, compiling notes, and writing; instead, she found conversations with Czech reporters and émigrés much more interesting (see Albright 2003, 90).

Albright accepted a position as national fundraising chair for Muskie's 1976 Senate campaign. She worked out of the family home in Georgetown and became known as a reliable, down-to-earth team player (see Dobbs 1999, 248–249). Once Muskie lost some of his staff members to Jimmy Carter's campaign, he offered Albright the post of chief legislative assistant. In August 1976, she began working on Capitol Hill.

Muskie by that point had served as governor of Maine for four years and as a US Senator for more than fifteen. His resume included unsuccessful bids for the Democratic presidential nomination in 1972 and for the party's vice-presidential slot in 1976. Albright assisted Muskie on issues ranging from the Panama Canal treaties to Jewish emigration from the Soviet Union. She learned that many US citizens and their elected representatives were deeply uninformed about the larger world (see Albright 2003, 93; Dobbs 1999, 250–257).

Muskie made a serious impression on the woman who became his protégée. Albright (1996, 38) calls him "my role model." In a eulogy delivered at his funeral in 1996, Albright insisted that without Muskie's mentorship, she would not have stood at a podium that day. As Albright

(1996, 38) concluded, "While we all had a good laugh when he sometimes slipped into political[ly] incorrect vocabulary or shielded his female staff members from some of his salted language, he was the man who earlier than others enabled women to take their place as public servants. Because he had faith in us, we had faith in ourselves."

Meeting Muskie was fortuitous because Josef Korbel, whom Albright (2003, 101) describes as "my greatest friend and advisor," died less than a year after she joined the Senate staff. In Josef's absence, Madeleine grew to rely on other men, including a former professor from Columbia. As national security advisor to President Carter, Zbigniew Brzezinski offered Albright the new role of congressional affairs liaison. Joseph Albright, an experienced political journalist by 1978, understood the importance of the post to his wife's upward mobility and, in her words, "was urging me on" (Albright 2003, 99).

Joining the staff of the White House National Security Council (NSC) meant that Madeleine could see not only how Congress looked from the outside, but also how Washington politics operated at the other end of Pennsylvania Avenue. Among the few NSC employees with experience on Capitol Hill, she focused on trying to improve relations between Carter and the legislative branch. During the president's meetings with members of Congress, Albright heard their complaints that American policies in the Middle East were decidedly anti-Israel. As a refugee from Central Europe, she understood that the administration was open to criticism once Carter (as quoted in Albright 2003, 104) urged Americans to get over what he termed an "inordinate fear of Communism."[3]

Albright hosted frequent social gatherings at her home in Georgetown and farm in Virginia. Inviting guests became a practice that not only deepened her network, but also reduced interpersonal tensions in a competitive work environment (see Dobbs 1999, 269–271). More than a decade before she joined the Clinton administration, Albright was well acquainted with strains between the NSC and the State Department. Brzezinski and Carter's secretary of state, Cyrus Vance, differed on issues including the Soviet invasion of Afghanistan and the Iran hostage crisis. Once an effort to rescue the hostages failed, Vance resigned and Muskie became his successor. Albright (2003, 111–114; see also Dobbs 1999, 278–279) saw relations between Brzezinski and Muskie enter the same downward spiral.

Albright's long hours at the NSC probably played a role in the breakdown of her marriage. With his wife at the White House by 7:30 each weekday morning, Joseph Albright assumed responsibility for family meals and homework (see Albright 2003, 115). His failure to move up in the family media empire, combined with Madeleine's success as a foreign policy advisor, made Joe Albright a likely candidate for midlife crisis. Madeleine was devastated by his decision to leave her for a younger woman (see Albright 2003, 120–121) but, as her family history had demonstrated, resilience was what mattered in tough times.

After the divorce, Albright became inaugural director of a new program in Georgetown University's School of Foreign Service that was designed to recruit more women to careers in international relations. The appointment placed Albright at the hub of liberal feminist networks in the nation's capital, and gave her an opportunity to encourage women students to "Speak up!" "Interrupt!" and always hold out a ladder for future cohorts (Albright 2003, 127; see also Dobbs 1999, 316). One program graduate, Nancy Soderberg, joined the Clinton transition team following the 1992 election and developed a list of nominees who might serve in the new administration. She included Albright's name, Clinton underlined it, and wrote "good" in the margin. Soderberg later became a member of Albright's staff at the United Nations (see Albright 2003, 160).

Deepening connections to other women extended Albright's personal network well beyond the web of men she knew from the Senate and the NSC. As director of the Georgetown program, she hosted potluck dinners for female faculty members who shared experiences of lower pay, more administrative responsibility, and less institutional recognition than their male peers. Albright began to understand from the lives of other women that the problems they confronted had systemic rather than individual or personal origins (see Dobbs 1999, 319–320).

Teaching at Georgetown University made Albright a lively communicator—since she could not know in advance what questions students would ask. When a dean invited her to participate in his regular PBS television panel, Albright accepted. She asked friends with media backgrounds to comment and took their advice seriously. In particular, she learned to make and reiterate her own points using crisp, clear language (see Dobbs 1999, 318–319).

That background was put to good use once Walter Mondale chose Geraldine Ferraro, a three-term member of the US House of Representatives from New York, as his 1984 running mate. Albright became Ferraro's foreign policy tutor and traveled with her throughout the campaign. She prepared Ferraro for difficult interviews, including one with Marvin Kalb on *Meet the Press*. When Kalb asked if Ferraro could "push the nuclear button," the candidate replied as follows: "I can do whatever is necessary in order to protect the security of this country" (Schanberg 1984). On *Nightline*, Ted Koppel asked about arms control: "Do you think that in any way the Soviets might be tempted to try to take advantage of you simply because you are a woman?" (Koppel, as quoted in Jamieson 1995, 107).

Ferraro debated the Republican vice-presidential candidate, George H. W. Bush, in October 1984. As a former UN ambassador, envoy to China, and CIA director, Bush had just spent four years at the heart of the Reagan administration—briefed on every major world event and privy to all foreign policy deliberations. Bush and Ferraro agreed before the debate that he would be addressed as "Vice President Bush" and she as "Congresswoman Ferraro." He broke the deal repeatedly by using the phrase "Mrs. Ferraro." Bush suggested that his opponent had trouble distinguishing between attacks on US embassies in Lebanon versus Iran (see Schanberg 1984). She responded by telling Bush, "I almost resent your patronizing attitude that you have to teach me about foreign policy" (Ferraro, as quoted in Raines 1984). Albright's advice paid immediate dividends: the debate was widely seen as a draw and, among women voters, as a victory for Ferraro (see Friedenberg 1994, 139–140).

Early in the 1988 presidential campaign, Albright announced that she would support Massachusetts governor Michael Dukakis. She became his top foreign policy advisor, and met Arkansas governor Bill Clinton when he visited Boston to assist Dukakis before the 1988 debate with Bush. According to Albright (as quoted in Dobbs 1999, 336), she and Clinton "hit it off right away." Clinton (2005, 344) writes that he "was very impressed with her intellectual clarity and toughness, and resolved to keep in touch with her."

The Dukakis campaign taught Albright that successful public engagement requires not just detailed policy knowledge, but also a bold personal presence. Dobbs (1999, 335; see also Albright 2003, 131) explains this realization as follows:

> In Madeleine's view, Dukakis was never taken seriously, not because he was wrong on substance but because he lacked a sufficiently macho image. . . . His failure, according to her, lay in his inability "to project himself as a strong national security figure." In her own career, she would do everything she could to avoid this mistake. She consciously cultivated the image of someone who can be relied upon to face down dictators and stick up for American interests.

Given her firsthand knowledge of what happened to Ferraro and Dukakis, Albright developed in the mid-1980s a forceful approach that emphasized the primacy of national interests in international affairs.

The fall of the Berlin Wall and the rise of new governments across Central and Eastern Europe increased demand for Albright's expertise.

Who better to interpret change from the perspective of America's security than someone who knew the region and its languages? In 1990 and following, Albright traveled extensively in the former Soviet bloc, meeting Czech president Václav Havel and conducting field research for the Times Mirror organization. Both Havel's insights and the results of her Times Mirror project predicted that the end of European communism would inflame older ethnocultural divisions (see Albright 2003, 153–154; Dobbs 1999, 342–344).

Albright became convinced that winning the Cold War had generated a smug, unthinking euphoria inside the United States. She grew concerned that celebrations of victory, indeed triumph, over the Soviet Union could prompt a return to isolationism and ultimately make the world more dangerous (see Albright 2003, 156).

MADAM AMBASSADOR

Albright returned to the White House in the fall of 1992 to work on transferring NSC operations to the incoming Clinton administration. She saw an unstable international environment in which East/West rivalries had been replaced in many regions by waves of social unrest and disintegrating states. Taken together, these patterns signaled what Albright (2003, 177) called a "new world (dis)order."

Although her name was on a list of potential appointees, Albright did not know what position, if any, Clinton would offer.[4] New barriers faced women seeking senior positions because the scrutiny of nominees' financial and legal affairs was especially thorough for mothers—who typically organized child care in homes where both parents worked.[5] Among the few mothers to pass the screening process, Albright met Clinton in Little Rock. He offered her the position of UN ambassador with cabinet rank, along with seats on the NSC and the Principals Committee (created in the Bush years to replace the National Security Planning Group). As Jeane Kirkpatrick had learned a decade earlier, frequent shuttling between Washington and New York would become a fact of life for an emissary who wanted to participate actively in both the UN and the administration.

Albright presented the broad lines of her approach to international affairs at a Senate Foreign Relations Committee hearing in early 1993. Asked about ethnic strife in the former Yugoslavia, she told legislators she was "totally horrified" by reports of Serb attacks against Bosnian Croats and Muslims, and advocated a more pro-active American stance: "I think how, years ago, as a student of history, when I studied the League of Nations,

I would say, 'How could they have stood around and done nothing?' We cannot sit around and wait to be judged on this issue 50 years from now." She went on to express "some amazement that the Europeans have not taken action. I believe that we must . . . press our European allies on this" (Albright, as quoted in McManus and Meisler 1993).

Albright told senators she would not hesitate to push European leaders to respond to the crisis in Bosnia. Journalists covering the hearing reported that Albright "was lavishly praised by both Democratic and Republican members" of the committee (McManus and Meisler 1993). They predicted her nomination would sail through, which it did (McManus and Meisler 1993).

Rather than viewing UN member states as friends or enemies of the United States, as Kirkpatrick had, Albright (2003, 175) employed a more complex typology. It distinguished among established liberal democracies, states emerging from a period of autocracy, poor and sometimes conflict-ridden countries with weak governments, and hostile rogue nations such as North Korea. Her approach saw some players as mixtures of more than one type and others as movements (rather than states) seeking international influence. Albright used her framework to educate American lawmakers and members of the general public about specific ways she planned to deal with each category:

> We had to forge the strongest possible ties among the first group, so that there was a solid foundation upon which to build; we should help the second group succeed, so that democratic trends would continue; we should aid those in the third group who were most willing to help themselves, so that areas of conflict and lawlessness diminished; and, finally, we should strive to protect ourselves by reforming, isolating, or defeating those in the fourth group. (Albright 2003, 175)

Albright thus projected an optimistic but hard-headed view that most international actors could be brought into the fold as allies.

She called her approach to international affairs "assertive multilateralism" (see Albright 2003, 222; Dobbs 1999, 349ff., 356). The adjective formed the more significant part of the phrase, since it outlived the noun by many years. "Assertive" remained important throughout the Clinton years because it rejected views that the United States could relax on a proverbial chaise lounge after the fall of the Berlin Wall. Democrats like Albright believed that sustaining and extending American power demanded international engagement. Taking the lead would sometimes be necessary. At no point could the country wallow in passivity or inaction.

Multilateralism proved more troubling, since to conservative critics it meant surrendering sovereignty to the United Nations or some other supranational institution (see Blood 1997, 161). To Albright, the concept was a positive one, grounded in cooperative efforts to promote some causes and stop others. She saw joint action as offering the US significant budgetary, diplomatic, and military advantages because the country could often accomplish more by operating in concert with others than on its own (see Albright 2008, 79, 92). She spoke less of multilateralism as time passed, however, once events in Somalia and elsewhere showed that too much collaboration and not enough direction produced disastrous results (see Albright 2003, 222).

The first major crisis of Clinton's first term involved Somalia—a failed or at best fragile state in the Horn of Africa. Administration actions provided a lesson in the perils of blending excessive compromise with minimal coordination, limited resources, and changing goals that were in some cases too ambitious. The United States had tried since the Bush years to provide basic food aid to Somali civilians. Bush's advisors, as well as the incoming Clinton team, wanted to shift responsibility for this humanitarian mission to the United Nations, whose secretary-general claimed his organization lacked the capacity to deliver aid. At the same time, both Bush and Clinton resisted pressure from the United Nations to neutralize a key Somali militia leader named Mohamed Aidid (see Albright 2003, 178–184).

As UN ambassador, Albright helped to broker a March 1993 deal that was, in retrospect, entirely unworkable. The United States would keep about 4,000 soldiers in Somalia under its own command, while the United Nations recruited a force of close to 30,000 peacekeepers. The secretary-general's special representative on the ground was a retired US navy admiral. United Nations troops, according to Albright (2003, 179), had a sweeping mandate that included taking arms away from local militias, creating regional governments, and fostering cooperation among leaders who had little history of working together.

The massacre of about two dozen Pakistani peacekeepers in June led the UN Security Council to call for the arrest of those responsible. That decision began a process of mission creep that saw more US troops and armaments shipped to the Somali capital, Mogadishu, at the request of the retired admiral in charge of UN forces. Aidid, who was seen as having caused the Pakistani deaths, remained at large for months—which in turn frustrated US legislators, who had yet to authorize military action. The UN ambassador turned her attention to settling the Somali civil war through diplomatic channels (see Albright 2003, 179–184; Dobbs 1999, 355–356).

Albright (2003, 182) admits that the decision to pursue a peaceful reso-lution was not communicated to US troops in Mogadishu, who attempted in the fall of 1993 to capture Aidid. Clinton (2005, 552–553) maintains he "did not envision anything like a daytime assault in a crowded, hos-tile neighborhood" when he "approved the use of U.S. forces to appre-hend Aidid." Nearly twenty American soldiers died and more than seventy were injured in an attack on the militia leader's compound. Not only were US forces attacked in the streets of Mogadishu, but also two Black Hawk helicopters were shot down and burned in the densely populated city. At least 1,000 Somalis were killed or wounded in the carnage (see Bowden 1999; Dumbrell 2009, 67).

Events in Somalia sparked congressional and public outrage. While supplying humanitarian aid to civilians might have been a defensible goal, did compelling reasons exist to dispatch US ground forces? Was the in-ternal chaos in Somalia so severe that it threatened international peace and security? In particular, the Black Hawk incident ignited simmering un-ease with supranational institutions. In their rush to frame the event as proof that the United Nations could not be trusted, critics forgot that US Army Rangers in Mogadishu operated under an American commander (see Albright 2003, 183; Clinton 2005, 550–551).

By the spring of 1994, provisions under discussion since the Bush years came into effect that sharply constrain American engagement in mul-tilateral operations. The rules are lengthy and detailed, covering nearly thirty single-spaced pages. They respond to criticisms of the Somali mission by ensuring that US participation will only occur following a de-cision "that the operation's political and military objectives are clear and feasible; and when UN involvement represents the best means to ad-vance U.S. interests" (National Security Council and National Security Council Records Management Office 1994, 2). The document imposes a "specified timeframe" on peacekeeping efforts including a "sunset provi-sion" to shut them down (National Security Council and National Security Council Records Management Office 1994, 5). It requires that Congress be "regularly and fully briefed on such operations, and, wherever possible, consulted about the participation of U.S. armed forces in them" (National Security Council and National Security Council Records Management Office 1994, 3). A series of sections under the heading "Strengthening the UN" detail how the international organization will better train and manage its peacekeeping efforts. In another bow to critics, the directive caps American contributions at one-quarter of overall costs for each opera-tion (see National Security Council and National Security Council Records Management Office 1994).

Given this climate, Albright and other members of the administration became exceedingly cautious about pursuing any form of international intervention. As she admits, they did little to stop the organized killing of Tutsis by Hutus in Rwanda. The initial steps toward genocide unfolded mere hours after the Black Hawk incident in Mogadishu. Failing to act on the Rwanda crisis remains Albright's (2003, 185) "deepest regret" from her years in public life (see also Clinton 2005, 593).

The UN Security Council authorized a peacekeeping mission to Rwanda in October 1993 to oversee a Hutu/Tutsi ceasefire. Beginning in January 1994, the Canadian in charge of UN forces warned of an imminent break-down in civil order and of rumors that Belgian troops under his command would be attacked because they were perceived to be pro-Tutsi. General Roméo Dallaire was correct in that the Rwandan president, prime minister, and ten Belgian peacekeepers were murdered in the next few months (see Dallaire 2003).

Belgium pressed the United States to end the UN mission in Rwanda, which contained no American soldiers. By contrast, Dallaire and African leaders wanted to reinforce the UN contingent, which was difficult for Clinton and his team given the new rules of multilateral engagement. Without evidence that vital national interests were at stake, no American president could hope to intervene.

By April, accounts from Dallaire and others suggested that premeditated ethnic slaughter was occurring on a mass scale (see Dallaire 2003; Orbinski 2008, Chapter 3). Albright contested instructions coming from the State Department by calling her NSC contacts in Washington. She asked not to side with the Belgians, but rather to vote for retaining a small UN presence. In the end, a Security Council resolution calling for reduced peacekeeping operations was approved unanimously (see Albright 2003, 192–193; Dobbs 1999, 357). Albright's vote and that of other ambassadors meant that genocide continued for months in Rwanda under the eyes of a limited peace-keeping contingent.

ASSERTIVE LEADERSHIP

Events in Somalia and Rwanda led Albright to insist on a reset of admin-istration foreign policy. She advanced two key arguments: (1) given both debacles in Africa, a more strategic approach was necessary in Central Europe; and (2) women's equality was crucial to national interests on the international stage. Albright's second pivot was explicitly feminist in that it sought to prioritize the rights and autonomy of women, including by creating networks of women leaders to advance that cause (see Blood 1997, 183–184; True 2003).

From its first month in office, the Clinton administration responded directly to feminist movement claims. The president signed legislation establishing unpaid family and medical leave. Clinton reversed a ban on abortion counseling in federally funded health clinics. In the domain of foreign policy, he issued an executive order overturning restrictions dating from the Reagan era on aid to agencies that approved of either contraception or abortion. Another order instituted public funding for abortions in US military hospitals located overseas (see Bashevkin 1998, 214–215).

As the senior woman in Clinton's foreign policy team, Albright advanced a pro-equality agenda by underlining the need for political and economic reform in newly democratizing states. She saw international stability after the Cold War as contingent on more than just open markets. In her view, the chaos then upending the old communist order held specific and frequently dangerous consequences for women (see Lippman 2000, 218). Speaking in December 1996, Clinton agreed. In his words, "We cannot advance our ideals and interests unless we focus more attention on the fundamental human rights and basic needs of women and girls" (Clinton, as quoted in Garner 2012, 122).

In particular, Albright stands out for converting an awareness of violence against women in the Balkans into tangible policy action. As historian Jelena Batinic argues, media and nongovernmental organizations were reporting in detail during the early 1990s on atrocities in Bosnia. By themselves, however, these accounts could not address the problem. Thanks to insiders like Albright, Batinic writes, "For the first time, rape in war found its place on the international agenda and in legal and human rights discourses; it was a crucial moment for feminists to try to make critical interventions into these discourses and to struggle for a feminist reconceptualization of violence against women [as a violation of human rights]" (Batinic, as quoted in Garner 2012, 128). Albright (2003, 232) encouraged her staff to assist a new tribunal that was created to investigate events in the former Yugoslavia. Established by the UN Security Council in early 1993, the International Criminal Tribunal for the Former Yugoslavia (ICTY) gathered testimony from witnesses and victims in order to document organized attacks on women during the Bosnian War. Conducted primarily by Serb militias against Bosniak women, cases of rape during the conflict numbered in the tens of thousands. Evidence that Serb soldiers forcibly enslaved Muslim women and girls, some of them in their early teens, led the tribunal to identify rape and sexual violence not only as crimes against humanity, but also as specific war crimes (see Allen 1996; Arbour 2002).

Albright (2003, 247) served as one of only seven female ambassadors to the United Nations from the more than 180 member states with permanent representatives. Given that they constituted less than 4 percent of UN ambassadors, she created a network of women emissaries. The group met monthly and pressed for the appointment of Canadian jurist Louise Arbour, the first woman chief prosecutor on the ICTY. Arbour, whom Albright (2003, 247) describes as "tenacious," went on to indict Serb leader Slobodan Milošević. Albright later brought together about fifteen women foreign ministers to press for UN action to stop trafficking in women and girls (Albright 2003, 433; True 2003, 380). According to Albright (2003, 434), none of the matters raised by female diplomats was easy to move forward; in her words, "We had, it seemed, to work doubly hard to be taken seriously, and triply hard to actually push our agendas through."

Albright's effort to bring together female diplomats merged the networking skills she learned at home, particularly from her father, with insights gleaned from her own political involvement. Albright (2003, 276) describes male bonding practices in Washington as follows:

> Ties are forged as early as prep school or college, or later in entry-level positions in law firms or on Capitol Hill. As careers progress, these networks broaden. Friendships are cultivated over drinks, cigars, steaks, Redskins games, and rounds of golf. Favors are exchanged for friends and relatives. Problems are solved and deals arranged through quiet phone calls and conversations, with outsiders none the wiser. Washington women also have networks, but until recently these networks were primarily social or philanthropic. Men focused on power. Women focused on everything except power.

Albright attributes many slights she experienced as UN ambassador and secretary of state to her gender. She notes that on one occasion when she telephoned Washington from New York, her call was directed to a junior member of the NSC staff rather than to someone at the appropriate level of responsibility (see Albright 2008, 58). During a visit to Kosovo, Serb men greeted her motorcade by exposing their genitalia. According to Albright (2003, 543), the point of the performance was simply to clarify their views about her.

In 1996, when two unarmed US civilian planes were shot down in international airspace, Albright's awareness of gender dynamics arrived in the international limelight. According to a transcript Albright released at the United Nations, Cuban military pilots flying MiG fighter jets launched

Figure 4.1. UN Ambassador Madeleine Albright releases transcript of Cuban pilot communications, 1996.
AP Photo; photo by Richard Drew.

a missile that killed all four men on board. At the press conference she held as UN ambassador, depicted in Figure 4.1, Albright used the same expression the MiG pilot employed when the missile he fired struck its target: "Cojones! We hit him! Cojones! We busted his cojones!" (pilot, as quoted in Albright 2003, 256). In a comment that President Clinton (as quoted in Albright 2003, 261) termed "probably the most effective one-liner in the whole administration's foreign policy," Albright (2003, 259; italics in original) announced: "I was struck by the joy of these pilots in committing cold-blooded murder. Frankly, this is not *cojones*. This is cowardice."

By using the Spanish word for testicles and impugning those of a fighter jet pilot, Albright breached both diplomatic protocol and prevailing gender norms (see Albright 2009, 19). Yet the comments reinforced her standing as a leader who could speak and act decisively (see Clinton 2005, 701). As

Figure 4.2. Secretary of State Madeleine Albright flattens four dictators in *Miami Herald* cartoon.
©Jim Morin, Morintoons Syndicate.

shown in Figure 4.2, a cartoon published in the *Miami Herald* revealed how Albright was perceived given her tough talk toward Cuba and her firm hand in other regions. The upper section of the caricature features a row of self-satisfied male dictators commenting on Albright as cute (Fidel Castro) or willing to make them a cup of tea (Saddam Hussein). The lower segment shows her knocking over four shocked men with one swift punch (see Albright 2003, 423).

Albright chaired the US delegation to the Fourth World Conference on Women, held in 1995 in Beijing. She flew to China with Hillary Clinton, a fellow graduate of Wellesley College. Both delivered eloquent remarks to the assembled delegates, but Clinton's address stands in the annals of public speaking as "a stunner" (Albright 2003, 250). It explained in forthright terms why women's experiences are important not only to feminists, but also to international public debate. Before the eyes and ears of the world, Clinton insisted, "Human rights are women's rights, and women's rights are human rights" (Clinton 1995). Following the Beijing conference, the administration convened a series of international meetings on the theme of women's involvement as a sine qua non of democratic politics (see Garner 2012, 135).

The trip to China forged a crucial link between Albright and Hillary Clinton. The timing was fortuitous: Warren Christopher resigned as secretary of state the same day as Bill Clinton won his second term. Albright had by then served more than three years as UN ambassador. Once Christopher announced his departure, Albright was deluged with encouragement, primarily from other women, to seek the post (see Albright: 2003, 275–281; Clinton 2003, 392–393; Dobbs 1999, 371–373).

Attempts to promote her candidacy faced major challenges. She faced strong competition from Holbrooke, who was supported by Gore (see Blood, 1997, 15; Talbott 2011, 16). Even though Albright had demonstrated a flexible, practical approach to crucial foreign policy choices—particularly as compared with Jeane Kirkpatrick—she was described by men on the Clinton team as overly ideological and tangential to the directions of administration decision-making (see Dobbs 1999, 363). This focus on her presumed failings led Albright (as quoted in Dobbs 1999, 369) to tell confidantes that, when it came to a woman at the top of Foggy Bottom, "The boys will never let it happen."

Bill Clinton nevertheless nominated Madeleine Albright as his second secretary of state. Months later, he revealed that his wife had strongly recommended her appointment. The president (quoting Hillary Clinton in Albright 2003, 280) recalled Hillary's advice as follows: "Only if you pick Madeleine will you get a person who shares your values, who is an eloquent defender of your foreign policy, and who will make every girl proud."

TOP DIPLOMAT

Albright appeared again before the Senate Foreign Relations Committee in January 1997. Her opening statement spoke of people around the world who looked toward "American institutions and ideals" as a shining model (Albright 1997). She argued that US leadership "must be sustained if our interests are to be protected around the world" (Albright 1997). In a pointed rebuttal to anyone who might have confused her with Kirkpatrick, Albright (1997) said US foreign policy was not about "geopolitical abstractions" but instead involved making the world safer and more prosperous.

The shadow cast by the crisis in Bosnia weighed heavily on the mind of the secretary designate. She told senators that a disorderly, vacillating, and distracted foreign policy imperiled American interests. In her words, "To defeat the dangers and seize the opportunities, we must be more than audience, more even than actors, we must be the authors of the history of our age" (Albright 1997).

Albright presented the varied sources of instability that, in her view, threatened international order. They included terrorism, ethnic wars within countries, and environmental change. As "the indispensable nation" in a disorderly world, the United States required both military and diplomatic strength to address them:

"That is why our armed forces must remain the best-led, best-trained, best-equipped and most respected in the world. And as President Clinton has pledged, and our military leaders ensure, they will. It is also why we need first-class diplomacy. Force, and the credible possibility of its use, are essential to defend our vital interests and to keep America safe. But force alone can be a blunt instrument, and there are many problems it cannot solve. To be effective, force and diplomacy must complement and reinforce each other. For there will be many occasions, in many places, where we will rely on diplomacy to protect our interests, and we will expect our diplomats to defend those interests with skill, knowledge and spine" (Albright 1997).

Albright assured legislators that as secretary of state, she would place cooperation with Congress at the top of her priority list.

The nominee then quoted a statement by Republican Senator Richard Lugar to the effect that America's international presence was "underfunded and understaffed" (Albright 1997). Albright asked lawmakers from both parties to support her plan to help new democracies, aid less affluent countries, and settle a balance owing at the United Nations. Reminding senators that she had arrived in America as an eleven-year-old refugee, Albright said she wanted to fulfill the yearnings of people like herself and her family. She asked legislators to join her in responding to "the prayer for peace, freedom, food on the table and what President Clinton once so eloquently referred to as 'the quiet miracle of a normal life'" (Albright 1997). The Foreign Relations Committee voted unanimously to confirm her nomination (see Albright 2003, 289).

As America's top diplomat, Albright faced circumstances that resembled earlier pressures in Bosnia. A crisis loomed in Kosovo, also in the former Yugoslavia, as the same nationalist leader in Belgrade who had targeted Muslims in Bosnia worked to extend Serbian control in Kosovo. Slobodan Milošević wanted to reverse an Ottoman victory dating from the 1300s that offered a measure of autonomy to the ethnic Albanian population of southwestern Serbia.

Like Bosnia, the Kosovo situation also pre-dated the Clinton administration. Milošević was told late in the George H. W. Bush years that the United States would intervene militarily if Serbia instigated trouble in Kosovo. Known as the "Christmas warning," the December 1992 declaration issued under a Republican president was reiterated by Democrats after they returned to the White House (see Albright 2003, 481–483; Dumbrell 2009, 92).

Yet important differences marked the two conflicts. When Serb militias attacked ethnic Albanians in Prekaz in early 1998, Madeleine Albright was a higher-ranking, more seasoned diplomat than five years earlier. As secretary of state, she issued an unambiguous statement: "We are not going to stand by and watch the Serbian authorities do in Kosovo what they can no longer get away with in Bosnia" (Albright, as quoted in Dobbs 1999, 403; see also Albright 2003, 485).

Stopping the bloodshed was complicated by the fact that Muslims made up about 90 percent of the population of a province inside Serbia. In Prekaz and elsewhere, ethnic Albanians organized a militia under the banner of the Kosovo Liberation Army (KLA) that could transport arms over the border from Albania. The KLA became a more radical faction of the Muslim community than the moderate stream represented by Kosovo's ethnic Albanian president, Ibrahim Rugova (see Albright 2003, 483–484).

In Prekaz, Serb forces killed dozens of civilians, as well as two brothers who were KLA commanders. No coordinated international response followed, since some European allies worried that Muslims in the Balkans were becoming radicalized. Italy, for instance, endorsed an arms embargo against the ethnic Albanians. Russia resisted any effort to sanction the Serbs (see Albright 2003, 486). Given these differences, debates inside what was known as the Contact Group consumed a great deal of Albright's time and energy (see Albright 2003, 485–488).

In Washington, the secretary of state championed swift action (see Clinton 2005, 850). She faced opposition from such colleagues as Secretary of Defense Bill Cohen and the chairman of the Joint Chiefs of Staff, General Hugh Shelton, who defined conflict as a declared war against a sovereign enemy state (see Dumbrell 2009, 92). Situations like the one in Kosovo diverged from that model because a humanitarian disaster was unfolding inside the boundaries of a country that opposed foreign intervention (see Daalder and O'Hanlon 2001; Judah 2002).

Albright presented her initial position at a White House meeting in April 1998. National Security Advisor Sandy Berger opposed arguments by Albright and the US envoy to the Balkans, Bob Gelbard, that said Milošević would only negotiate under a credible threat of NATO military intervention. Berger cut off Gelbard as follows: "You can't just talk about bombing in the middle of Europe. . . . It's irresponsible to keep making threatening statements outside of some coherent plan. The way you people at the State Department talk about bombing, you sound like lunatics" (Berger, as quoted in Albright 2003, 488).

Berger's tone offered Albright a chance to use the strategy she had taught in her courses. In dealing with belligerent men, she advised women students, adopt a leadership style that is at least as assertive as theirs. Albright (2003, 488) writes that she followed the course of action she had urged in the classroom, which was to interrupt and refuse to be silenced. Albright recalled being cut off five years earlier by Tony Lake in debates over Bosnia. As secretary of state, she would not defer to others and would insist on holding a full discussion of the options in Kosovo.

Once Britain raised the possibility of NATO intervention at the UN Security Council, that body passed a resolution declaring that the Kosovo crisis was a threat to peace and security (see Albright 2003, 494; Blair 2010, 230). Albright emphasized two key points in administration debates. First, stability in Europe was integral to American interests. Second, Serb aggression in Kosovo endangered the entire continent. In her words, "if we did not act, the crisis would spread, more people would die, we would look weak, pressure would build, and we would end up resorting to force anyway under even more difficult and tragic circumstances" (Albright 2003, 493).

Serb attacks in the summer of 1998 undermined the KLA and imperiled thousands of civilians. In late September, the New York Times published photographs and eyewitness testimony showing that Serbs had massacred dozens of ethnic Albanians in villages including Gornje Obrinje. Jane Perlez (1998) describes how entire families, including a ninety-five-year-old man, were burned to death after soldiers and police set fire to their houses. Bodies of a mother and her two young daughters, each shot at close range, lay on a rocky path where they had tried to escape. Nearby was another dead relative, her pregnant belly sliced open (see Perlez 1998).

Perlez (1998) links these events to Milošević's effort to weaken the KLA and terrorize the majority population. She cites Serb actions, including the looting of homes and attacks against Muslim civilians, as evidence that Belgrade planned to force about 250,000 ethnic Albanians to leave the area. Survivors of the massacres said the Serbs dominated the KLA in Gornje Obrinje and elsewhere because of their edge in troops, guns, and heavy equipment, including armored personnel carriers (see Perlez 1998).

On the recommendation of the Principals Committee, President Clinton sent Richard Holbrooke to Belgrade to convince Milošević that NATO was serious about using force to defend Muslims in Kosovo. The visit proved fruitless, in Albright's view because the Serbs had found ways to manipulate both Russia and US allies. It took until mid-October for Albright and Holbrooke to win support from France, Germany, and Italy for NATO intervention. Serbia then signed an agreement to allow Muslim refugees to return home under the eyes of international observers. The October accord obligated Milošević to negotiate the future autonomy of Kosovo province and reduce the Serb military and police presence in the area (see Albright 2003, 494–497).

Despite the deal, Serb leaders continued their ethnic cleansing program. Albright argued vigorously at a mid-January meeting of the Principals Committee that Kosovo was on the verge of becoming the Bosnia of five years earlier. Her memoir indicates that these comments were not well received (see Albright 2003, 499).

Serb forces massacred about forty-five ethnic Albanian civilians that same week in Račak, a small village in Kosovo. An American member of the international observer team that visited Račak found human bodies separated from heads and faces with empty eye sockets, indicating gunshots fired at close range (see Daalder and O'Hanlon 2001, 63–64). Albright eventually gained the support of Cohen and Shelton for US participation in a NATO peacekeeping mission (see Albright 2003, 502–503; Dumbrell 2009, 93). To reinforce her position further, members of Congress from both parties endorsed a plan to send troops to Kosovo if necessary (see Albright 2003, 516; Riley 2015).

Aware that Albright was serious about using force, Russian foreign minister Igor Ivanov pressed Serbia to participate in peace talks with multiple ethnic Albanian representatives. Discussions began in February 1999 in Rambouillet, France, where the various sides debated how independent Kosovo would be in the future (a central concern for the KLA) and whether foreign troops could intervene in the affairs of a sovereign state (highly troubling for the Serbs; see Albright 2003, 505–515).

As the talks continued, evidence suggested that Milošević was preparing to push more Muslims, possibly as many as half a million, out of Kosovo. Albright traveled back and forth to European capitals, and convened daily conference calls with NATO colleagues.[6] Given that air raids might not prove sufficient to deter the Serbs, she ensured that plans were in place to employ ground forces. Albright also secured Clinton's support for a reconstruction plan for postwar Kosovo (see Albright 2003, 523–524, 528–529; Dumbrell 2009, 96).

NATO air strikes beginning on March 24, 1999 marked the first step in what *Time* magazine called Madeleine's War (see Albright 2003, 522; Isaacson 1999). Designed to undermine the Milošević regime, allied bombs targeted electrical plants, bridges, military installations, state communications facilities, and factories—all of them critical to the Serb campaign. Two months after the NATO air war started, the ICTY announced the indictment of Slobodan Milošević and four other Serb leaders for crimes against humanity. For the first time ever, international criminal charges had been leveled against a sitting head of government (see Albright 2003, 533).

Support for the Milošević regime crumbled with the ICTY indictments plus the damage caused by NATO bombs. Reports emerged of troops abandoning their units, and of efforts by Serb soldiers to sell arms to the KLA (see Albright 2003, 533). Caught in a diplomatic, military, and domestic political vise, Milošević withdrew his forces from Kosovo in early June; NATO then suspended air strikes and the UN authorized a peacekeeping mission (see Albright 2003, 534–535; Dumbrell 2009, 96).

Some ethnic Albanians who returned to Kosovo were ready to exact revenge. In July, Muslims killed fourteen Serb civilians on a farm near Gracko (see Hedges 1999). Albright visited the region that month to warn the Albanians they had nothing to gain and a great deal to lose by emulating the behavior of the Serbs. She then traveled to a Christian monastery to tell members of the Serb minority that the international community wanted to see a multi-ethnic Kosovo. Outside the Eastern Orthodox retreat, Serb men displayed their genitals for the secretary of state (see Albright 2003, 543).

EVALUATING IMPACT AND REPRESENTATION

Madeleine Albright traveled an enormous distance from her European childhood to leading an international response to crises in the Balkans. Not only was she the first woman to reach the top rung of a highly competitive foreign policy ladder in the United States, she also ascended to that rank despite having immigrated as an adolescent. In other respects, however, Albright's experiences hewed close to her origins. Her father had worked as a Czech press attaché and, later on, as his government's ambassador in Belgrade—not far from the sites of tragedy in Bosnia and Kosovo that made headlines through the 1990s. Those events echoed circumstances the Körbel family had faced in the late 1930s: ethnic intolerance fanned by dictators broke countries apart, and provoked barbarous acts that placed masses of civilians in harm's way.

Given her own background, Madeleine Albright opposed silence in the face of humanitarian disaster. In particular, her knowledge of the history of Central Europe underpinned decisions to endorse two separate military interventions in the former Yugoslavia. She convinced administration colleagues of the wisdom of that approach using a persuasive, forceful interpersonal style. Her actions not only helped to stop the bloodletting at Europe's heart, but also challenged the impression that US foreign policy was waffling and inchoate. Albright effectively rescued America's international relations from the charge of being as disorganized as the world they sought to shape.

Compared with Jeane Kirkpatrick's record, Albright's foreign policy career is distinguished by both pragmatism and consistent efforts to elevate the status of women on the global stage. In the Kosovo crisis, for example, Albright understood that Russia could press Serbia to end the conflict. Albright (2003, 504–505) thus invested considerable energy in building close ties with her counterpart Igor Ivanov, to ensure that Russia would not veto Contact Group efforts to find a solution. Within the US administration, she resisted Pentagon claims that war is necessarily fought using massive ground forces and heavy battlefield equipment. Instead, she advanced and ultimately confirmed a more nuanced argument which said that crises in the Balkans could be addressed via air strikes alone. Not all wars, in short, would end up like Vietnam.

This flexible approach also had its limits, however. If Kirkpatrick's foreign policy was open to charges of being too doctrinaire, then Albright's ran the risk of being seen as overly hopeful, elastic, and what one observer termed "opportunistic" (Doug Bennet, as quoted in Dobbs 1999, 356). Critics point to efforts to capture a Somali warlord, which led to violent chaos in the streets of Mogadishu and, in turn, inaction in the face of genocide in Rwanda (see Hyland 1999, 56–57; Rodman 2009, 219). Hyland (1999, 119–122) presents Albright's emphasis on improving human rights in China as not just narrow but also ineffective. Neither intervention in the former Yugoslavia, according to Hoff (2007, 129–130), produced "much more than tense apartheid arrangements." The inability of two consecutive Clinton administrations to conclude a nuclear deal with North Korea or reach a comprehensive peace in the Middle East can also be read as evidence that Albright's approach did not yield constructive results.

Neither the North Korea nor Middle East failure was unique to the Clinton team, though, since the subsequent Bush and Obama administrations fell short of settling both conflicts. It is therefore hard to sustain the argument that Albright's orientation was by itself a problem during the 1990s. Instead, it seems reasonable to view her presence as having made measurable contributions to the resolution of significant crises, notably those in Central Europe.

In particular, Albright's record stands out in the area of gender representation. She formed new networks of female diplomats, promoted women's advancement as a key US foreign policy goal, and repeatedly raised issues related to the autonomy of women and girls. Her efforts to press for international action against trafficking in women and girls, for example, led to the adoption of a new UN protocol in 2000 (see Raymond 2002). Unlike

Kirkpatrick, she did not hesitate to advocate for equality, including when the issues at stake, such as rape as a weapon of war, were raised by interests operating outside formal state and supranational channels. As discussed in Chapter 7, Albright's contributions are consistent with those of a feminist critical actor in that she created structures and initiated policy proposals to advance women's independence, which in turn emboldened others to take similar steps (see Childs and Krook 2008; Dahlerup 1988).

For Albright, taking charge of the new world disorder went hand in hand with a strong pro-equality agenda. Since she conceived of international relations as a set of evolving relationships, Albright (2009, 20) believed that nurturing those ties and ensuring that women benefited from economic and political reforms constituted integral parts of American diplomacy. Her career thus reveals the impact of the engaging interpersonal style recommended in Kirkpatrick's (1974) account of state lawmakers, when that approach is mapped onto a sustained but practical defense of US interests and women's rights.

Although the Clinton administration could not on its own fix the new world disorder of the 1990s, it is clear that much of the order it did foster emerged thanks to Albright.

CHAPTER 5

Preemption in the Wake of 9/11

Condoleezza Rice became the first female national security advisor to a US president following the election of George W. Bush in 2000. She then served during his second mandate as secretary of state, the only African American woman to date to reach that position.

In some respects, Rice resembled her pioneering predecessors. Like Jeane Kirkpatrick and Madeleine Albright, she arrived in the senior ranks of the executive branch with an academic background in political science and experience as a foreign policy advisor. Rice reflected many of the same character traits in that she was a confident, determined woman who communicated her views in direct and forceful terms.

Yet Rice's personal outlook, approach to leadership, and understanding of international affairs were clearly distinguishable from those of both Kirkpatrick and Albright. Rice saw individual will as the engine of human advancement. This philosophy echoed that of her parents, who assured their daughter she could become president of the United States—despite all the evidence to the contrary facing an African American girl born in Birmingham, Alabama in 1954 (see Mabry 2007, 35). Writing nine years later, Martin Luther King, Jr. (1963, 3) described Birmingham as the "most thoroughly segregated city in the United States." Compared with Albright, whose father was a Czech social democrat, Rice was far more conservative and individualistic.

Like her parents, Rice was guided by reliance on a divine spirit. She joined religious communities everywhere she lived; Christian congregations provided social networks that paralleled what protest groups offered other blacks and women of her generation. For Condoleezza, belonging to a community of faith created an extended family for an only child who never married and had no children of her own. Rice thus stood out from

Kirkpatrick in that her individualism was more strongly imbued with religious content.

The centrality of individual, family, and Christian doctrine to Rice's outlook created an exceptionally close tie with George W. Bush—who relied on the same anchors (see Alexander-Floyd 2008). As detailed in the sections that follow, Rice built a warm relationship with the Bush family beginning in the 1980s, which afforded her significant political access as well as influence. She served as George W. Bush's main foreign policy tutor before his candidacy for president was publicly declared, then as his lead advisor on the campaign trail and closest confidante through two executive mandates (see Kessler 2007; Mann 2004, 315, 367; Woodward 2004, 23). On the night following the attacks of 9/11, only Rice and the presidential couple slept in the White House family quarters (see Rice 2011, 77). As national security advisor and secretary of state, she spent considerable time at Camp David, the Bush family compound in Maine, and the Bush ranch in Texas (see Woodward 2004, 23). Bush (2010, 90) later wrote of Rice, "After six years together in the White House and on the campaign, I had grown very close to Condi Rice. She could read my mind and moods. We shared a vision of the world, and she wasn't afraid to let me know when she disagreed with me."

To what extent did Rice shape the main lines of US foreign policy during the George W. Bush years? Was she a transforming actor? How did Rice operate with respect to military force and gender politics? Did she adopt stereotypically masculine norms of behavior at the point of entering executive office, or rely on repertoires from an earlier time?

This chapter addresses each question using memoir, biographical, and other public sources that include Rice's own writings. It concludes that parallel with Kirkpatrick, Rice created the scaffolding that framed foreign policy. Like Kirkpatrick's (1979) indictment of the Carter administration, Rice (2000) dissects decision-making in the Clinton era. Similar to her predecessor, Rice (2000) develops the next president's international doctrine. Early in Bush's first term, following the attacks of 9/11, Rice formulated the rationale for preemptive military intervention that became the core of the US "war on terror."

Although studies of the George W. Bush years recognize Condoleezza Rice as a central actor, they see her as both underpowered and overpowered for the role she played. On one side, she is criticized as unqualified, indecisive, and incompetent—particularly by analysts who argue that personal loyalty to Bush impeded not only her assessment of intelligence information, but also her management of the policymaking machinery (see Charles-Philippe 2010; Clarke 2004, 229–230; Woodward 2004, 414–415). According to Charles-Philippe (2010, 54), Rice failed as national security advisor to coordinate the State and Defense departments, which meant that Bush was controlled by the latter: "Overly eager to keep Bush's ear and preserve her status, Rice placed the NSC at the service of the President's desire, not the government's needs." Charles-Philippe (2010, 54) concludes that "[w]hen it comes to the US blunders in Iraq, Rice was arguably one of the worst advisors on national security" (see also Rumsfeld 2011, 328–329).

By contrast, other sources suggest that Rice authoritatively steered the ship of state. These analysts attribute the decision to invade Iraq to her willingness to embrace idealistic values alongside national interests as the drivers of foreign policy. Simply stated, Rice convinced Bush to overthrow Saddam Hussein as part of a plan she developed to spread democracy across the Middle East (see Logevall 2010, 96; Mann 2004, 315–316). As the first African American woman to reach the heights of foreign policy responsibility, Rice's influence is often presented in highly sexualized terms—notably in videos and cartoons from the Bush era that portray her as a dominatrix or, in the words of Alexander-Floyd (2008, 439, 440, 444), a "vulture," "sexualized warrior princess," and "emasculating neo-jezebel" with romantic ties to the president. The photograph of Rice wearing a long, military-style coat and high boots when she met US troops in Germany in 2005, presented in Figure 5.1, tended to reinforce such images.[1] As

Figure 5.1. Secretary of State Condoleezza Rice greets US troops at Wiesbaden Army Airfield, 2005.
AP Photo; photo by J. Scott Applewhite.

discussed in Chapter 1, these tropes resemble views dating from the Renaissance era and earlier of women as wily, deceptive connivers rather than proper diplomats.

Regardless of how she is described, Condoleezza Rice shaped Bush-era foreign policy in identifiable ways. What distinguishes her from earlier leaders is an unusually close personal tie to the president and his family, which afforded opportunities to shape foreign policy directly and with less interference from other actors. Rice's (2000, 48–49) blueprint for the new administration thus became official practice: it merges an emphasis on unilateral military action in the national interest with a celebration of "America's special role" in spreading democracy and prosperity. This intermingling of power with value considerations diverges in stark terms from Kirkpatrick's (1979, 2007b) insistence on a prudent, more narrowly defined understanding of national interests.

Rice was connected with Albright in that they shared the same world politics mentor: Josef Korbel, Albright's father. After he died in 1977, Albright returned to Denver, where she found the family home filled with generous tributes. One arrived inside a piano-shaped flower planter. Mandula Korbel explained that it came from Josef's favorite student, Condoleezza Rice, who had entered the University of Denver with plans to become a concert pianist (see Albright 2003, 102).

Rice, however, projected little of the nuanced internationalism that Korbel imparted to his daughter. What she did absorb were his emphases on advancing American interests and values, and building social networks. She applied those lessons by forging a more norms-based foreign policy than Kirkpatrick (2007b) advocated, alongside what was arguably the closest relationship between a president and a foreign policy advisor in recent American history. Parallel with the cases of Kirkpatrick and Albright, the assertive approach to world affairs that she crafted—known as the Bush doctrine—diverges clearly from a "beautiful souls" view of women as pacific creatures who avoid conflict at all costs (see Elshtain 1995).

Like her understanding of national security, Rice's views about women's equality were firmly established and publicly known before her appointment to senior office. She elevated individual rights and personal will above group claims when it came to both gender and race, as reflected in the following statement:

> As an educated person, you have tools to change your own circumstances for the better whenever you find them stifling and along the way to change the lives of others, too. But you have to believe—like many who had less reason to have

faith in tomorrow but nonetheless did—that the locomotive of human progress is individual will. And then you have only to act on it, confident that you
will succeed. (Condoleezza Rice, 1994 commencement speech delivered at the
University of Alabama, as quoted in Mabry 2007, 39)

Beyond a circle of family, friends, and political contacts, Rice (2010,
48) was disinclined to join or identify with groups to the point that
she rejected demands by "victims" for what she saw as preferential
treatment. Since Rice conceived of America as a land of opportunity for
ambitious people from all backgrounds, she maintained that the best
way to address discrimination was through education, religious faith,
and hard work.

Rice put these beliefs into practice prior to becoming national security advisor. As the first woman and the first black to serve as provost of
Stanford University, she was widely recognized as a trailblazer. Yet in substantive terms, her commitment to conservative individualism served to
weaken equity programs on campus (Lusane 2006, 77). As detailed in this
chapter, even though her decisions as a university leader were extremely
contentious, Rice refused to compromise.

Later, Rice joined a Republican presidential team that was lauded for
appointing her and other women to senior posts, even though both Rice
and the party disparaged ideas of group belonging (Flanders 2005, 10–11,
71–72). Moderate voters were swayed not just by Bush's appointment record but also by administration rhetoric that said millions of women and
girls in Afghanistan and Iraq could go to school because they had been "lib-
erated" by US military intervention (George W. Bush, as quoted in Flanders
2005, xiii). Claims about protecting and freeing women, which Rice used
less than other members of the Bush inner circle, were voiced at the same
time as the administration curtailed access to abortion and contraception
in the global South (see Finlay 2006). This track record means that Rice
cannot be considered a critical actor for feminist interests.

This discussion opens by examining Bush-era foreign policy, in order
to evaluate Rice's status as a transformative leader. The following sections
then consider the personal background that informed her approaches to
war and women's equality.

SHAPING THE WAR ON TERROR

Accounts of Bush-era foreign policy focus on how the administration
responded to the attacks of 9/11. Naftali (2010, 86) maintains that the

decision to prosecute what the president and his advisors called the war on terror produced "decidedly mixed" results. On the positive side, al-Qaeda was prevented from mounting a further assault on American soil and was weakened by efforts to freeze the group's assets and dislodge the Taliban from power in Afghanistan (see Naftali 2010, 69, 77–78, 86; Schier 2009, 131–132). On the negative side, Bush's decision to invade Iraq is widely seen as a critical error. Schier (2009, 135; see also Logevall 2010; Woodward 2004) contends that the regime of Saddam Hussein posed little danger to US national security, given that the administration failed to prove either that Iraq was involved in the attacks of 9/11 or that it possessed weapons of mass destruction. Naftali (2010, 87) argues that rather than neutralizing the threat of insurgency, the invasion "created a petri dish for massive amounts of terrorism in Iraq between 2003 and 2007." Whether because of poor planning and intelligence (Schier 2009, 140–142) or a willful rejection of warnings about the likely consequences of overthrowing Saddam (Charles-Philippe 2010, 34), US actions in Iraq seriously damaged American interests.

Moreover, scholars present the Bush administration's goal of eliminating terrorism as both unrealistic and dangerous. On one level, it raised expectations that American military force could create a world free of extremist threat. Schier (2009, 134), for instance, posits that the preemption doctrine adopted by Republican leaders to justify invading Iraq reduced both American authority on the global stage and domestic confidence in the president. On another, decision-makers who endorsed the war on terror ignored the possibility that their actions would heighten, rather than eliminate, the prospects of violence (see Naftali 2010, 66; Schier 2009, 146).

Key directions of administration foreign policy are consistent with Rice's status as the most loyal and trusted advisor to George W. Bush (see Kessler 2007). Similar to Kirkpatrick's work with Reagan in 1980 and Albright's with Dukakis in 1988, Rice prepared a presidential candidate for the prime-time spotlight. The nominees her predecessors coached were also state governors who needed to demonstrate their foreign policy capabilities. Yet George W. Bush stands out because he was both substantively reliant upon and personally close with his tutor. Taken together, these patterns help to explain why Rice's influence proved so pivotal.

The partnership between Condoleezza Rice and the man who won the White House in 2000 grew out of a single telephone call. Former president George H. W. Bush contacted Rice in August 1998 to invite her to the family compound at Walker's Point, Maine. In Rice's (2011, 1) words, the prospective presidential candidate and prospective foreign policy teacher chatted on the back porch before a lobster supper, "just so we could get to know each other better."

The ties between George W. and Condoleezza dated from his father's presidential term. Rice first visited the retreat in Maine as a staff member at the National Security Council (NSC). After assembling a group of academic specialists to brief George H. W. Bush on the looming breakup of the Soviet Union, she became a high-profile member of his foreign policy team. Bush (as quoted in Rice 2010, 262; see also Mabry 2007, 122) senior, in fact, presented Rice to Mikhail Gorbachev as the woman "who tells me everything I need to know about the Soviet Union." Toward the end of H. W.'s term, Barbara Bush invited Rice for tea at the White House. The first lady predicted that the paths of the NSC assistant and her family would cross again (see Rice 2010, 270).

In 1995, Rice accompanied George H. W. to the opening session of the Texas legislature. His eldest son, George W., was a new state governor who spent an hour "talking life, politics, and baseball" with Rice at his office (Mabry 2007, 151). They met a few years later in former secretary of state George Shultz's living room, where the discussion lasted for hours and, according to Shultz, the connection between George W. and Rice—then provost of Stanford University—was palpable. In Shultz's words, "He and Condi really clicked, you could see it—on a human level" (Shultz, as quoted in Mabry 2007, 151).

The ties between candidate and advisor strengthened during the summer 1998 weekend in Maine. As Rice recalls, "we spent a lot of time out on the boat and in different places, talking about what you would face in foreign policy if you were president" (Rice, as quoted in Mabry 2007, 152). Mabry (2007, 152) writes that "[w]hile fishing, playing tennis, and working out side by side (she ran on a treadmill while he rowed and biked), Condi and W. bonded." She joined Bush's exploratory committee, traveled with him, and played the lead role in creating his foreign policy advisory group. Named after a cast iron statue of the Roman deity of fire that stands above her hometown, the team was called the Vulcans (see Mann 2004).

Like Kirkpatrick, Rice built her public profile as an outspoken critic of Democratic foreign policy. In "Promoting the National Interest," published in *Foreign Affairs*, Rice (2000) argues the Clinton administration missed multiple chances to advance American prestige. She portrays Democratic leaders as too undisciplined to develop a strategic approach to world politics, and misguided in their attempts to secure international consensus by operating through multilateral institutions. Democrats, in short, ignored the core purpose of US foreign policy.

That purpose, according to Rice (2000), is promoting the national interest. Clinton-era decisions to sign the Kyoto protocol on the environment or ban the testing of nuclear weapons reveal an inability to champion

US primacy. Such choices stand in stark contrast to the preeminent aim of a future Republican administration. Rice (2000, 46) identifies that priority in sharp, forceful terms: "to ensure that America's military can deter war, project power, and fight in defense of its interests if deterrence fails." Rice (2000, 50) rejects Democratic efforts to limit military spending, arguing that "the Clinton administration witlessly accelerated and deepened" cuts begun after the fall of the Berlin Wall. In her view, spending reductions deplete morale as well as fighting capacity. Moreover, she draws a clear distinction between humanitarian versus strategic policies, claiming that efforts to help civilians are in some cases antithetical to national interests. Rice (2000, 53) cites Clinton administration actions in Somalia as one example of what can go wrong when troops are dispatched to deal with problems in a faraway land. From her perspective, intervening in the Horn of Africa not only cost American lives, but also gravely damaged the international reputation of the United States.

By contrast, Rice (2000, 52) views intervention in Kosovo as having been necessary because a small-scale regional war threatened NATO allies. She disagrees, however, with Clinton administration claims that violence in the Balkans by itself justified US involvement. In her view, providing food and other necessities of life is potentially part of an interests-based foreign policy. What matters for Rice (2000, 53) is differentiating between the core motivations of humanitarian aid versus national interests. Her essay condemns how the United States acted in Kosovo. In Rice's (2000, 52) words, "The Kosovo war was conducted incompetently, in part because the administration's political goals kept shifting and in part because it was not, at the start, committed to the decisive use of military force." Without a clear sense of either ends or means, she maintains, the Clinton team was unable to develop an exit strategy.

Rice (2000, 48) places the defense of American power above any temptation to "do good" in the international arena; for example, she criticizes multilateral responses to humanitarian crisis because they privilege "illusory 'norms' of international behavior" and undermine American prestige. Above all, Rice (2000, 46) insists that leaders must understand the mandate of the country's armed forces. She maintains that the US military is a lethal brigade designed to serve national interests rather than the priorities of the UN or other supranational organizations. Heavy reliance on multilateral engagement risks turning American troops into what she terms "the world's '911'" (Rice 2000, 54). As Rice (2000, 53) declares, the US military "is not a civilian police force. It is not a political referee. And it is most certainly not designed to build a civilian society."

The final sentences of the essay reveal an ambitious and potentially reckless reading of national interests. In Rice's (2000, 62) words, "America can exercise power without arrogance and pursue its interests without hectoring and bluster. When it does so in concert with those who share its core values, the world becomes more prosperous, democratic, and peaceful. That has been America's special role in the past, and it should be again as we enter the next century." The approach she advocates thus begins with national interests, but stretches the concept such that it recognizes a "special role" or universal mission to spread freedom and economic growth.

As the closest advisor to Bush, Rice's willingness to embrace multiple foreign policy motives proved crucial. On the morning of September 11, 2001, as the president showcased his public education and literacy agenda by reading a story with second graders in Florida, he learned early details of the attack from Rice—who was in Washington that day (see Padgett 2011; Rice 2011, 72). Bush remained with the schoolchildren for a few minutes before moving to a nearby room, where he announced the following:

> Today, we've had a national tragedy. Two airplanes have crashed into the World Trade Center in an apparent terrorist attack on our country. I have spoken to the Vice President, to the Governor of New York, to the Director of the FBI, and have ordered that the full resources of the federal government go to help the victims and their families, and—and to conduct a full-scale investigation to hunt down and to find those folks who committed this act. Terrorism against our nation will not stand. (Bush 2001b)

After requesting a moment of silence, Bush (2001b) offered the following statement: "May God bless the victims, their families, and America."

The president spoke that evening from the Oval Office. He condemned the attacks as "evil, despicable acts of terror" and "acts of mass murder," and reiterated his promise to find and prosecute those responsible (Bush 2001c). He then reinforced his morning statement on the importance of keeping faith in times of crisis. In announcing his determination to win what he termed "the war against terrorism," Bush (2001c; see also Rice 2011, 77) used a sentence recommended by his national security advisor: "We will make no distinction between the terrorists who committed these acts and those who harbor them." His formal address concluded with a values-based call to "go forward to defend freedom and all that is good and just in our world" (Bush 2001c).

Rice (2011, 77) reports that "the President nicely invited me to stay in the [White House] residence" that night. As shown in Figure 5.2, she focused in the next hours and weeks on gathering information and finding common

Figure 5.2. President George W. Bush reviews briefing paper outside the Oval Office with Vice President Dick Cheney and National Security Advisor Condoleezza Rice, 2001.
Courtesy George W. Bush Presidential Library and Museum.

ground in the foreign policy team. It included Vice President Dick Cheney and Defense Secretary Donald Rumsfeld, who wanted to prosecute the war on terror in both Afghanistan and Iraq. By comparison, Secretary of State Colin Powell preferred to exhaust diplomatic options first—especially with respect to Iraq. Rice (2011, Chapter 12) describes herself, President Bush, and CIA director George Tenet as somewhere in the middle: neither convinced by claims that Saddam Hussein was directly linked to al-Qaeda, nor optimistic about UN efforts to press the Iraqi leader to change.[2]

Rice's bridge across the factions began with a proposition she had advanced in discussions with Bush on the fateful day. If no distinction were made between the attackers and those who sheltered them, then waiting for another strike by al-Qaeda or others with similar motives was not an option. The United States needed to address potential sources of danger in order to prevent further attacks.

Bush's (2002a) State of the Union address expands on Rice's equation between terrorists and their havens. It singles out regimes that shelter extremists by asserting that North Korea, Iran, and Iraq, together with "their terrorist allies, constitute an axis of evil, arming to threaten the peace of the world. By seeking weapons of mass destruction, these regimes pose a grave and growing danger. They could provide these arms to terrorists, giving them the means to match their hatred. They could attack our allies or attempt to blackmail the United States. In any of these cases, the price of indifference would be catastrophic" (Bush 2002a).

The "axis of evil" phrase drew a direct link between weapons ostensibly possessed by Iraq and other countries, and their potential use by groups hostile to the United States. It explicitly raised the possibility of military action against named enemy states.

Consistent with views she expressed prior to the 2000 election, Rice fused an interests-based response to 9/11 with considerations grounded in the spread of American values. She worked with Bush to craft a Freedom Agenda, which saw the absence of democratic rights in regions like the Middle East as an incentive for young men to join al-Qaeda and other similar groups. Bush's (2002a) State of the Union message outlines a plan to spread liberal values in predominantly Muslim countries:

> America will always stand firm for the non-negotiable demands of human dignity: the rule of law; limits on the power of the state; respect for women; private property; free speech; equal justice; and religious tolerance. America will take the side of brave men and women who advocate these values around the world, including the Islamic world, because we have a greater objective than eliminating threats and containing resentment. We seek a just and peaceful world beyond the war on terror.

Consistent with Rice's (2000) intermingling of interest- and value-based approaches to foreign policy, Bush thus signaled within months of 9/11 a readiness to use military force to uphold liberal democratic ideals—including "respect for women" living outside the United States. The latter phrase was more nuanced than women's equality, since it "is not threatening to those U.S. allies who do not fully recognize women's rights but who do claim to respect women" (Ferguson 2007, 202). Using the language of taking sides, his text not only defends armed intervention in the service of various norms, but also justifies preemptive action.

A few months later, in an address to West Point graduates, the president stated that threats to national interests would be eliminated at their point of origin. Once again, Rice shaped a key sentence in Bush's prose. It reads as follows: "Our security will require all Americans to be forward-looking and resolute, to be ready for preemptive action when necessary to defend our liberty and to defend our lives" (Bush, as quoted in Rice 2011, 152).

By the spring of 2002, the main markers of Bush-era foreign policy were in place. First, consistent with Rice (2000), the administration had not hesitated to act unilaterally. Second, the national security advisor ensured that the president's Oval Office statement on 9/11 affirmed that those who shelter terrorists would be held to account. Third, Bush's 2002 State of the Union address asserts the US will not just defend its interests, but also pursue a values-based approach to international affairs. The last fulcrum of the Bush doctrine was clarified in Rice's contribution to the West Point text, which said that military action would be undertaken in anticipation of threats to US security and values.

A year after the al-Qaeda attacks, Rice released a new National Security Strategy. Like her earlier statements, the document combines values with interests by insisting that the core aim of national security policy is "to promote a balance of power that favors freedom." Rice (2002a) maintains that poor, corrupt countries without democratic institutions need to be changed in order to make life better for their citizens, stop the growth of international terror networks, and ensure America's security. If necessary, the strategy confirms, the United States will defend its interests on its own and in advance of an attack.

Rice (2002b) includes a detailed discussion of rogue states, defined as countries governed by dictators who oppress their own people; ignore international law; seek "to acquire weapons of mass destruction" (WMD) such as nuclear, biological, or chemical agents that can cause widespread death and destruction; support terrorism; and oppose the United States and its values. Unlike former enemies such as the Soviet Union, rogue states are difficult to contain because they pursue risky, often unpredictable actions to attract attention. In a section titled "Prevent Our Enemies from Threatening Us, Our Allies, and Our Friends with Weapons of Mass Destruction," Rice (2002b) asserts that preemptive action against rogue nations is necessary: "The overlap between states that sponsor terror and those that pursue WMD compels us to action."

Rice (2002b) thus provides a rationale for the most significant and controversial element of George W. Bush–era foreign policy: the invasion of Iraq beginning in March 2003. Although the national security advisor was far from alone in promoting that action, she was Bush's closest confidante in the deliberations leading up to it and the lead administration voice who foreshadowed and defended the decision in media interviews (Flanders 2005, 68–69). From the time Bush began to consider a presidential run through her authorship of the 2002 National Security Strategy, Rice guided his thinking about world affairs and, above all, her words provided the main justification for invoking military force.

The next sections explore the background to her development as a transformative foreign policy leader.

As the only child of two African American teachers, Condoleezza Rice (2010, 187) was expected to be a top achiever—a "striver," in her own words. She developed exceptional poise and confidence by working hard to meet the high standards set by her family. They encouraged her to feel proud of herself despite the circumstances (see Rice 2010, 47, 70). In the Birmingham of Rice's youth, white supremacists controlled major public institutions, including city hall, the police and fire departments, and the local school board. Neighborhoods were divided by race, as were schools at all levels. The city had one black-owned restaurant.[3]

Rice's family background crossed multiple races, ethnocultural groups, and social classes—which explains in part her attraction to individualist rather than collectivist ideas. Rice (2010, 4) recalls her maternal grandmother's "rich brown skin and very high cheekbones, exposing American Indian blood that was obvious, if ill-defined." Her grandfather, Albert Ray, had such light skin that he was assumed to have at least partial Italian ancestry. Rice (2010, 4) suggests that this element forms the basis for the first names of various members of the family, including herself and her mother, Angelena.

Mattie and Albert Ray dug a well and built a house on land they purchased outside Birmingham. Albert worked as a miner by day and blacksmith by evening. Mattie saved so she could buy mahogany furniture and the piano she used for teaching music. As upwardly mobile blacks, the Rays tried to shield their offspring from visible signs of racial discrimination; for instance, they banned their children from using segregated public toilets and buses (see Mabry 2007, 22; Rice 2010, 8).

Angelena and her sister played piano and organ for black churches. Both completed undergraduate degrees at a nearby college. Angelena was a fashionable woman whose light skin was seen as attractive by African Americans in the area (see Rice 2010, 13). She found work at Fairfield Industrial High School, opened in the 1920s for the children of black workers at a local steel plant.

John Rice, Jr. became athletics director at the same school after earning degrees in history and divinity. His paternal grandparents were slaves and, later, sharecroppers on an Alabama cotton farm. His grandmother worked in the main plantation house, learned to read, and was reputed to be the owner's daughter (see Mabry 2007, 18–19; Rice 2010, 13). John's father was a minister with a network of churches and schools across the South, while his mother came from a half-Creole background in Louisiana. John Jr. used income from his teaching job to create the Westminster

Presbyterian Church, a branch of his father's organization, in the middle-class black neighborhood of Titusville. The church became a hub of not just religious and social activity, but also a focal point for efforts to lift African Americans out of poverty through education.[4]

John and Angelena shared a belief that personal motivation, learning, and religious faith made it possible to build a meaningful life in unjust circumstances. Rice (2010, 47) recalls one clear message that her parents and other teachers conveyed: "'To succeed,' they routinely reminded us, 'you will have to be twice as good.' This was declared as a matter of fact, not a point for debate." Rice (2010, 48) summarizes the individualism of middle-class adults in Titusville as follows: "We love you and will give you everything we can to help you succeed. But there are no excuses and there is no place for victims."

As an expectant father, John Rice bought a football for what he assumed would be a son. Undeterred, he coached Condoleezza in the practice and analysis of the sport, and turned her into a lifelong NFL fan. Rice (2010, 75) describes herself as a "tomboy" who enjoyed bowling with her dad and watching football and hockey games with him (see also Rice 2010, 10, 29, 33, 44).

Angelena created what relatives and neighbors describe as a "fiercely protective bubble" around Condoleezza (Mabry 2007, 30). She and John read to her every night; they bought a miniature organ and later a piano, and arranged for Grandma Ray to teach their daughter. Condoleezza gave her first public piano recital when she was four. Rice (2010, 74) recalls being enrolled in "all kinds of lessons: ballet, gymnastics, and even baton twirling, of all things." When Condoleezza was eight years old, Angelena hired a private tutor for weekly French lessons (see Rice 2010, 74).

The couple also created a politically engaged environment at home. The Rices developed various rituals, including the secret ballot election of a household president. Condoleezza relied on her mother's vote to win the race (see Rice 2010, 36). As Chet Huntley and David Brinkley delivered the evening news, John sat at his daughter's side to answer her questions and explain in detail the background to stories, including the Cuban missile crisis (see Mabry 2007, 38; Rice 2010, 38).

Rice's early social network included mostly relatives and other educators. In her words, "my parents kept their distance from the white world and created a relatively placid cocoon of family, church, community, and school" (Rice 2010, 24). Rice's (2010, 58) memoir describes a "parallel universe" of middle-class black society that, for the most part, remained intact until the ground literally began to shake in the early 1960s. Before that point, as Rice

(2010, 86) maintains, "we found a way to live normally in highly abnormal circumstances."

Racial tensions escalated with the arrival in Birmingham of Martin Luther King, Jr. In early 1963, civil rights activists targeted the seat of Jefferson County, Alabama because its white leaders refused to desegregate schools, stores, restaurants, or buses—even after court orders had been issued and significant progress had been achieved elsewhere in the South. As Rice (2010, 86) recalls, "Birmingham eclipsed every other big American city in the ugliness of its racism."

Although John Rice did not march in civil rights protests, he rejected efforts by the school board to punish students who did participate. In May 1963, Rice took his nine-year-old daughter to the city fairgrounds, which Birmingham police had turned into a holding area for students under arrest. About a week later, together with Angelena, John walked Condoleezza through the charred wreckage of a race riot. After the Ku Klux Klan had attacked a black-owned motel in order to kill King—who by that point had left the city—blacks torched an armored personnel carrier they believed was carrying the police chief (see Rice 2010, 96).

A few months later, on a quiet Sunday morning, Birmingham quaked with the force of what was thought to be a mining disaster. A powerful firebomb had exploded at the Sixteenth Street Baptist Church while Condoleezza and her parents prayed a couple of miles away. Klansmen had concealed dynamite under a shrub beside the black church, and killed four young girls ranging in age from eleven to fourteen. Denise McNair and Condoleezza had played dolls together. Cynthia Wesley had participated in the youth fellowship at John's church. Addie Mae Collins had been a student of Angelena's brother (see Mabry 2007, 40; Rice 2010, 98). The force of the blast blew open a wall of the church, injuring dozens, including a man who was thrown into the air from his car as he drove by (see Mabry 2007, 39). Bombing a church and murdering children proved, in Rice's (2010, 97) view, that her hometown remained "a city of appalling hatred, prejudice, and violence."

John Rice told members of his family that he opposed the nonviolent strategy of some civil rights leaders (see Mabry 2007, 48). While the motto of King's Southern Christian Leadership Conference asserted, "Not one hair of one head of one person should be harmed," John Rice advocated a biblical "eye for an eye" approach that recognized unmitigated evil on the segregationist side. John's perspective helps to explain the firm support his daughter later voiced for the right to bear arms. Rice (2010, 93; see also Mabry 2007, 85) notes that in her childhood, public officials in Birmingham were allies of the same whites who bombed black churches. As the city's Public Safety Commissioner, Bull Connor would not have permitted men such as John Rice to own, let alone use, the weapons they carried in self-defense.

Consistent with their values, Angelena and John found an independent route out of Jefferson County. In 1966, graduate studies John had begun at the University of Denver led to his appointment as dean of students at Stillman College. The family moved to Tuscaloosa, an academic center with integrated restaurants and greater openness to the outside world. Condoleezza began grade eight at the age of eleven, two years ahead of the norm. John continued to study each summer in Denver, where Condoleezza awoke at 4:30 a.m. to practice figure skating (see Rice 2010, 121, 128).

Once John received an offer to join the administrative staff of the University of Denver, the family left Alabama. Condoleezza entered a private school in Denver and continued to study figure skating and piano (see Rice 2010, 125, 130). Tennis lessons and a new grand piano were added to the mix (see Mabry 2007, 73; Rice 2010, 139). As in Alabama, she showed great determination to excel, but realized for the first time that perseverance was not always enough. Her plan to combine the last year of high school and first year of a music degree at the University of Denver left little spare time; moreover, she recognized that the stars did not align for a career as an outstanding figure skater. Rice (2010, 151; see also Mabry 2007, 75) explains her decision in simple declarative terms: "So I quit competitive skating."

After investing two years in a music performance program, Rice reached a similar conclusion about piano: conscientious work habits were insufficient. One summer at the Aspen Music Festival School revealed that young prodigies could master pieces in a single sight reading and play them with greater interpretive depth than she could muster after months of preparation. In Rice's (2010, 161; see also Mabry 2007, 73–74) words, "I'd never be good enough to rise to the top of the profession."

Consistent with the resilience her family had demonstrated for generations, Condoleezza started over. She drew on the example of her mother's experiences in the same period: after discovering a lump in her breast when Condoleezza was fifteen, Angelena underwent cancer treatment in Denver. She insisted that the family's life would go on without interruption—and it largely did (see Rice 2010, 142–146).

DOING INTERNATIONAL RELATIONS

The spring of Condoleezza's junior year at Denver marked her initial exposure to the study of international relations. In a course taught by Josef

Korbel, the father of Madeleine Albright, she was intrigued by lectures on Eastern and Central Europe and, in particular, the rise of Stalin (see Mabry 2007, 80; Rice 2010, 163). Korbel encouraged Rice to study the Russian language and pursue an advanced degree. She graduated at the age of nineteen as the outstanding woman in the senior class (see Mabry 2007, 86; Rice 2010, 165).

Rice followed Korbel's advice by enrolling in an MA program at the University of Notre Dame—a decision that took her away for the first time from the city where her parents lived. She enrolled in a variety of politics and economics courses, built a network of friends, and dated an array of football players. According to Mabry (2007, 90–91), she nearly married Denver Broncos wide receiver Rick Upchurch. Mabry (2007, 90) reports that the two were engaged until Rice realized they were entirely unmatched. Rice successfully applied to law schools but was not enthusiastic about becoming a lawyer (see Mabry 2007, 91; Rice 2010, 176).

With no clear road map for the future, Rice consulted the man she called "her second father" (Mabry 2007, 80). Josef Korbel urged her to consider doctoral studies, so Condoleezza entered the PhD program in international relations at Denver. Korbel's health deteriorated, however, to the point that he asked Rice to take responsibility for one of his undergraduate courses (see Rice 2010, 179). In the summer of 1977, while Rice held a State Department internship in Washington, Korbel died.

Rice floundered until her parents offered to fund a visit to the Soviet Union (see Rice 2010, 184). The trip not only improved her language skills but also helped to clarify plans for her dissertation. She chose to focus on the place Korbel had left, postwar Czechoslovakia. Her thesis examined tensions between Moscow and Prague over the allegiance of the Czech military (see Rice 2010, 186).

Travels in Eastern Europe opened Rice's eyes to the daily grind of life under communism. Initially resistant to the idea that US foreign policy should concern itself with the internal politics of other countries, she came to see America as a "beacon of democracy" to people around the globe (Rice, as quoted in Mann 2004, 148). This perspective gradually meshed with her emphasis on strategic power considerations such that for Rice, liberal values and US interests intertwined in a single tapestry.

Rice's next steps up the career ladder benefited directly from affirmative action efforts of the early 1980s. Given that relatively few women, African Americans, and especially African American women studied Soviet bloc militaries, she won a Ford Foundation fellowship based at Stanford University (see Mabry 2007, 94–96). Rice had neither completed the dissertation at that point, nor had she studied at an institution that approximated Stanford's elite status (see Rice 2010, 186, 195, 197).

Yet Rice had learned enough about strategic studies to apply basic theories to practice. As a visitor in Palo Alto, she presented her thesis findings to multiple audiences, including the international security research center and the political science department. She held meetings with campus leaders, one of whom recalls Rice in her mid-twenties as a woman who "had a very self-confident manner without being overbearing or arrogant" (David Kennedy, Associate Dean of Humanities and Sciences at Stanford, as quoted in Mabry 2007, 97). Stanford's Department of Political Science offered a tenure-track faculty position, which she accepted.

Rice needed to demonstrate that she deserved lifetime employment from a university that typically tenured only about a third of its entry-level recruits. Rice once again worked to beat the odds: she developed a network of senior scholars willing to comment on her work, advise her on future projects, and include her in their research conferences. Those efforts paid off when Princeton University Press agreed to publish a revised version of the dissertation (see Rice 2010, 207).

Rice built a circle of friends that included other professors and members of the Presbyterian community. It provided valuable support to her as a single woman and only child when Angelena died in Denver in 1984. John moved to Palo Alto, where he later remarried.

The ideas Condoleezza had learned from Josef Korbel favored the Democratic Party and superpower détente. Like Jeane Kirkpatrick, however, she grew frustrated with Jimmy Carter's seeming naïveté toward the Soviet Union. In Rice's (2010, 187) words,

> I had this narrative in my head about reconciliation of the North and South; he was going to be the first southern president. Now I watched him say that he had learned more about the Soviet Union from this Afghanistan invasion than he had ever known. "Whom did you think you were dealing with?" I asked the television set. When Carter decided that the best response to the invasion was to boycott the Olympics, he lost me. I voted for Ronald Reagan in 1980, and a few years later I joined the Republican Party.[5]

Rice's distrust of Soviet expansionism first became relevant to policymaking in 1986, when she began a fellowship at the Joint Chiefs of Staff in Washington. At the Nuclear and Chemical Division, charged with developing plans for full-scale war between the United States and the Soviet Union, Rice met senior military officers including General Colin Powell, then deputy national security advisor in the Reagan administration (see Rice 2010, 232–233).

Her profile as a conservative foreign policy expert took off the following year, when *ABC News* invited her to serve as a national commentator. Once George H. W. Bush won the 1988 presidential election, Rice received offers to join the State Department, Pentagon, and National Security Council. Rice (2010, 243; see also Mabry 2007, 112; Rice 2011, 4, 13) decided "there was nothing like being a member of the White House staff" and became NSC special assistant for Soviet and East European affairs. Rice's work habits resembled those of Brent Scowcroft, the national security advisor who recruited her. She arrived at the office by 6:30 most mornings and generally did not leave until after nine at night (see Rice 2010, 246).

Given tumultuous changes unfolding in the region for which Rice was responsible, Scowcroft asked her to assemble a group of experts who would meet the president at the family compound in Maine. Since the only heated room on a snowy day in early 1989 was Bush's bedroom, that's where the briefing took place. Bush then commissioned a thorough review of US policy toward the Soviet bloc (see Rice 2010, 248–250).

Rice produced a report that found central control had measurably weakened in both Russia and its satellite states. As a result, she argued, Washington could no longer rely on domino theories that sought to deter Soviet expansionism (see Rice 2010, 250; Mabry 2007, 114). Rice identified the looming challenge for the United States and its allies as integrating post-communist states into a post–Cold War international system. She captured the future in two words: "beyond containment" (Rice 2010, 251; Mabry 2007, 114).

The phrase catapulted Rice from a relatively obscure special assistant at the NSC into a respected presidential advisor. She accompanied Bush when he delivered major foreign policy speeches, including in Hungary and Poland, and served as White House representative on the international negotiating team charged with sorting out German unification. Her strong advocacy for bringing East and West Germany together quickly inside NATO helped to ensure that outcome. Bush asked Rice to travel to Palo Alto with Mikhail and Raisa Gorbachev when they visited in 1990. She sat in Scowcroft's office while Bush held an unannounced meeting with Russian opposition leader Boris Yeltsin (see Rice 2010, 254–268).

In her role at the NSC, Rice helped to develop, communicate, and implement US policies toward the post-Soviet world. She established that record inside an administration that pursued markedly conservative positions on matters of gender and race—positions she would later uphold as an academic leader at Stanford University. George H. W. Bush vetoed the 1990

Civil Rights Act, for example, arguing that the legislation imposed an unfair burden on businesses by establishing hiring quotas. The revised law he signed a year later weakened protections for workers by permitting companies to use tests and other tools in recruitment and promotion decisions (see Bashevkin 1998, 77).

Bush reinforced these directions with the appointment of increasingly conservative judges and, in particular, nominated Clarence Thomas to the Supreme Court. A conservative black, Thomas was named by Bush to serve on the District of Columbia appeals court. Given his staunch opposition to civil rights and feminist claims, Thomas faced a vigorous campaign by progressives to block any further promotions (see Hill 2007; Thomas 2007, 239–240).

Once Bush nominated Thomas to the high court in the summer of 1991, University of Oklahoma law professor Anita Hill alleged that Thomas had sexually harassed her. Hill told the Senate Judiciary Committee that as her supervisor in Washington, Thomas had made inappropriate sexual advances on multiple occasions. The Bush White House responded in ways that effectively put Hill on trial in the court of public opinion. Thomas secured his judicial appointment, and the conflict between supporters and opponents of group-based remedies to inequality became even more polarized (see Black and Allen 2001, 36–37).

Toward the end of her term at the NSC, Rice accepted an invitation for tea in the White House residence. First Lady Barbara Bush (as quoted in Rice 2010, 270) told Rice that as "such a good friend of the Bushes," she and the nation's first family were sure to meet again.

Those who observed Rice after she returned to Stanford University in 1991 saw a highly motivated and well-connected political actor. As author of the "beyond containment" doctrine, she had molded the contours of post–Cold War foreign policy. In the words of a colleague, Rice came back as "a different person: more confident, more able to deal with outside demands and criticisms, more ambitious" (Daniel Okimoto, as quoted in Mabry 2007, 122).

Rice's standing was revealed in the decision of George Shultz to invite her to join his lunch group as well as the board of Chevron. More board offers arrived from Hewlett-Packard, Transamerica, and other firms (see Mabry 2007, 123–124). The governor of California appointed Rice to the state's electoral boundaries commission. She resumed her work as a commentator for *ABC News* (see Rice 2010, 272–274).

Together with her father and stepmother, Rice established a charity in Palo Alto called the Center for a New Generation. Funded by many of the same donors who supported Stanford University, it offered reading, mathematics, music, and other programs for disadvantaged blacks and Hispanics. Condoleezza thus put into action the family philosophy, which said that individuals who invested in learning could improve their lives (see Mabry 2007, 142–143; Rice 2010, 278).

ACADEMIC LEADERSHIP

In 1992, Rice was named to the search committee for a Stanford University president. The institution faced serious problems once the federal government cut transfers in the wake of a financial scandal. The campus also needed physical renewal after a major earthquake (see Rice 2010, 283–284). Gerhard Casper, a legal scholar from the University of Chicago, accepted the position.

Casper and Rice were conservative academics who believed that universities were best insulated from external social pressures. From their perspective, the primary aim of top-ranked academic organizations was to advance research and teaching. In Casper's words, "A university did not have a political mission as such." Casper and Rice also shared a frustration with the typically slow pace of campus decision-making. Casper felt "completely impatient with all of these processes" and sensed that when it came to lengthy consultations, Rice "was perhaps even more impatient" (Casper, as quoted in Mabry 2007, 125).

Casper's success at Stanford depended on recruiting a decisive provost—effectively, the chief operating officer of the university. As a thirty-eight-year-old with no experience managing her own department, Rice was not an obvious choice. Yet if Casper sought someone who was determined to reform the institution, then she fit the bill perfectly. During six years as provost, Rice turned Stanford's more than one-billion-dollar budget from deficit to surplus. She introduced small undergraduate seminars taught by top scholars and oversaw the construction of an entirely new science complex (see Mabry 2007, 146; Rice 2010, 309). In short, Rice applied an unrelenting emphasis on results to her academic leadership career.

Rice confronted obstacles, however, at the levels of both substance and process. As provost, she asked every division to plan for a 5–10 percent budget cut. Black and aboriginal student groups opposed both the funding reduction and her decision to impose it from the center. Rice announced her modus operandi in an open meeting with faculty members. Her summary statement (as quoted in Mabry 2007, 294) was as follows: "I don't do committees. I'll consult widely. But someone will have to make decisions, and that will be Gerhard and me."

Rice thus told critics that their priorities would not be protected from budget cuts. At one meeting, a student accused Rice of not caring enough about "the plight of minorities." The provost replied, "You don't have the standing to question my commitment to minorities. I've been black all of my life, and that is far longer than you are old" (Rice 2010, 295).

The position held by Cecilia Burciaga, a veteran Latina staff member who managed Stanford's affirmative action program, was on the chopping block. Among the faculty appointments she had played a role in creating was the slot in political science held by the provost. Burciaga's supporters mounted what Rice (2010, 296) describes as "a massive protest." Students began a hunger strike and built a tent encampment outside her office. When colleagues asked how she felt, Rice (2010, 296) said she was committed to implementing her course of action; as she told Stanford's Faculty Senate, "I am sleeping and eating just fine. They can stay out there until hell freezes over. My decisions stand."

After Burciaga's job ended and a number of women professors were denied tenure, the provost became embroiled in another dispute. Rice argued that Stanford's situation resembled that of other elite universities: an over-whelmingly white male professoriate was becoming more mixed with the re-cruitment of new female assistant professors. She cited her own provostial appointment as evidence that glass ceilings were being shattered for the categories of sex and race as well as age. Rice said she approved of efforts to recruit more women and minorities as assistant professors. She opposed, however, any dilution of institutional standards at the point of tenure. She insisted her policy represented no change from practices that had applied in her own case. According to Rice, she had been offered a chance to prove herself worthy of tenure and promotion at Stanford (see Mabry 2007, 134–141; Rice 2010, 300–305).

The controversy heated up once Stanford's past leaders said that diversity considerations had figured in the tenure process (see Mabry 2007, 138–139). Rice's critics questioned whether she deserved tenure given her absences from campus and what they saw as a modest research record.[6] Rice's refusal to budge led one close observer to describe her as "despotic" (anonymous source quoted in Mabry 2007, 147; see also Mabry 2007, 133).

In 1999, sixteen female academics who held past or present affiliations with Stanford lodged a formal complaint with the US Department of Labor. It alleged that "they had been unfairly denied tenure or promotions or had been wrongfully terminated, at least in part because of their gender" (Wilson 2008). Casper claimed the Clinton administration's willingness to investigate the grievance was politically motivated (see Mabry 2007, 147). The process dragged on to the point that eleven of the complainants dropped out. In 2008, when the Labor Department concluded that evidence of systemic discrimination was not clear in the remaining five cases, a new team of university leaders announced that their institution had been vindicated (see Sturrock 2008; Wilson 2008). What remains noteworthy is that sixteen accomplished women filed discrimination complaints against Stanford during the term of its first female provost.

Rice, however, was unmoved by their grievances. Since early childhood, she had been taught that motivated individuals rise to the top despite their circumstances. Moreover, she likely did not equate the tenure hurdle for female professors at Stanford with the barriers she had faced in Birmingham. Rice's refusal to bend in the face of campus protest reinforces this point. As a senior decision-maker at a respected university, she ranked balancing the budget and defending academic standards above concerns for faculty or curriculum diversity.

Holding a major institutional leadership position before she joined the George W. Bush administration made Rice distinctive among foreign policy leaders. Prior to their appointments by Presidents Reagan, Clinton, and Obama, respectively, neither Jeane Kirkpatrick, Madeleine Albright, nor Hillary Clinton had grappled with the scale of bureaucratic complexity that Rice confronted as provost. In that post, she developed and executed a controversial strategic plan that reshaped the university's internal operations, thus gaining extensive hands-on experience in managing a large organization. Above all, Rice demonstrated unwavering commitment to proceed despite concerted opposition.

Once she returned to Washington, Rice employed a similar approach to getting things done. After the 2000 election, she nurtured a close relationship with a chief executive who shared the same core beliefs and, assured of his support, focused her energies on realizing their joint agenda. At the level of gender politics, she joined a presidential team that, like the Gerhard Casper administration at Stanford, talked about opportunities for women but refused to adopt policies demanded by feminist groups.

Rice's time as Stanford provost offers clear signals as to her behavioral repertoire. She communicated using assertive, blunt language. Her approach when challenged was to be forceful and uncompromising, rather than diffident and malleable. Contrary to claims that women adopt new and stereotypically masculine approaches in order to be taken seriously in senior foreign policy roles, Condoleezza Rice arrived in the top echelons of the George W. Bush administration with firm ideas about what considerations should drive decision-making, and no support for what she saw as "victim" responses to gender, racial, or other inequalities.

In early 1999, Rice joined George W. Bush's campaign committee and set about organizing his foreign policy advisory group. Bush and Rice faced an impending race against a strong Democratic nominee: Al Gore was in many respects the antithesis of Bush, who only won the Texas governorship in 1994. By 2000, Gore had served two terms as a highly engaged vice president, plus more than fifteen years in the Senate and House of Representatives. His knowledge of subjects including arms control and climate change seemed unassailable.

Neither Bush nor Rice, however, was easily deterred. Rice assembled a group of experts known as the Vulcans who were overwhelmingly white and male, and heavily tilted toward experience in the George H. W. Bush administration. She scheduled regular consultations among them and with George W. to sort out policy differences, and to ensure that the campaign platform reflected his relatively centrist or "big tent" orientation (see Mann 2004).

Rice recruited Paul Wolfowitz as advisory group co-chair. A specialist on arms control and a fervent anti-communist, Wolfowitz had worked in diplomatic and defense positions for presidents from both major parties. Like Jeane Kirkpatrick, he had been a "Scoop" Jackson Democrat who migrated to the neoconservative movement. Inside that stream, Wolfowitz was unusually hawkish and unpredictable. Before a congressional committee in 1998, for instance, he criticized George H. W. Bush's decision seven years earlier not to depose Saddam Hussein. At the time Bush made that choice, Wolfowitz served as a policy undersecretary to Secretary of Defense Dick Cheney (Mann 2004, 198). The views of Wolfowitz, Cheney, and others that unfinished business remained from the first Gulf War, which had pushed Iraqi troops out of Kuwait—but left Saddam in power in Baghdad—directly shaped the foreign policy actions of the George W. Bush administration.

As well, Wolfowitz co-authored a 1992 defense planning document which said the US should confront any new competitor for global power through, if necessary, the use of preemptive unilateral force (Mann 2004, 199). President George H. W. Bush chose to rely instead on the more moderate strategy Rice proposed as an area specialist at the NSC, known as "beyond containment." Ultimately, the events of 9/11 led Rice to see preventive action as a useful way of containing and eliminating groups such as al-Qaeda.

Arguably the greatest challenge for George W. Bush was demonstrating foreign policy competence. During the New Hampshire primaries, a journalist asked Bush to name the leaders of four global hot spots. Bush could correctly identify one, the president of Taiwan, and then tried to turn the tables by asking the reporter to name the foreign minister of Mexico. The remainder of their exchange unfolded as follows: "The reporter replied, 'No sir, but I would say to that, I'm not running for president.' Bush said, 'What I'm suggesting to you is, if you can't name the foreign minister of Mexico, therefore, you know, you're not capable about what you do. But the truth of the matter is you are, whether you can or not'" (see Johnson 1999). Media accounts of the interview were overwhelmingly negative, as reflected in a *Washington Post* headline that read "Bush Fails Quiz on Foreign Affairs."[7]

Rice used the opportunity to intensify her schedule of one-on-one tutorials with the Texas governor. Bush then acquitted himself well in a key foreign policy debate with Gore. Borrowing a page from Reagan's performance twenty years earlier that relied heavily on Kirkpatrick (1979), Bush presented an abridged version of Rice (2000). He explained that the guiding principle behind his international decision-making would be the best interests of America. Troops would only be committed when strategic priorities were at stake. In cases such as Somalia, he argued, the Clinton administration's decision to pursue armed intervention was not defensible on the basis of national interests.

Bush defined the purposes of the US military in terms that clearly echoed those of Rice (2000): "Our military is meant to fight and win war. That's what it's meant to do" (Commission on Presidential Debates 2000). He underlined the limits of American power by telling PBS anchor Jim Lehrer, "We can't be all things to all people in the world" (Commission on Presidential Debates 2000). As Bush discussed issues ranging from Third World debt to genocide in the Balkans, it became clear that Rice's coaching had imparted capable insights into international politics. Consistent with Reagan's strategy to weaken Carter, Bush spoke in relaxed, folksy terms that made him seem more conversant with the field than Gore—who appeared stiff and formal.

Immediately after the debate, Bush understood the significance of what he and Rice had accomplished. He gave her a hug outside his hotel room. As Rice (2011, 8) writes, he "said, 'Oh, baby!' I translated that as 'Job well done.'" Bush's comment reveals both the extremely close bond that had evolved between candidate and tutor, and the risks posed by her gender, race, and age. Using the phrase "oh, baby" rather than a more generic expression such as "wow" signaled that her contributions as an international affairs expert could be trivialized in an environment of primarily older white men.

Even as the results of the 2000 election were being contested, Bush named Rice as his national security advisor. She observed on her own as he took the presidential oath of office, just a few weeks after her father had died. Rice felt deeply alone because the parents who had shared their commitments to faith and learning, had nurtured her every ambition, and had provided for her in ways that tapped their resources to the fullest were both gone. Demonstrating her resilience once again, Rice (2010, 324) refused, in her own words, "to be debilitated by my grief."

She set about building an agency that would assist the president and, at the same time, interact smoothly with the State Department and the Pentagon. Her model was Brent Scowcroft's National Security Council of the late 1980s, a place where she had worked for Bush senior. Rice (2011, 15) saw herself as a policy coordinator, or, in her words, an "honest broker" who would improve both the content and style of decision-making in the executive branch.

Despite being a woman, an African American, and only forty-six years old, Rice held an edge over other members of the administration. Her strong personal ties with the Bush family, and especially with George W., were widely known. Rice (2010, 4) notes that she managed the various "personalities and egos" inside the Vulcan group during the election campaign such that "in general, we got along well." This sense of camaraderie, Rice (2010, 4) writes, was grounded in an obvious fact: "they all knew that I was the one who was closest to the governor. I was the point of access."

As President Bush's national security advisor, Rice traveled with him to meet his Mexican counterpart and the heads of the G8 countries, then on her own to confer with Vladimir Putin. She convened frequent meetings of the Principals Committee to defuse internal tensions, notably between the State Department and Pentagon (see Leffler 2013, 210; Woodward 2004, 23). As top diplomat in the administration, Colin Powell had served during the Clinton years as chairman of the Joint Chiefs of Staff. He saw shadings of meaning in the actions of others, advocated the judicious use of force, and preferred to respond to international crises with allies and through multilateral institutions (see Charles-Philippe 2010, 46, 53).

By contrast, Defense Secretary Donald Rumsfeld took a bold and often tempestuous approach to foreign policy (see Baker 2015; Rice 2011, 20). In 1997, Rumsfeld, along with Wolfowitz and Cheney, signed a statement of principles by the neoconservative Project for the New American Century; it condemned the Clinton administration for lacking strategic vision and failing to invest in a strong military. Rumsfeld and Wolfowitz also endorsed a subsequent open letter to President Clinton arguing that the United States needed to effect regime change in Iraq and could no longer "be crippled by a misguided insistence on unanimity in the UN Security Council" (Abrams et al. 1998).

Early signs suggested that Rice was unable to coordinate the president's advisors. In a statement Cheney delivered to senators in March 2001, Bush (2001a) said the United States opposed the Kyoto deal on greenhouse gas emissions as "an unfair and ineffective means of addressing global climate change concerns." Rice was not consulted on the wording, nor was Powell (see Rice 2011, 42). Yet she confirmed Bush's stance the next day by informing European ambassadors that "Kyoto is dead on arrival" (Rice 2011, 42; see also Mabry 2007, 173).

Amidst these tensions, Rice used the leverage afforded by closeness to Bush to consolidate her position. When Bush was away, for example, Cheney tried to usurp the role of the national security advisor as chair of the Principals Committee. Rice (2011, 17; see also Mabry 2007, 171) met privately with the president to argue that committee leadership was integral to her job. Cheney backed off.

Unlike Albright's (2003) account of Clinton-era skirmishes that sees gender as a key factor, Rice (2011) presents conflict in the Bush administration as involving strong individuals with disparate institutional interests. According to Rice (2011, 19), Rumsfeld viewed Principals Committee meetings as taking him away from the job of directing the US military. He may also have missed an older interpersonal dynamic in which she was his protégée rather than his peer. In Rice's (2011, 21) words, "A relationship between equals was much harder for him." Although Rice does not probe the gender dimension of these interactions, she notes that Bush behaved in ways that spoke to factors other than her status as his national security advisor. During a summit meeting with European Union leaders, for instance, she indicated to Bush that she wanted to intervene in the discussion. As Rice (2011, 43) tells the story, "Much to my astonishment, he announced to the group, 'Condi, you got something to say real quick.' I was furious because his offhand tone seemed to belittle my participation."

Had Albright experienced this treatment, she probably would have evaluated it with respect to women's long exclusion from political power and, in particular, the relative novelty of female foreign policy leadership. Yet Rice (2011) does not explore the extent to which dismissive and marginalizing actions by Cheney, Rumsfeld, or Bush are typical of males asserting dominance over females. Had her identification with civil rights groups been stronger, Rice (2011) might also have commented on efforts by Cheney and Rumsfeld to undermine both her standing and that of Powell.

As a staunch individualist, Rice (2011) is silent on how the privilege that comes with being white rather than black, or older rather than younger, can overlap with and reinforce the authority associated with being a man rather than a woman. In particular, the attempt by Cheney (then age sixty) to displace Rice as chair of the Principals Committee suggests a modest thought experiment. Could the reverse scenario have unfolded, whereby a young black woman in a public leadership position attempts to undermine an older white man and then, having lost the battle, continues in her job and suffers no measurable consequences? The scenario is hard to imagine.

RESPONDING TO 9/11

On the night of September 11, 2001, Rice's apartment in the Watergate complex had no Secret Service detail. The president's invitation to stay in the White House family quarters was more attractive than a backup plan to sleep by her desk. Rice (2011, 82, 103) recalls spending long periods at work, up to seventeen hours a day, in the subsequent weeks. Together with Bush, she visited the burned-out Pentagon building and attended memorial services for victims of the attacks. Within days, she felt "a sense of rising defiance" (Rice 2011, 83).

Rice played an integral role in designing, explaining, and ultimately expanding what became the "war on terror." She supported proposals to dislodge the Taliban regime in Afghanistan that "condoned and at times supported bin Laden's efforts to establish al Qaeda training camps and recruit extremists to his cause" (Rice 2011, 85). Setting aside the folk wisdom that this was "the place where great powers go to die," Rice (2011, 84) believed "a successful campaign in Afghanistan could help redraw the map of the region." Consistent with Rice (2000), she saw military intervention in Central Asia as serving US interests and, at the same time, entrenching democratic values in an area where they were weak. In fact, her post–9/11 account of musing at Camp David about freeing the people of Central Asia reflects a belief that changing norms and political systems in various parts of the world is necessary in order to protect the United States. As time passed, this stress on ideals whereby America is a "beacon of democracy" meshed with a proposal that Wolfowitz and others had long championed—namely, that military force should be employed against Iraq (Rice, as quoted in Mann 2004, 148, 198).

Consistent with Powell's advice, the administration decided to target al-Qaeda in Afghanistan only after the Taliban government was offered a chance to resolve the dispute diplomatically (see Schier 2009, 130). Once Afghanistan refused demands that al-Qaeda leaders be turned over and the group's training camps closed, the United States and the United Kingdom initiated an air war known as Operation Enduring Freedom. Over time, it expanded to include a ground campaign (see Mann 2004, 308).

In assessing how to prevent future attacks, Rice (2011, 67–68) maintained that what had been distinct internal and external intelligence-gathering machineries needed to be better coordinated. She attributed the failure to apprehend al-Qaeda operatives in part to a rigid separation between the domestic policing remit of the FBI and the international work of the CIA. She believed those watertight divisions would blur in a constructive way via a newly formed Office of Homeland Security.

Rice also worked on determining how information would be obtained from detainees held in Guantanamo Bay, Cuba, and other offshore locations. The administration ultimately approved activities such as waterboarding, which entailed pouring water over the face of a bound prisoner to create the effect of suffocation or drowning. Unlike the physical scars left by fists, whips, and electric shock, waterboarding leaves fewer and possibly no marks on a captive's body. Even though Rice and others viewed waterboarding as an enhanced method of interrogation that could lead them to top al-Qaeda operatives, critics viewed it as torture, plain and simple (see Bush 2010, 171; Senate Select Committee on Intelligence 2014).

Rice (2011, 113) strongly defends legislation known as the PATRIOT Act, signed by President Bush in late October 2001.[8] The law promised to intercept and obstruct terrorists by expanding government access to the records of individuals and companies. Advocates saw the provisions as critical to learning how al-Qaeda and other similar organizations functioned, what they planned for the future, and which communication and funding channels could be blocked. Under the terms of the act, court orders were no longer necessary to monitor the email, telephone, or banking activities of citizens of any country. The law provided more funding for counterterrorism, border security, and surveillance by federal agencies and permitted the US government to detain immigrants for indefinite periods.

Rice (2011, Chapter 8) maintains that each measure was essential. By contrast, civil libertarians challenged administration efforts to undermine rights protections enshrined in the US Constitution. Whether their target was the offshore detention facility in Guantanamo, the use of waterboarding techniques, or the invasive reach of data gathering permitted under the terms of the PATRIOT Act, critics raised serious objections that were in some cases upheld by judicial decisions. Yet Bush's national security advisor remains unswerving in her view that the purpose of each action was entirely defensible. As Rice (2011, 120) writes, "I do not regret the decisions we made."

The administration's initial rationale for military action in Afghanistan was to defend national interests by disabling al-Qaeda. This message began to change, however, when for the first time in US history the president's wife spoke for the full duration of her husband's weekly radio address. Laura Bush's (2001) comments in mid-November focused on barriers facing women and girls who lived under what she described as "the al-Qaida terrorist network and the regime it supports in Afghanistan, the Taliban." Her speech maintained that al-Qaeda and the Taliban went beyond "legitimate religious practice" as understood by most Muslims around the world. They restricted access to education, employment, and health services by making it impossible for adult women to circulate freely outside their homes. Taliban leaders threatened to rip out the nails of those who dared to use finger polish. Laura Bush (2001) argued that American military action would reverse "the severe repression and brutality against women in Afghanistan." In her words, "The fight against terrorism is also a fight for the rights and dignity of women."

According to Flanders (2005, 268), claims that military action helped women were politically useful, since they attracted female voters who otherwise tended to oppose armed intervention. The same rationale meant that administration policy gained support from American women's groups, including the Feminist Majority Foundation (Cohn and Jacobson 2013, 114). Moreover, coming from a first lady who had daughters of her own, the strategy was far from radical: it reinforced views in the United States and elsewhere that Western militaries operated as chivalrous defenders of vulnerable civilians and promoters of democracy (see Brenner 2009; Ferguson 2007, 199, 205–206; Ferguson and Marso 2007, 3). What remains notable about this rhetoric is that Rice employed it much less than others. When she mentioned protecting women, "it has been only a passing reference in a speech focused on some other matter . . . [Rice] was never the one who introduced any new policies or initiatives on women" (Ferguson 2007, 198–199).

Talk about improving women's lives in other parts of the world allowed members of the Bush administration to obscure regressive changes that Republicans had made since the Reagan years. These initiatives rolled back rights legislation and court decisions, dismantled enforcement mechanisms in the federal government, and denied funds for contraception and abortion services both inside the country and internationally (see Bashevkin 1998). As well, pro-women rhetoric served to blunt the sharp edge of other directions in American foreign policy—including the detention and torture of prisoners in the "war on terror," and distracted listeners from the deterioration of women's circumstances in places such as Afghanistan and Iraq (see Kandiyoti 2007). Above all, Rice's position as a young African American woman in an administration that was full of older white men afforded the Bush team a visual diversity that, in turn, gave credence to claims that Republican actions were creating opportunities for women and girls in places like Afghanistan. As Flanders (2005, xi) reflects, "the Bush administration's genius lies in presenting many different faces to different constituencies" such that moderate as well as traditionalist interests could all find something to support in the policy array.

PREEMPTIVE ACTION IN IRAQ

By the end of 2001, Operation Enduring Freedom had removed the Taliban from the formal seat of power in Afghanistan. Another terrorist attack in the skies was avoided when explosives hidden in the shoe of an al-Qaeda agent who boarded a US-bound plane did not detonate, thanks to quick action by flight attendants and passengers. With these immediate successes in hand, members of the Bush administration began to develop the next phase of the "war on terror."

The broad outlines of their plan can be traced to 1998, when Congress passed and President Clinton signed the Iraq Liberation Act. The bill declared the leadership of Saddam Hussein in need of replacement by a democratic government, and authorized US aid, including military training and equipment, for opposition groups. Passed by a wide margin in the House of Representatives and unanimously in the Senate, the act justified regime change on the basis of Saddam's failure to abide by terms agreed to at the end of the Persian Gulf War in the early 1990s. By creating barriers for UN weapons inspectors, the Iraqi leader had impeded efforts to assess the chemical and biological agents in his arsenal. Knowing what Saddam possessed mattered, since in the 1980s he had used lethal toxins against both Kurds in Iraq and Iranian troops in the Iran-Iraq War. In 1991, Iraq fired more than three dozen Scud missiles toward both Israel and Saudi Arabia. Beginning in 2000, Saddam's government sent $25,000 payments to relatives of Palestinian suicide bombers who participated in the second intifada uprising against Israel (see BBC News 2003).[9]

According to Rice (2011, 86), Deputy Defense Secretary Paul Wolfowitz promoted the idea of invading Iraq rather than Afghanistan at a meeting at Camp David on September 15, 2001 (see also Bush 2010, 189; Rumsfeld 2011, 359; Solomon 2007, 75). He stressed the greater significance of the Middle East, as compared with Central Asia, to US interests. Moreover, Rice (2011, 86) writes, Wolfowitz maintained that "Saddam was clearly an enemy of the United States and had supported terrorism. The war in Afghanistan would be so much more complicated than a 'straightforward' engagement against a real army such as Saddam's."

The decision at Camp David was to use military force in Afghanistan because the 9/11 attacks could be traced to al-Qaeda's base of operations in that country. Yet Wolfowitz's position hardly fell off the foreign policy agenda. Rice (2011, 172) reports that Bush asked Rumsfeld to develop a battle plan for regime change in Iraq (see also Bush 2010, 234; Rumsfeld 2011, 425). The secretary of defense conveyed that request to the military commander responsible for the Middle East on December 1, 2001. Rice's (2011, 172) timeline thus indicates that the Bush administration commissioned a road map for the use of force against Saddam Hussein less than three months after planes struck New York and Washington.

In developing the ideational defense for invading Iraq, Rice (2011, 153) fused power considerations related to national interests with value-based priorities that involved the spread of democratic norms; in particular, she aimed to enforce militarily "the United States' view of how the world ought to be." In February 2002, she suggested that Bush use the phrase "coercive diplomacy" to describe US policy toward Iraq. America would press Saddam to open the doors to weapons inspectors by reinforcing diplomatic pressure with the threat of military intervention. According to Rice (2011, 172, 180), the president "loved the term" and "decided on a policy of coercive diplomacy."

Rice signaled plans to go to war in a series of interviews with prominent media outlets. She stated on the BBC in August 2002 that with respect to Iraq, "We believe the case for regime change is very powerful." She described Saddam Hussein as "an evil man who, left to his own devices, will wreak havoc again." She reminded viewers of the "miserable life" of civilians in Iraq, and maintained that the situation in Afghanistan had measurably improved since military action began ten months earlier. Echoing Laura Bush's address of the previous fall, Rice said Afghans no longer faced "the repressive regime that they had, where girls couldn't go to school, where women were punished severely for allowing their steps to be heard. You can't say that the people of Afghanistan are not better off." Rice insisted that from the perspective of threats to national security coming from Iraq, "We certainly do not have the luxury of doing nothing" (BBC4 2002).

Speaking with CNN's Wolf Blitzer a month later, she advocated the use of preemptive force. In Rice's words, "There is no doubt that Saddam Hussein's regime is a danger to the United States and to its allies, to our interests. It is also a danger that is gathering momentum, and it simply makes no sense to wait any longer to do something about the threat that is posed here." After reiterating that passivity was not an option, Rice told Blitzer that in the near future the Bush administration would ask Congress to approve military action against Iraq. As she stated, "the president thinks it's best to do this sooner rather than later and in this session of Congress" (CNN 2002).

Blitzer interrupted Rice to ask for clarification. Did evidence show that Saddam Hussein was behind the al-Qaeda attacks? "No," she replied, "we do not know that he had a role in 9/11. But I think that this is the test that sets a bar that is far too high." The Iraqi leader was known to support international terrorism. He had plotted to kill the father of the current US president. And, she continued, "We know that he is acquiring weapons of mass destruction, that he has extreme animus against the United States." Rice claimed Iraq had procured aluminum tubing of a type that was "only really suited for nuclear weapons programs, centrifuge programs" (CNN 2002).

Blitzer turned to the events of 9/11, noting that Rice had been the first to inform Bush of the attacks. He asked what conclusions could be drawn from that day. Rice said the main lesson learned was the preemption doctrine. In her words, "you should not wait to be surprised by evil people who may wish you real harm with weapons of mass destruction that would make September 11 look small in comparison. History shows us that inaction is the problem, and the vulnerability of the United States is really what came home very, very clearly on 9/11" (CNN 2002).

Speaking at the United Nations just after the first anniversary of the attacks, Bush revised slightly the point Rice had made with Blitzer. Unlike his advisor's claim that Iraq already had specific weapons parts in hand, Bush (2002b) said the following: "Iraq has made several attempts to buy high-strength aluminum tubes used to enrich uranium for a nuclear weapon. Should Iraq acquire fissile material, it would be able to build a nuclear weapon within a year."

The drumbeat toward war grew louder in Bush's (2003a) State of the Union address, which declared, "The British government has learned that Saddam Hussein recently sought significant quantities of uranium from Africa." That sentence became infamous after the US invasion, when extensive searches failed to unearth any weapons of mass destruction. Even more damaging to American credibility were CIA documents that showed the agency wanted the claim about uranium removed from Bush's text because it was not verifiable (see Mabry 2007, 196).

In February 2003, Bush and Rice watched together at the White House as Powell presented the case for war at the UN Security Council (see Mabry 2007, 192). The secretary of state spoke for an hour and a half. He played tapes of Iraqi officials speaking with each other, and offered translations indicating the officials were consorting to hide not only documents, but also material evidence from arms inspectors. He displayed aerial photographs of what were deemed to be biological, chemical, and nuclear weapons facilities, as well as decontamination vehicles. Powell offered technical details about the aluminum tubes Iraq had allegedly sought, and said other evidence pointed toward Iraqi efforts to procure the equipment needed to enrich uranium.

Immediately after the speech, Bush called Powell to congratulate him (see Mabry 2007, 192). Both the president and Rice were accurate in seeing the long, detailed presentation by a decorated military leader as highly influential. Surveys conducted after Powell stepped down from the UN podium show that Americans were overwhelmingly convinced that Saddam Hussein possessed weapons of mass destruction. Influential columnists who had hesitated to endorse the march to war said that Powell's address had won them over (see Mabry 2007, 192).

Six weeks later, George W. Bush (2003b) announced the start of what he called "a broad and concerted campaign." His address identified the goals of American military action as the same three objectives his national security advisor had flagged in interviews the previous summer: "to disarm Iraq, to free its people, and to defend the world from grave danger" (Bush 2003b). The president thus set in motion a foreign policy calculus that meshed value considerations with national interests—the same combination Rice (2000) had promoted prior to reaching top office.

EVALUATING THE RECORD

Cauldrons of ink have been spilled over Bush administration foreign policy. Rice (2011, 120, 198) defends the choices made, maintaining that the use of force was justified in the wake of 9/11 and the track record of Saddam's regime. Critics argue that justifications for the invasion of Iraq in particular were false, exaggerated, or willfully ignorant of the consequences of overthrowing Saddam (see, for example, Schier 2009).

As time passed, the condemnations of Rice in particular grew louder. The national security advisor was accused of failing to vet properly Bush's (2003a) allegation that Iraq had sought uranium in Africa (see Mabry 2007, 196). When pressed by reporters, Bush maintained that he was responsible for his own statements. He then defended Rice to the point of hyperbole, insisting, "Dr. Condoleezza Rice is an honest, fabulous person. And America is lucky to have her service. *Period*" (Bush, as quoted in Mabry 2007, 197; emphasis in original). It is difficult to conceive of Bush or any other president endorsing the "fabulous" personal qualities of a male advisor.

Rice was not alone in distorting the threat posed by Saddam. Nor was she the only insider who failed to interrogate fully Pentagon plans for postwar reconstruction in Iraq (see Mabry 2007, 194–195). Where she does stand out is in violating her own key test of foreign policy decision-making, which asks whether choices are made on the basis of national interests (see Rice 2000).

If measured with respect to international prestige and credibility, then America's standing declined markedly as coalition troops searched without result for weapons of mass destruction. At the level of national security, invading Iraq seemed far from defensible. How could one weak state in the Middle East endanger US interests? Among those who pressed for answers was Jeane Kirkpatrick (2007b, Chapter 6), who portrays the decision to intervene in Iraq as imprudent and impractical.

As Iraqi opposition to the invasion became an organized insurgency, Rice provided values-based justifications for the continued US presence. Her emphasis on remaining in order to create "a balance of power that favors freedom" was difficult to reconcile, however, with the daily experiences of Iraqi civilians (Rice 2002a). What freedom did they enjoy under circumstances of not just foreign control but also social chaos? Once divisions between Sunni and Shia Muslims turned into a civil war, how could American leaders maintain that Iraq was on the road to orderly liberal democracy?

Rather than liberating Iraqis, critics charged, the invasion produced a costly morass. Approximately 4500 American soldiers died and more than 32,000 were wounded within nine years. Although the number of Iraqi civilian casualties is disputed, US military estimates place the figure above 66,000 (Leigh 2010). Direct US Treasury expenditures for the war, setting aside major indirect costs such as care for returning veterans, reached about $815 billion (Belasco 2014, 15). These results echo what Powell had predicted when he met Bush in the summer of 2002 to ask him not to sign off on plans for invading Iraq. In the secretary of state's words, "You are going to be the proud owner of twenty-five million people . . . all their hopes, aspirations, and problems. . . . It's going to suck the oxygen out of everything" (Powell, as quoted in Woodward 2004, 151).

The publications of Professor Condoleezza Rice, who specialized in the study of military/civilian relations, provide one reason why Iraq imploded. Rice (2000, 53) explains that the US military "is not a civilian police force. It is not a political referee. And it is most certainly not designed to build a civilian society." President Bush's decision in his second term to shift primary responsibility for Iraq's reconstruction from the Pentagon to the State Department reflects a belated recognition of that point.

As Bush's foreign policy confidante, Rice tutored and directly influenced a chief executive who faced daunting challenges. The president responded to the events of 9/11 in a manner fully consistent with the views she promulgated: he asserted the right of the United States to find the parties responsible, to punish those who offered them shelter, and, if necessary, to act unilaterally as well as preemptively against threats to national security. Particularly in his approach to the Middle East, Bush embraced what Rice (2000, 49) called "America's special role" in spreading democracy and prosperity. Given this confluence between Rice's perspectives and crucial administration actions, she fits our definition of a transforming policy actor.

Rather than adopting a masculine repertoire on her appointment to top office, Rice became national security advisor with a track record of muscular, unyielding leadership. As Stanford provost, she implemented controversial decisions, no matter how heated the opposition. The pattern of seeking consensus in order to stake out common ground with critics and opponents thus did not feature in her outlook before she assumed senior public office.

Once appointed to an official position, Rice activated much of the foreign policy game plan she had proposed as Bush's campaign advisor. Rice (2000) conflates national interests with the spread of democratic ideals. Consistent with her outlook, the invasion of Iraq was justified under the terms of a Freedom Agenda that highlighted moral or value-based imperatives for military intervention. Where the academic analyst diverged from the decision-maker is in what armed force can accomplish: while Rice (2000) establishes clear limits on the role of the US military, her actions in office vastly stretched those terms of engagement.

Given the principles she had absorbed since early childhood, Rice's worldview saw individual will as the motor of human advancement. She may have believed that resolving international crises was analogous to managing academic budgets and rebuilding a crumbling campus: an educated, motivated person could succeed by dint of concerted effort and strong faith. Rice's outlook made her a committed crusader or moralizer, as well as a problem-solver, according to Kirkpatrick's (1974, 175) rubric. In addition, the emphasis Rice placed on retaining Bush's approval suggests what Kirkpatrick (1974, 175) describes as personalizer tendencies. Yet for Rice, the disadvantages of each approach were minimal given her proximity to and similarities with the president: George W. was also a moralizer who wanted to solve problems and retain her support. Together, they forged ahead with a shared *weltanschauung*.

In terms of gender politics, Rice identified closely with people like herself—achieving individuals in liberal democratic societies. Her refusal to join movement-based responses to discrimination came from family teachings that elevated hard work, study, and faith. As a foreign policy appointee, she reiterated statements made by Laura and then George W. Bush to the effect that US military action promised to widen educational opportunities for women and girls in such places as Afghanistan and Iraq. Although Rice voiced these claims and believed in spreading liberal values, at no point did she assume a leadership role in the promotion of women's rights. Nor can the administration in which she served be said to have acted in ways that resonated with a progressive feminist agenda.

The concept of preemption that underpinned Bush's foreign policy doctrine thus served as Rice's personal credo. She tried from her earliest years to be "twice as good" as those around her, refused to be what she called a victim, and asserted herself at every turn (Rice, as quoted in Mabry 2007, 37). Her modus operandi was consistent with the idea of acting first—and acting decisively.

CHAPTER 6

Women's Security as National Security

Hillary Rodham Clinton served four years as secretary of state following Barack Obama's swearing in as president in 2009. Before her, no American woman had risen from White House spouse to elected legislator to top diplomat. Clinton capped her ascent in 2016 as the first female presidential candidate for a major US political party.

As first lady, Clinton traveled the globe to meet not just world leaders, but also local citizens in small, often remote communities. She then served two terms in the Senate, losing to Obama in the 2008 race for the Democratic presidential nomination. Neither Jeane Kirkpatrick, Madeleine Albright, nor Condoleezza Rice had sought, let alone won, national elective office, meaning that Hillary Clinton stood alone as international advisor to a president who had defeated her on the campaign trail.

Clinton's approach to life resembled in many respects that of her predecessors. She demonstrated iron-willed determination and strong personal resilience, including in her ability to grab victory from the jaws of defeat. For example, Clinton (2003, 256, 258) describes Democratic losses in the 1994 midterm elections as a "full-blown disaster" that led her and her husband to "develop a new strategy for a new environment." Congressional Republicans undertook lengthy investigations of subjects including President Clinton's relations with other women. Hillary responded by escaping Washington; she visited cities and villages around the globe, learning firsthand about efforts to improve women's health, to build schools for girls, and to enhance the economic security of families through micro-credit projects. As biographer Carl Bernstein (2007, 9–10) suggests, fleeing the capital helped to lessen the pain and humiliation awaiting her at home. At the same time, becoming a world traveler established Clinton's credentials as an active participant in global politics.

Unlike her counterparts, Hillary Clinton had a long history of engagement in civil society protest, including organized feminism. She demonstrated against the Vietnam War as an undergraduate, became a pioneering advocate for children as a law student, and helped to establish rape crisis services as a young law professor. In 1995, Clinton's speech to delegates at the Fourth World Conference on Women in Beijing made international headlines.

As secretary of state, Clinton was distinctive in that she explicitly merged the rights of women and girls, on one side, with the promotion of American interests, on the other. Her "Hillary doctrine," as articulated in the following quotation, posited a direct tie between US security, international stability, and opportunities for women and girls in all regions to reach their full potential (see Hudson and Leidl 2015):

> I believe that the rights of women and girls is the unfinished business of the 21st century.... This is a big deal for American values and for American foreign policy and our interests, but it is also a big deal for our security. Because where women are disempowered and dehumanized, you are more likely to see not just antidemocratic forces, but extremism that leads to security challenges for us. (Hillary Rodham Clinton, as quoted in Lemmon 2011)

In addition to operating as a critical actor in the field of gender equality, Clinton was a hawk on matters of foreign policy. The attacks of 9/11 unfolded during her first year in the Senate. Compared with other Democratic lawmakers in that period, including Senator Barack Obama, her statements and actions were unusually forceful. Clinton (as quoted in Gerth and Van Natta 2007, 241) vowed on September 12, 2001 that those who had assisted al-Qaeda would feel America's "wrath." Clinton endorsed Bush administration responses to the attacks, including military intervention in Afghanistan, the PATRIOT Act, the use of armed force against Iraq, and supplementary funding for military operations in Afghanistan and Iraq (see Clinton 2001, 2004; Davis 2013).

Like the three women who preceded her, Clinton proved as a top decision-maker to be anything but a pacifist angel (see Elshtain 1995). She pressed for the use of "all necessary measures" to protect civilians in Libya in 2011 and, after overcoming opposition from Obama's male advisors, worked to forge a multilateral military coalition. Given strong counter-pressures inside the administration, she was unable to win support in 2012 for a proposal to arm rebels seeking to unseat the Assad regime in Syria.

Even though some elements of her career were distinctive, Clinton shared important commonalities with Kirkpatrick, Albright, and Rice. She, too, was the first child of politically involved parents who expected their daughter to succeed, and who encouraged her in ways that built personal confidence, poise, and focus. Clinton evidenced razor-sharp concentration and ambition from an early age. Like Kirkpatrick and Rice, she participated in athletic and distinctly "tomboy" activities in her youth. Clinton immersed herself in practical politics, studied political science, and taught at the university level. Hillary regularly crossed paths with other accomplished women like herself: while living in Arkansas, for instance, Clinton met Albright at a Washington fundraiser for Children's Defense Fund (see Albright 2003, 245–246). When Chelsea Clinton was ready to apply to colleges, Rice was the Stanford University provost who welcomed her and the first lady to the campus (see Clinton 2003, 372; 2014, 717).

Like Kirkpatrick and Rice, Clinton was born in the United States. Yet her upbringing in a "sheltered" Chicago suburb stood in stark contrast to Rice's childhood in Birmingham (Clinton 2003, 50). Particularly as compared with the challenges facing Albright, Rice, and their families, Clinton grew up in a place that was insulated from massive public upheaval. To wit, Clinton's family was not uprooted in her youth because of war, communism, or racial strife.

Clinton's (2003, 1) early years in "a fortunate time and place" made her part of a baby boom generation that was restless for other reasons. If postwar America seemed content in its affluence and triumphalism, then that sense of self-satisfaction was a source of concern rather than comfort to her and many of her contemporaries. Clinton showed an interest in changing what she observed from a very young age. Her emphasis would remain largely the same as she grew older: defending the rights of disadvantaged groups, notably women and children, by holding public leaders to account for their actions. Unlike Kirkpatrick, Albright, and Rice, Clinton engaged with New Left politics of the 1960s and following, including by protesting US intervention in Indochina.

This sense of purposeful mission grew from the Methodist stream of social gospel Protestantism, which sees earthly life as perfectible if human beings take concerted action. Clinton's awareness of the many difficulties her mother faced made the claims of children's rights and women's rights campaigners meaningful in a very immediate way. The fact that Hillary Rodham met Bill Clinton at the peak of campus ferment provides a significant dimension to this story, since it illustrates how a sturdy partnership was formed in the cauldron of 1960s activism. Taken together, this background helps to explain Hillary's belief in the ability and, indeed, the responsibility of individuals to work together to improve their world.

Following the 2008 election, Barack Obama struck a cabinet that resembled Abraham Lincoln's "team of rivals." He asked Hillary Clinton to serve as secretary of state because she had been a formidable competitor in the nomination process. By appointing her, Obama was assured of support from the Clintons' domestic political network. Moreover, Hillary arrived with an array of international contacts dating from her time as first lady (see Purdum 2012).

To what extent did Clinton shape foreign policy during the first Obama mandate? Can her role be considered transformative? What are the main hallmarks of Clinton's actions with respect to armed force and women's equality? Did her behavior as secretary of state reflect a newfound adoption of masculine norms or, instead, a continuation of earlier practices?

Autobiographical, biographical, and other sources on the public record indicate that Clinton made significant contributions to foreign policy. Echoing Albright's interventions in debates over the Balkans, Clinton argued successfully for the use of multilateral military force in Libya, despite opposition from men in the Obama administration. Also in parallel with Albright, Clinton was a critical actor who assumed a leadership role in highlighting human rights and especially women's rights in international politics. As reflected in her summary of the Hillary doctrine that is quoted in the preceding, she insisted that national security relied on the stability of the rest of the world, which in turn depended on ensuring that women and girls in all regions were empowered to reach their full potential. As she told an enthused audience in South Korea, "[No democracy] can exist without women's full participation. No economy can be truly a free market without women involved" (Clinton, as quoted in Ghattas 2013, 40). Clinton spread her vision as secretary of state with exceptional energy, traveling to 112 countries and flying close to a million miles in four years—records that eclipsed those of her predecessors (see Hudson and Leidl 2015, 52).

In accounts of 2009 and following, Clinton has been assessed as both lacking clout and as overly influential. The main theme of the former trope is that Barack Obama relied primarily on his own foreign policy counsel and that of his White House advisors (see Dueck 2011, 18; 2015, 146; Mann 2012, 10; Rothkopf 2014, 49). Dueck (2011, 18) writes, "Secretary of State Clinton is the public face of American diplomacy, a role she plays well, but she does not appear to be at the true center of decision making on multiple issues Obama deems vital. . . . Obama is his own grand strategist, and whatever tactical adjustments he makes on either process or substance, he is not about to relinquish that role." Mann (2012, 6) claims that Clinton was a political rival whose modest assets were purposefully deployed inside rather than outside the proverbial tent: "Over the long run, Hillary Clinton's appointment would work out much better than Obama's early supporters had feared. It would also work out well for Clinton, who would eventually come to be viewed as loyal, competent, and (most important of all) independent from her husband."

Other authors depict Clinton as a potent, possibly dangerous operator. According to Bader (2013, 11), Clinton commanded "international rock star qualities" both at home and abroad. In the words of Milne (2012, 940), she numbered among the very few "big hitters" in the first Obama cabinet. Mann (2012, 84) observes that policies after 2009 more closely resembled Hillary Clinton's campaign positions than Obama's, as reflected in a hawkish approach to China. Above all, the decision to intervene militarily in Libya was a "decisive step" that Clinton promoted and Obama pursued (Mann 2012, 290). The fact that Clinton's proposal to use force in North Africa was supported by other senior females and opposed by top male defense appointees led to speculation about "fierce women" and "militaristic muses" in the administration, and to concerns that Obama was "a ditherer chased by Furies" (Dowd 2011).

Did Clinton's record as secretary of state deviate from her earlier directions? This argument is hard to sustain given her Senate record in the months after 9/11. Moreover, Clinton's view that national security depends on women's security resonates closely with statements she made more than ten years earlier as first lady.

The next section outlines the main foreign policy directions of Obama's first term, in order to assess Clinton's leadership. The discussion then considers the background that underpins her stances on armed force and gender politics.

INTERVENING IN THE MIDDLE EAST

Like presidential candidates before him, Barack Obama promised to right the wrongs of his predecessors. Obama (2007, 4) advanced a "partnership" approach that was distinct from the policies of George W. Bush: "We can neither retreat from the world nor try to bully it into submission. We must lead by deed and by example." Obama said he would end the conflicts in Afghanistan and Iraq, and reduce overseas troop commitments. In stressing the use of "soft power" diplomacy and other approaches that would engage rather than isolate the United States, Obama stressed the capacity of institutions such as NATO to frame cooperative responses to international crises. Moreover, he maintained, the United States could not impose democracy in distant locations using such top-down means as coercive force (see Obama 2007, 14).

Obama's nomination of Hillary Clinton as secretary of state helped to ensure that these priorities would be converted from ideas into action. From her years as first lady, Clinton had shown a strong preference for spreading American influence through unofficial, often informal channels, including contact with nongovernmental actors. She had traveled during the 1990s to more than eighty countries, where she practiced direct, people-to-people diplomacy and championed local forms of grassroots empowerment, including micro-credit enterprises for women (see Clinton 2003, 268–286, 298–310, 353–362, 397–419).

At her Senate confirmation hearing, Clinton (2009a) outlined a pragmatic but principled approach to international relations—one that she contrasted with the orientation of the Bush years. Clinton (2009a) described her strategy as one of "smart power:" "I believe that American leadership has been wanting, but is still wanted. We must use what has been called smart power, the full range of tools at our disposal—diplomatic, economic, military, political, legal, and cultural—picking the right tool or combination of tools for each situation. With smart power, diplomacy will be the vanguard of our foreign policy."

Early in her term as secretary of state, Clinton (2009b) told the Council on Foreign Relations that the United States was adopting "a new mindset" for a "new era of engagement." In her words, America would work with other actors to foster "common interests, shared values, and mutual respect." The "different global architecture" Clinton described echoed her background as a social activist and advocate for empowering women: "We'll go beyond states to create opportunities for non-state actors and individuals to contribute to solutions. . . . In short, we will lead by inducing greater cooperation among a greater number of actors and reducing competition, tilting the balance away from a multi-polar world and toward a multi-partner world." At the same time, Clinton (2009b) warned, "We will not hesitate to defend our friends, our interests, and above all, our people vigorously and when necessary with the world's strongest military."

Obama voiced populist and feminist views similar to those of Clinton when he visited Egypt within six months of taking office. Speaking at Cairo University, he announced "a new beginning between the United States and Muslims around the world, one based on mutual interest and mutual respect." He highlighted commonalities between America and Islam in arguing that "they overlap, and share common principles—principles of justice and progress; tolerance and the dignity of all human beings." The speech called for greater understanding between the two sides, and referred explicitly to the need to foster democracy and religious freedom in the Middle East. In particular, Obama identified women's equality as a major driver of economic growth, asserting that "countries where women are well educated are far more likely to be prosperous" (Obama 2009a).

Scholars disagree as to the impact of Obama's first four years in office. Some maintain that the new administration restored the United States' damaged international reputation. These observers present the pivot toward Asia as a sensible recognition that China and India had become major players in world economics and politics, and deserved to be treated as such (see Indyk, Lieberthal, and O'Hanlon 2012, 31; Milne 2012, 942). Indyk, Lieberthal, and O'Hanlon (2012) and Milne (2012) commend the handling of unprecedented uprisings across the Middle East in 2010 and following, known as the Arab Spring; they see resisting the temptation to engage in Tunisia and Egypt while bringing NATO forces to bear in Libya as deft responses to unanticipated developments in a high-conflict region. Indyk, Lieberthal, and O'Hanlon (2012, 34) see decisions to draw down US military forces in places where Bush had intervened as "signature achievements" that showed Obama was serious about alternatives to troops on the ground.

Other analysts read the administration's reliance on multilateralism and restraint as signs of foreign policy weakness (see Dueck 2011; Kaufman 2014). Attempts to reach out to China and Russia did little to address such challenges as Iran's nuclear program, while cuts to military funding and decisions to withdraw US troops from Iraq undermined earlier gains (see Kaufman 2014, 453; McCormick 2011, 11). Dueck (2011, 103–104) and Rothkopf (2014, 47) maintain that the administration waited too long before responding to Arab Spring events, and failed to show that international alliances were necessarily conducive to national interests. Critics thus present Obama's emphases on caution and collaboration as generating policies that, particularly in the Middle East, were "incoherent" and "floundering" (Dueck 2011, 23, 24).

Despite these divergent perspectives, commentators tend to agree that Hillary Clinton was influential in shaping the US pivot toward Asia and actions in the Middle East (see Bader 2013; Mann 2012; Milne 2012). According to Clinton (2014), what stands out with respect to the latter is that she and Obama differed in meaningful ways over how to address changes in Egypt, Libya, and Syria. The fast pace of events on the ground, combined with Obama's stress on reversing the precedents of the Bush years, led to what Clinton (2014, 360) terms "imperfect compromises."

The content of Clinton's contributions is at least as significant as their weight. With respect to the Middle East, Clinton seems to have employed a more force- and interests-based calculus than the chief executive who appointed her. As detailed later in this chapter, she played a major role in debates over Libya: Clinton convinced administration colleagues of the need to create an international military coalition to protect civilians once the government of Muammar Gaddafi began to reverse rebel advances. By contrast, she failed to stop Obama from calling for Hosni Mubarak to step down immediately as Egypt's president and was unable to secure military aid for rebels fighting the regime of Bashar al-Assad in Syria. The fact that Clinton successfully pressed for the main military intervention of Obama's first term demonstrates her clout as secretary of state. At the same time, the president's willingness to follow other advice on Egypt and Syria reveals the limits of her influence, and made him vulnerable to the charge of failing to advance US priorities in a decisive manner.

The view that foreign policy deliberations needed to be infused with not just national interests and liberal values, but also explicit recognition of civil society voices, proved especially challenging once popular uprisings swept through the Middle East. Clinton (2014) summarizes debates over waves of protest in Egypt that sought to end the rule of a long-standing US ally. Along with Vice President Joe Biden, Defense Secretary Robert Gates, and National Security Advisor Tom Donilon, Clinton (2014, 341, 343) advised caution: the United States needed to offer Mubarak time to reform since prolonged instability in Egypt and the larger region was the most likely consequence of removing him from power right away (see also Gates 2014, 504–505; Landler 2016, 160; Mann 2012, 266).

Clinton (2014, 341) recognized, however, that "the President wasn't comfortable sitting by and doing nothing while peaceful protesters were beaten and killed in the streets." Instead of urging a "peaceful, *orderly* transition to a democratic regime," as Clinton (2014, 341; italics in original) had in her public statement of January 30, 2011, Obama announced two days later that he had told Mubarak that political change must happen immediately. Egypt's president left office within ten days of Obama's statement.

Clinton (2014, 346) traveled weeks later to Cairo, where she met protesters who seemed very "disorganized" and inexperienced relative to the two main pillars of power in Egypt: the Muslim Brotherhood and the armed forces. As Clinton had predicted at the start of demonstrations in Egypt, political control lurched over the next three years from the military to the Brotherhood and back to the military. Given that millions of civilians suffered in the ensuing turmoil, Obama's rush to remove Mubarak arguably endangered both democratic values and the liberals who supported them in

Egypt. Whether US influence and, in particular, the partnerships doctrine fared any better remains an open question. The optics of an American president instructing a loyal ally to leave office "*now*" were likely detrimental to national interests and particularly to relations with friendly powers in the Middle East and elsewhere (Obama, as quoted in Clinton 2014, 343; italics in original). As noted in the following discussion, Obama's treatment of Mubarak during this period contrasted with Russian leader Vladimir Putin's staunch support for Assad.

Where Clinton succeeded was in forging an approach to Libya that resonated with administration goals. By February 2011, street protests had broken out in areas including the eastern city of Benghazi. Demonstrators included many women whose husbands and sons were imprisoned by Gaddafi, who had governed in an erratic and often violent way since gaining power in a 1969 coup. Forces loyal to the regime threatened to reverse rebel advances (see ICAN 2013).

Clinton (2014, 366–367) opposed unilateral US action in Libya. The possibility of collective intervention arose, however, once the Arab League endorsed a UN-sanctioned no-fly zone in Libya and after countries including the United Arab Emirates, France, and the United Kingdom expressed willingness to participate in a military coalition (see Chollet 2016, 96; Clinton 2014, 367–368). In March 2011, Clinton (2014, 369) met the leader of the Libyan opposition, Mahmoud Jibril, who "told us that hundreds of thousands of civilians in Benghazi were in imminent danger as the regime's forces marched toward the city, raising the specters of the genocide in Rwanda and ethnic cleansing in the Balkans. He pleaded for international intervention."

Like Obama's military advisors, Clinton (2014, 366–367) saw a no-fly zone as unlikely to defeat the Libyan dictator (see also Chollet 2016, 97). Not only could Gaddafi's air defenses shoot down foreign planes, but civilians would be at risk from artillery shells fired by his troops. Clinton (2014, 370–372) therefore endorsed a more open-ended UN resolution authorizing "all necessary measures," including ground forces to defend civilians in Libya.

Speaking by telephone from Cairo, Clinton pressed her administration colleagues to support an "all necessary measures" resolution at the UN Security Council. In her view, the United States needed to protect civilians and operate in a manner that connoted international leadership (see Dueck 2015, 195). The other senior women on Obama's foreign policy team, UN ambassador Susan Rice and National Security Council staffer Samantha Power, agreed. Opponents included Vice President Biden, Defense Secretary Gates, and the chairman of the Joint Chiefs of Staff, Admiral Mike Mullen (see Chollet 2016, 99; Dowd 2011; Gates 2014, 515–516; Ghattas 2013, 269; Mann 2012, 292; Warrick 2011).

Obama asked to review detailed military plans for Libya. His options were no action, enforcement of a no-fly zone, or all necessary measures (see Chollet 2016, 98; Ghattas 2013, 270). He endorsed the third choice, which triggered a NATO-led campaign under the operational command of a Canadian, Lieutenant General Charles Bouchard. Obama administration rules of engagement prohibited the deployment of American ground troops. These provisions meant that the United States was widely seen as "leading from behind" in Libya, an image that Clinton (2014, 375) rejects as inaccurate. By the autumn of 2011, Gaddafi was no longer in power, and the conflict became known as "Hillary's war" (Warrick 2011). As shown in Figure 6.1, Clinton visited Tripoli to greet the forces that had replaced Gaddafi's army.

How would Libya emerge from decades of dictatorship? Clinton (2014, 378, 379) recalls her visit to Tripoli after Gaddafi's capture; she describes crowds of "armed and bearded militia fighters . . . exuberant and exultant men" who were benefiting from "the loose weapons now flooding the country." Young women at Tripoli University asked Clinton (2014, 380) how to encourage wider political participation and entrench such norms as freedom of speech. As time passed, the questions female students

Figure 6.1. Secretary of State Hillary Clinton with militia fighters in Tripoli, 2011.
AP Photo; photo by Kevin Lamarque.

posed became increasingly academic given the absence of an effective post-Gaddafi government that could limit the spread of jihadist arms and ideas. Within a year of Clinton's (2014, 383) trip, two US diplomats and two CIA officers were killed in Benghazi—in her words, "a crushing blow" for which she accepted full responsibility.

Multiple investigations of what transpired in Benghazi came to overshadow Clinton's larger contribution. In particular, they obscured the fact that as secretary of state, she had realized key elements of the administration's international strategy. In coordinating a response to events in Libya, Clinton had built international partnerships not just with NATO allies, but also with predominantly Muslim countries of the region. She had bargained hard with Russia's foreign minister to prevent his vetoing the "all necessary measures" resolution at the UN Security Council (see Clinton 2014, 371–372). In Libya, a dictator who had been unfriendly toward the West lost power without American "boots on the ground," unlike the scenario in Iraq during the Bush years. While neither liberal values nor a vibrant civil society blossomed after the fall of Gaddafi, both Obama and Clinton had upheld their commitment not to impose democracy via military means.

Clinton (2014, 461) later failed to convince Obama to support a plan to vet, train, and arm "moderate Syrian rebels" fighting the Assad regime (see also Rothkopf 2014, 47). A proposal that Clinton (2014, 464, see also 462) developed in 2012 with the director of the CIA, General David Petraeus, attracted "high-level support from the National Security Council" but opposition from senior military advisors (see also Chollet 2016, 141; Panetta 2014, 449). The plan sought to bolster US influence in a disintegrating Syria—where Russia consistently protected the existing government; Iran and Hezbollah channeled funds, fighters, and weapons to the same side; and Sunni Arab states including Saudi Arabia dispatched arms to the rebels. Having lost that debate, Clinton (2014, 464) worked to increase humanitarian aid and assist "activists, students, and independent journalists" who opposed Assad.

The United States intervened militarily in Syria after Clinton (2014, 465) left the cabinet in early 2013 (see Chollet 2016, 142). Obama's hesitation to act was notable because he had employed the phrase "red line" in 2012 in warning against any use of chemical weapons by the Syrian government (see Clinton 2014, 465; Panetta 2014, 450). Independent accounts later confirmed that such weapons had been used (see Gladstone and Chivers 2013). By the summer of 2016, unrest in Syria had claimed approximately 400,000 lives and created close to five million refugees (Powell 2016).

Clinton's advice to Obama concerning the Middle East indicates that she prioritized national interests and was prepared to use force to defend them. At the same time, her approach sought to build cooperative relations with other players and to advance democratic ideals in ways that differed from the practices of the Bush years. With respect to Egypt, her refusal to call for Mubarak's immediate removal demonstrates a willingness to take partnerships seriously and to consider the social consequences of sudden political change. President Obama pursued a different approach and, as Clinton had anticipated, the situation deteriorated to the point that the Muslim Brotherhood assumed power, only to be removed by military leaders. In short, the chaos that Clinton predicted came to pass.

On Libya, Clinton created an international coalition with UN approval that protected civilians from an unstable dictator, all without engaging American ground troops. In the case of Syria, she tried to secure military aid for moderate rebels in order to enhance US influence and democratic values in a fragmenting state. This approach found belated acceptance after Clinton had resigned as secretary of state.

Hillary Clinton thus breathed life into key foreign policy precepts that both she and Barack Obama had articulated. Obama did not implement all of Clinton's advice, but he permitted her as secretary of state to transform American international relations from the unilateralism of the George W. Bush years toward a multilateral "smart power" posture. The next sections consider the experiences that underpin her significant redirection of US foreign policy.

SUBURBAN BEGINNINGS

Born in 1947, Hillary Rodham grew up in a suburb of Chicago called Park Ridge that was predominantly white and middle class. Clinton (2003, 1–15) describes the area as full of young families with children, the offspring of veterans returning from military service and the women who stayed home to raise them. Her father, Hugh Rodham, was a Navy trainer during World War II (see Bernstein 2007, 15). His drapery business grew such that within a few years of Hillary's arrival, the Rodhams paid cash for a detached brick house on a corner lot (see Bernstein 2007, 18; Clinton 2003, 9).

Hillary's parents met in the early 1940s. Hugh Rodham was a traveling salesman visiting a Chicago textile plant at the same time as Dorothy Howell was applying for a secretarial job. According to Clinton (2003, 6), "She was attracted to his energy and self-assurance and gruff sense of humor." Hugh came from a Welsh immigrant family in Scranton, Pennsylvania, where his father rose from the factory floor to a supervisory position. His mother, Hannah Jones Rodham, bought and managed rental properties. Clinton (2003, 4) recalls her paternal grandparents as hard-working Methodists living in "a rough industrial city of brick factories, textile mills, coal mines, rail yards and wooden duplex houses." Her father's father "was a kind and proper man," while Hannah was a tough taskmaster (Clinton 2003, 7).

Clinton (2003, 4) describes her dad as "hardheaded and often gruff," much like his own mother. Carl Bernstein (2007, 13–16) concludes, based on interviews with family members and friends, that Hugh Rodham was not merely demanding, but also miserly and tyrannical. Rodham behaved in particularly mean-spirited and dismissive ways toward his wife, who was eighteen when the couple met. According to Bernstein (2007, 20, 25), Dorothy was aware of how Hugh affected those around him. She developed coping techniques that included retaining her own political beliefs and advising Hillary to resist pressures to think, act, and dress like others in her peer group (see Clinton 2003, 11, 20).

The independence Dorothy demonstrated inside her marriage built on a history of making the most of difficult circumstances. Hillary's maternal grandparents, Della and Edwin Howell, were teenagers who left Dorothy alone to fend for herself as a little girl in a five-story tenement on Chicago's South Side. Dorothy and her younger sister were later shuffled from relative to relative until their parents divorced in 1927. They were then sent alone by train, at the ages of eight and three, to Edwin's parents in California (see Bernstein 2007, 23; Clinton 2003, 2).

Resenting this imposition, Dorothy's grandmother confined the girl to her room when she was not at school and forced her to eat alone. Dorothy nevertheless became a strong student and, at the age of fourteen, found work as a mother's helper in the home of warm, loving parents. After ten years without any contact, Della called Dorothy back to Chicago. Dorothy returned, only to find she was expected to keep house for her mother and a property investor stepfather named Max Rosenberg. Max agreed to send Dorothy for vocational training but not to college (see Bernstein 2007, 23–24; Clinton 2003, 3).

As a mother, Dorothy stressed the importance of study, inner strength, and personal independence. Hillary recalls not wanting to venture outside at the age of four because she feared another little girl. Dorothy assured Hillary it was okay to hit back if the girl struck her. In Mrs. Rodham's words, "You have to stand up for yourself. There's no room in this house for cowards" (as quoted in Clinton 2003, 12). Hillary straightened her upper body and walked out the door to settle the score on her own (see Bernstein 2007, 28).

Hugh not only reinforced the stress on personal autonomy, but also instilled elements of economic responsibility and "tomboy" competitiveness (Clinton 2003, 15). He expected Hillary and her younger brothers to work in the family business even though they were not paid for their efforts (see Bernstein 2007, 18). Clinton (2003, 8) recalls spending weeks every summer at a family cabin in the Pocono Mountains where "we explored the surrounding countryside, hiking and driving the back roads and fishing and boating on the Susquehanna River. My father taught me to shoot a gun behind the cottage, and we practiced aiming at cans or rocks." Hugh taught her to play baseball and football while Dorothy worked on her tennis skills (see Bernstein 2007, 29; Clinton 2003, 22). As Clinton (2003, 12) writes, both parents "conditioned us to be tough in order to survive whatever life might throw at us."

Hillary sent a letter as a teenager in which she volunteered for America's space team. Given that she had been raised to believe in her own potential, Rodham found NASA's response infuriating. As Clinton (2003, 20) writes, "I received a letter back informing me that they were not accepting girls in the program. It was the first time I had hit an obstacle I couldn't overcome with hard work and determination, and I was outraged." What permeates her account of this episode and life's journeys in general is a sense that barriers are meant to be surmounted. Clinton (2003, 1) suggests that while discriminatory practices held back earlier generations of American women, their willingness to push back against obstacles inspired her whenever she faced challenges.

Without her parents' knowledge, Hillary offered at the age of thirteen to help the Republican Party track suspected voter fraud on Chicago's South Side. Hugh was a strong Republican who believed that the local Democratic machine controlled by Mayor Richard J. Daley had enabled John F. Kennedy to win the 1960 presidential election. He did not endorse, however, Hillary's trip to a gritty area to try to overturn what was, in his view, a *fait accompli* (see Bernstein 2007, 31; Clinton 2003, 17).

Clinton debated issues at home and with her friends, served on the high school student council, and participated in Young Republican activities. As Bernstein (2007, 30) writes, "Hillary seemed to be involved in almost every extracurricular activity featured in the Maine East yearbook: student government, school newspaper, cultural values committee, the Brotherhood Society, prom committee, member of the *It's Academic* quiz show team that competed on local television." She was invited in eleventh grade to speak on TV about efforts "to promote tolerance" at the local high school (Clinton 2003, 19).

Hillary was also encouraged to participate in politics by the Methodist minister in Park Ridge. Don Jones held sessions twice a week with young people to share the social gospel doctrine: that is, the ability of human beings to work together to make a difference in the here and now. As part of his youth group, Hillary visited minority congregations in other parts of the city and listened spellbound as Martin Luther King, Jr. addressed an audience at Orchestra Hall (see Clinton 2003, 23).

King's civil rights message reinforced values that Hillary had learned from her mother. Unlike Hugh Rodham, who Bernstein (2007, 18) says was quick to express bigoted views, Dorothy told Clinton (2003, 11) "that we were no better or worse than anyone else." Hillary describes going with church friends to babysit the children of migrant farmworkers. She told Dorothy that a seven-year-old Mexican girl named Maria had no First Communion dress. Dorothy took Clinton (2003, 48) to buy Maria "a beautiful dress."

Given the conservative tenor of Park Ridge, Jones lasted only two years as the local minister (see Bernstein 2007, 35–36; Clinton 2003, 23). Yet his support for civil rights and social activism more generally, together with Hillary's growing awareness of her mother's experiences, meant that she was imbued with reformist ideas at a tender age.

CAMPUS ACTIVIST

Clinton (2003, 24) understood she'd be going to college but, in her own words, "did not have a clue about where." Two student teachers, one from Wellesley College and the other from Smith, encouraged her to apply to their alma maters—both East Coast women's schools known for high academic standards. She selected Wellesley because a photo of the bucolic campus reminded her of the Poconos (see Clinton 2003, 25).

Hillary's years at Wellesley marked her transformation from Republican to Democrat, and from engaged student to high-profile social campaigner. When she ascended the podium as Wellesley's inaugural class graduation speaker in the spring of 1969, Hillary Rodham projected far more self-assurance and assertiveness than she carried in the car with her parents on the drive from Park Ridge. In turn, those traits would serve her well in the public spotlights of Little Rock, Washington, and elsewhere.

What's remarkable about her path is that Hillary Rodham initially wanted to quit Wellesley College. Much like Madeleine Korbel's experiences on the same campus ten years earlier, Rodham felt out of place among so many daughters of wealth and privilege. When she arrived from Denver,

Korbel was able to draw on her knowledge of multiple foreign languages and destinations—even if she had mainly traveled as an exile. By comparison, Hillary Rodham had studied Latin only briefly in high school and left the United States but once, to see Niagara Falls from the Canadian side (see Clinton 2003, 27).

Both relied in that transitional period on strong work habits, outgoing personalities, and curiosity about the larger world. Hillary built lasting friendships at college that were grounded in activity outside the classroom. In her first year, she led the Wellesley Young Republicans, but stepped down as her views about civil rights and the Vietnam War diverged from those of the party. By junior year, Rodham was at the opposite end of the spectrum from a father who detested hippies, beatniks, and other counterculture protesters against US engagement in Indochina (see Clinton 2003, 31, 36).

Rodham chose a political science major and focused her attention on campus governance. In discussing issues from curriculum reform to the creation of a Black Studies program to diversifying the student body, Rodham retained the support of college leaders because she identified moderate solutions to problems. When it came to protesting American involvement in Vietnam, she convened educational teach-ins, rather than confrontational and potentially violent demonstrations. In February 1968, fellow undergraduates elected her as president of their student government (see Bernstein 2007, 45–46, 56–57; Clinton 2003, 30–31, 34).

That same spring, Hillary volunteered in Senator Eugene McCarthy's presidential primary campaign in New Hampshire. McCarthy opposed US involvement in Vietnam, a topic that increasingly dominated public debate. Young men of Hillary's age faced a compulsory draft; their alternatives included trying to defer military service, becoming a conscientious objector, or fleeing to Canada. The massive and unexpected Tet offensive of early 1968, mounted by Viet Cong forces against South Vietnamese and American troops, undermined arguments by the Johnson administration that the war was both winnable and worth continuing with US boots on the ground (see Bernstein 2007, 54; Clinton 2003, 32–33).

Less than three weeks after nearly losing to McCarthy in the New Hampshire primary, President Johnson announced that he would not seek re-election. The idea that a chief executive who had swept to office in 1964 could be brought to his knees by a member of his own party seemed unthinkable. Even more disturbing were other events of the spring of 1968. Martin Luther King was felled by an assassin's bullet in Memphis. Robert F. Kennedy, who had entered the Democratic nomination race after the New Hampshire vote, was fatally shot in Los Angeles.

Clinton (2003, 33) recalls that she marched at a Boston protest in April and "returned to campus wearing a black armband" to commemorate King's life as well as deaths on all sides in Indochina. That summer, Hillary interned with Republican lawmakers in the House of Representatives. She joined Nelson Rockefeller's campaign to prevent Richard Nixon from securing the party's presidential nomination in Miami. Rockefeller's effort failed, and Rodham returned to Chicago in time to see police use tear gas and clubs against antiwar protesters outside the Democratic convention (see Bernstein 2007, 55–56; Clinton 2003, 37).

In Chicago, Rodham met community organizer Saul Alinsky. She wrote her senior thesis on his ideas, convinced that Alinsky had developed useful ways "of empowering people to help themselves." Where they differed was with respect to the best means of doing so. Alinsky pursued transformational change from outside established institutions, whereas Clinton (2003, 38) preferred an incremental approach that said "the system could be changed from within."

As head of Wellesley's student government, Rodham was pressed by her peers to demand that a representative of the graduating class address the 1969 commencement ceremony. Wellesley's president eventually agreed, and Rodham spoke after Senator Edward Brooke—a Republican from Massachusetts who was among the first and, at the time, the only African American in the US Senate. Brooke professed empathy toward what he termed "productive dissent," but rejected what he saw as "coercive," less constructive campus protests. He advised Wellesley graduates to celebrate American achievements such as declining poverty rates (Brooke 1969).

Hillary Rodham spent long hours, including all night before the ceremony, preparing her text. The address was powerful at a symbolic level, since never before had a student spoken at graduation. Rodham tried to give voice to a generation coming of age amidst both international and domestic conflict. Hillary commented briefly on Senator Brooke's remarks, but her most pointed rebuttal suggested—somewhat circuitously—that sympathy was an insufficient response to demands for meaningful social change (see Rodham 1969).

Turning to her own "little speech," as she referred to her address, Rodham spoke of efforts over the past four years to gain greater voice in college decision-making, to recruit more African American faculty members and students, and to create an Upward Bound program for low-income teenagers. She condemned the hollowness of the time, arguing that "there are some things we feel, feelings that our prevailing, acquisitive, and competitive corporate life, including tragically the universities, is not the way of life for us. We're searching for more immediate, ecstatic, and penetrating modes of living" (Rodham 1969).

Rodham said that some of her cohort's expectations had been met, notably in reforms to the Wellesley curriculum, while hopes for what she called "human liberation" remained unfulfilled. She underlined a sense of unfinished business by reading a friend's poem that ended as follows:

> It is well at every given moment to seek the limits in our lives.
> And once those limits are understood
> To understand that limitations no longer exist.
> Earth could be fair. And you and I must be free
> Not to save the world in a glorious crusade
> Not to kill ourselves with a nameless gnawing pain
> But to practice with all the skill of our being
> The art of making possible.[1]

It is hard to imagine a more potent distillation of the values Hillary Rodham had absorbed from her mother and Don Jones. At Wellesley, she announced a pragmatic intention to remake the world to the extent that human beings can, within the constraints they are prepared to recognize.

The speech propelled Rodham toward national prominence. As illustrated in Figure 6.2, *Life* magazine sent a reporter and a photographer to Park Ridge. *Life*'s feature article, titled "The Class of '69," showcases student commencement speakers from a handful of top private colleges. Dressed in striped jeans, a long-collared blouse, and sandals, Hillary poses beside bookshelves at home, gesturing and explaining in an earnest way the process she followed to prepare her text (see Cosgrove 2014).

Rodham moved to New Haven later that summer to begin law school at Yale. Her visibility only increased: the League of Women Voters, formed in 1920 to enhance civic participation among the newly enfranchised women of America, invited her to a fall conference on youth political involvement. In May 1970, Rodham spoke at the group's fiftieth anniversary convention. Wearing a black armband to recall antiwar protestors killed days earlier at Kent State University, Rodham explained her opposition to the Nixon administration's decision to bomb Cambodia. In Clinton's (2003, 46) words, campuses across the country were convulsed by "the unconscionable expansion of a war that should never have been waged." Consistent with the reformist ideas she had expressed at Wellesley, Rodham said American corporations were out of touch with the citizenry at large. What could the good ladies of the League do? Rodham urged women shareholders to demand accountability from the firms in which they invested. As Hillary (as quoted in Bernstein 2007, 70) asked her audience, "What do you do with your proxies? How much longer can we let corporations run us?"

Figure 6.2. Hillary Rodham as a recent Wellesley College graduate, 1969.
Getty Images; photo by Lee Balterman.

Marian Wright Edelman, an African American civil rights campaigner who had graduated from Yale law school in 1963, delivered the convention's keynote address. She spoke subsequently in New Haven about the need for an anti-poverty organization focused on children. Rodham introduced herself and arranged to serve as Edelman's intern in Washington during the summer of 1970. Hillary studied the health and schooling of migrant children in the United States and, after returning to Yale that fall, worked as a researcher for a book about children and the law (see Bernstein 2007, 72–75; Clinton 2003, 46–50).

Rodham's personal background, academic training, and passion for social reform began to intertwine closely. As Clinton (2003, 50) writes, "I realized that what I wanted to do with the law was to give voice to children who were not being heard." It was as if the legacy of young Dorothy Howell—whose neglected upbringing was only known in general terms to Hillary and her brothers in 1970—had been channeled directly into her daughter's career plans. Rodham gathered materials for a series of influential scholarly articles in outlets including the *Yale Law Journal* and *Harvard Educational Review*. Rodham's publications helped to map the emerging terrain of children's rights law and ensured that she was recognized in Wills (1992) as "one of the more important scholar-activists of the last two decades."

As she had at Wellesley, Rodham proved adept as a law student at reconciling divergent points of view. She moderated a campus debate on the Nixon administration's decision in spring 1970 to escalate the war in Indochina. The session was raucous, in part because nine Black Panthers were on trial for murder at the same time in New Haven. Civil rights and antiwar activists coordinated demonstrations around the country to coincide with May Day. As Bernstein (2007, 68) writes, Rodham "became a kind of mediator, damping down the vitriol of some of the heated presentations of various factions, restating rhetorical excess in less incendiary language, and more or less presiding in a Robert's Rules of Order fashion." The meeting she oversaw culminated in an overwhelming vote by Yale law students to go on strike.

This period was at least as significant for other reasons: Hillary Rodham first observed Bill Clinton. By her account, she passed the law student lounge as he waxed eloquent on his favorite subject, Arkansas's world-beating watermelons (see Bernstein 2007, 79; Clinton 2003, 52). On their first date, he persuaded striking caretakers at Yale's art gallery to let the couple enjoy an exhibition even though the building was officially closed (see Bernstein 2007, 80; Clinton 2003, 53; Bill Clinton 2005, 182). Bill demonstrated a compelling interpersonal style: he could immediately command other people's attention and convince them of his point of view. These skills contrasted directly with Hillary's more studied and methodical approach.

The couple lived one summer in Berkeley while she worked on child custody cases. Back in New Haven, they supported George McGovern's presidential bid and moved the following summer to Texas, where Bill ran the statewide McGovern campaign and Hillary registered Hispanic voters. A coworker in that campaign, Sara Ehrman, nicknamed Rodham "Fearless." Bernstein (2007, 86) observes that when it came to tracking down potential

Democratic voters, no neighborhood in San Antonio was too run-down for Hillary Rodham.

Despite his dedicated team, McGovern proved to be an electoral disaster. He won one state, Massachusetts, plus the District of Columbia. As detailed later in this chapter, Hillary Rodham's commitment to social reform remained intact despite those results.

PROFESSIONAL BEGINNINGS

Rodham took her first major trip outside the United States with Bill Clinton, who had traveled extensively when he was a Rhodes Scholar based at Oxford. After she graduated from Yale in 1973, Hillary and Bill visited the Houses of Parliament in London, cathedrals in the countryside, and the columns of Stonehenge. One evening in the Lake District, he asked her to marry him. Clinton (2003, 61) replied, "No, not now."

Rodham began work at Edelman's newly created organization, the Children's Defense Fund, at the time based in Massachusetts. She focused on such issues as separating juvenile from adult prisoners and ensuring that children with disabilities could attend public schools. Having taken the Arkansas bar exam at Bill's urging, she journeyed to see him in Fayetteville at the end of the year. Civil rights lawyer John Doar—recently named as chief counsel to the Judiciary Committee of the House of Representatives—phoned to ask Bill to join an inquiry into the activities of the Nixon White House. Since he planned to seek a House seat in Arkansas, Bill declined (see Bernstein 2007, 191–194; Clinton 2003, 64–65).

Rodham accepted a post with Doar, and began a detailed study of the terms under which presidents had been impeached. The assignment formed the foundation for a document that examined the meaning of constitutional language stating officials could be removed from office if they were convicted of "high crimes and misdemeanors." The knowledge Hillary gained of the intricacies of presidential impeachment in 1974 gave her confidence two decades later that Republican allegations would not derail her husband's administration (see Clinton 2003, 67).

Working for the Judiciary Committee revealed the informal face of power and, in particular, taught Rodham how skilled leaders could control the flow and presentation of information. Doar worked hard to shield the inquiry from Washington's gossip mill: staff lawyers toiled up to eighteen hours a day, could not discuss their assignments with anyone outside the unit, and were prohibited from compiling private notes or journals. He also imposed strict standards of nonpartisanship and legal thoroughness to protect the committee's integrity (see Bernstein 2007, 96).

Once recordings came to light showing the extent to which Nixon had orchestrated a coverup of the burglary at Democratic Party headquarters, House investigators developed a strong case against him. Aware that congressional support for removing him from office was growing, Nixon resigned in early August. His decision was conveyed in a one-sentence letter to Secretary of State Henry Kissinger—the same advisor who had served at Nixon's side to prosecute and escalate the war in Indochina (see Kimball 2006, 66; National Archives 1974).

The day Nixon waved goodbye from the door of his helicopter on the White House lawn, Hillary Rodham accepted a faculty position at the University of Arkansas law school. She was a star recruit: degrees from Wellesley and Yale, significant scholarly as well as activist contributions to the field of children's rights, and constitutional experience with the House impeachment inquiry. Although Ehrman (as quoted in Bernstein 2007, 106) urged her not to join a "hillbilly" law faculty, Hillary chose to test her relationship with Bill on his home turf.

Rodham and Ehrman drove south from Washington in the late summer of 1974. Hours after arriving, they watched Bill deliver an impressive stump speech to a campaign crowd in Bentonville, Arkansas. Much of Hillary's time was taken up with meeting new people and learning how things worked in Fayetteville, a college town at the cusp of the Ozark Mountains. Rodham taught criminal law and trial advocacy, and was responsible for the law faculty's legal aid as well as prison projects. She built a strong network of friends, including Diane Kincaid (later Diane Blair), a political science professor who defended the Equal Rights Amendment in a 1975 debate against Phyllis Schlafly at the state legislature. Although Kincaid was widely viewed as the victor, state lawmakers again refused to ratify the amendment (see Bernstein 2007, 108–112, 142; Clinton 2003, 70–72).

As reflected in that vote, neither feminism nor feminists were welcome in all corners of Arkansas society. Hillary faced criticism for her values, appearance, and decision to retain her surname after she and Bill married (see Bernstein 2007, 111–113, 165–167; Clinton 2003, 91–93). Yet the personal fortitude her parents had worked to instill from early childhood meant that Hillary did not back down from the challenges she faced in Arkansas.

As a university faculty member, Rodham secured state as well as federal government funding for a new legal aid clinic. She taught courses that pressed students to reach high professional standards. Together with Kincaid and others, Rodham worked to establish Fayetteville's rape crisis center (see Bernstein 2007, 127, 147; Warner 1993, 92). She served as Indiana field coordinator for the Carter/Mondale campaign, and was appointed by President Carter to the board and later the chair's post at the Legal Services Corporation. The agency funded legal representation for Americans who could not afford to pay for counsel (see Bernstein 2007, 134).

Bernstein (2007, 113) writes that Hillary was concerned during this period about Bill's infidelity. After banning one particular student volunteer from his 1974 congressional campaign, she assumed a larger role in the election team. She adopted the same approach after 1980, when he lost the governor's job after only two years. Hillary announced to journalists her decision to work full-time on a new gubernatorial bid. Moreover, Hillary (as quoted in Bernstein 2007, 166) continued, "I'll be Mrs. Bill Clinton. I suspect people will be getting tired of hearing from Mrs. Bill Clinton." Reinstalled as governor, Bill learned that his new chief of staff was Betsey Wright, Hillary's close friend from the McGovern campaign in Texas. Wright literally sat as an enforcer outside his office door (see Bernstein 2007, 175).

After Bill became Arkansas attorney-general in 1976, Rodham moved to Little Rock. As Clinton (2003, 78) tells the story, the state capital was too far away from the university campus for her to continue teaching law. Moreover, his modest salary and the fact they wanted to start a family led her to enter private practice with the area's most prestigious legal group. In 1980, Hillary gave birth to a daughter, Chelsea Victoria.

The Rose Law Firm, as the organization she joined was known, had a roster of clients that included giants of Arkansas business, such as Walmart and meat processor Tyson Foods (see Bernstein 2007, 128). Not only did Clinton begin to represent the kind of major business interests she had questioned in her speeches to the Wellesley convocation and the League of Women Voters, but she also joined an extremely small cadre of elite women lawyers. Hillary Rodham had begun at Yale in 1969 in a class of 235 students, of whom about 11 percent were women (see Clinton 2003, 44). John Doar's team of forty-four lawyers on the House impeachment inquiry included three women, or less than 7 percent of the professional staff. In Little Rock, Clinton became the first female lawyer at the city's premier firm (see Bernstein 2007, 96, 128).

The years at Rose were crucial to Hillary's development for two main reasons. First, as in her work with Doar, she learned a great deal from observing and emulating the skills of others. According to Bernstein (2007, 131), Hillary learned from senior partners at Rose how to speak comfortably in front of jurors. She took on increasingly tough assignments for her husband, becoming the state governor's chief political strategist and troubleshooter on health care and education reform (see Bernstein 2007,

144–147; Clinton 2003, 93–95). She learned, in short, how to survive a relentless, often malicious public spotlight that was in many respects a microcosm of the national stage the Clintons faced in 1992 and following.

Second, Clinton raised her profile as a civic volunteer—a role that imparted balance to her day job in corporate law. Hillary offered pro bono counsel in a number of child advocacy cases. She volunteered with the local Methodist church as well as the Arkansas Children's Hospital, and chaired the board of Children's Defense Fund (see Bernstein 2007, 150, 154; Clinton 2003, 83–84).

As her prominence grew, Clinton demonstrated that she was a savvy, pragmatic operator who could get things done. She chaired the Education Standards Committee that her husband created, and traveled the state to hear from citizens. The upshot of the committee's work, according to Bernstein (2007, 171), was "largely predetermined by Hillary and the experts with whom she was working." Arkansas adopted a statewide curriculum as well as mandatory teacher testing, which civil rights groups said put many African American educators out of work (see Bernstein 2007, 173).

What her years in the Deep South did not foreshadow was diplomatic leadership. Professor Hillary Rodham did not specialize in international law or its trade, tax, communications, or transportation aspects—each of which involves the application of legal remedies across national boundaries. Instead, she engaged in domestic policy debates ranging from legal aid and children's rights to violence against women and education reform.

Moreover, once they settled in Arkansas, Hillary and Bill traveled little outside the country. They took brief trips to Mexico, Spain, England, and Canada's West Coast. The journeys were far less extensive than what Hillary had imagined as a student at Wellesley, when she speculated about taking a year off to explore Africa (see Bernstein 2007, 103).

Yet Clinton learned in Arkansas to thrive in the public limelight. During the 1992 presidential campaign, she held her own in intense interviews with journalists, including *60 Minutes* reporter Steve Kroft, who wanted to know what kind of marriage the Clintons had (see Clinton 2003, 107–108). On the brink of becoming first lady, she seemed intent on maximizing opportunities and minimizing the chances of defeat.

TRAVELING FIRST LADY

The 1992 presidential race focused primarily on matters of domestic public policy. Consistent with strategist James Carville's reminder that what mattered most to Americans was "the economy, stupid," the Clinton/Gore team adopted a slogan of "Putting People First" (Clinton 2003, 113, 115). Discussions with voters during the campaign convinced Bill Clinton to make health-care reform the "signature initiative" of his first mandate (Clinton 2003, 144).

He asked Hillary to lead a health-care task force and named Ira Magaziner, a graduate of Brown University who also had been featured in *Life* magazine's story on student commencement speakers, as its operations manager (see Bernstein 2007, 285; Clinton 2003, 120, 143). Clinton's judgment in appointing his wife to such a contentious post was questioned along with his ability to deliver, as promised, a reform plan to Congress within one hundred days. The task force spent nearly two years developing a complex public/private scheme that failed to win legislative approval (see Clymer, Pear, and Toner 1994; Panetta 2014, 132). Hillary Clinton (2003, 248) summarizes the loss as follows: "Bill and I were disappointed and discouraged. I knew I had contributed to our failure, both because of my own missteps and because I underestimated the resistance I would meet as a First Lady with a policy mission." Yet she remained convinced that trying to provide health coverage to all Americans was the right thing to do (see Clinton 2003, 248–249).

Republicans took control of the House of Representatives and Senate, as well as multiple state governors' offices in the fall 1994 mid-term elections. Linked to the main debacle of her husband's first two years as president, Hillary sought new outlets. She nurtured a close friendship with UN Ambassador Madeleine Albright (2003, 246), who writes that in this period she "learned how informed [Hillary] was and how interested in foreign policy." In March 1995, Hillary and Chelsea traveled at the invitation of the State Department to five countries in South Asia. Clinton (2003, 270) recalls that "[t]he point of my mission was to meet rural as well as urban women, to jettison the predictable itineraries and get into the villages where most people lived." The visit covered many bases: Hillary had lunch with Pakistani Prime Minister Benazir Bhutto, spoke at girls' schools in India and Bangladesh, and learned firsthand about micro-credit support for women farmers and entrepreneurs across the region (see Clinton 2003, 271–285; Gerth and Van Natta 2007, 149–151).

Clinton (2003, 278) discovered immediately that media coverage of her trip was far more favorable than what she typically garnered in Washington. Having experienced the benefits of international travel as a people-to-people ambassador for the United States, Hillary reached out for the chance to do more. She joined the US delegation to the Fourth World Conference on Women in 1995 in Beijing, where she delivered a speech that Albright (2003,

250) describes as such "a stunner" that one American reporter termed it "a home run." A *New York Times* editorial said the address "may have been her finest moment in public life" (as quoted in Clinton 2003, 306). On the advice of Albright and others, the text made explicit reference to the use of rape as a weapon of war and the plight of women refugees fleeing conflict. The perspectives Clinton advanced were seen by some observers as contentious, especially for a first lady speaking at an international gathering (see Clinton 2003, 303–306; Gerth and Van Natta 2007, 151–152).

Clinton (2003, 305) asserted that "it is no longer acceptable to discuss women's rights as separate from human rights." In her view, matters related to the health, education, and legal status of women and girls should be integrated into international agendas so that, in Clinton's (2003, 304) words, "we may help bring new dignity and respect to women and girls all over the world—and in so doing, bring new strength and stability to families as well." Her argument that a lack of opportunity for women and girls held significant consequences—to the point that it stymied not just families, countries, and regions, but also America's security, became a core pivot of US foreign policy during the first Obama presidency. As the quotation in the introduction to this chapter shows, the approach known in 2009 and following as the Hillary doctrine extends the key point of Clinton's 1995 speech (see Hudson and Leidl 2015).

Clinton continued to travel extensively during the remainder of her husband's first term and through his second mandate. She visited about eighty countries in Central and South America, Europe, Asia, Africa, and Oceana, and made a point of following a populist itinerary that went beyond official meetings and receptions (see Hudson and Leidl 2015, 20). In Clinton's (2003, 388) words, she was able "to meet with women in their homes and workplaces, tour hospitals that used innovative approaches to expanding health care to children and families and visit schools, especially those educating girls." After a trip to Thailand, she began to press for administration action on sex trafficking in women and girls (see Clinton 2003, 389–390).

Clinton's emphasis on the significance of gender to US national interests was a perspective she shared with Albright, as well as other senior diplomats who were appointed after 1992. The group launched a project known as the Vital Voices Democracy Initiative in Vienna in 1997. Drawing together US government, nongovernmental organization (NGO), and corporate representatives, Vital Voices focused on assisting women and girls in postcommunist societies as well as sites of political transition, including South Africa and Northern Ireland (see Clinton 2003, 414–415; Garner 2012; Hudson and Leidl 2015, 25–26, 29).

The positive headlines that Clinton generated bore little resemblance to the embattled state of her husband's presidency. Through 1998, the Lewinsky scandal and Republican threats to impeach Bill Clinton were subjects of saturation coverage in the domestic media. Yet Clinton (2003, 477) realized her "own approval rating was nearing an all-time high and would eventually peak somewhere around 70%."

The celebrity globetrotter status that Hillary Clinton attained after the defeat of health-care reform made her a compelling choice as Democratic candidate for the seat vacated by Daniel Patrick Moynihan, a veteran senator from New York. Moynihan had served prior to his political career in major diplomatic posts, including ambassador to the United Nations. Once Moynihan announced his decision not to seek re-election, Democrats began a concerted campaign to "draft Hillary." Clinton (2003, 501–502) explains her decision to run as follows:

> After years as a political spouse, I had no idea whether I could step from the sidelines into the arena, but I began to think that I might enjoy an independent role in politics. All over the United States and in scores of countries, I had spoken out about the importance of women participating in politics and government, seeking elective office and using the power of their own voices to shape public policy and chart their nations' futures. How could I pass up an opportunity to do the same?

Following a hard-fought campaign, Hillary Clinton won by a margin of 12 percent over her Republican opponent, Congressman Rick Lazio (see Clinton 2003, 523; Gerth and Van Natta 2007, 213).

This outcome made political history, since no White House spouse had ever sought—let alone secured—elective office. Moreover, Hillary Clinton's victory in November 2000 contrasted with the fate of the man who had served two terms as her husband's vice president, Al Gore—who lost the presidential race to George W. Bush. Clinton began her Senate service at an unusual moment, when Democrats and Republicans each held fifty seats, so that tie-breaking control rested with Bush's vice president, Dick Cheney.

From the perspective of foreign policy contributions, the legacy of Clinton's time as first lady proved crucial. She emerged from the shadow of health-care reform by reconstructing her reputation in hospitals, schools, and village squares far from Washington, D.C. In substantive terms, Clinton cooperated with Albright and others who shared the same priority, namely the advancement of women and girls around the globe. Buoyed by a network that extended to international NGOs, Clinton used the accolades from her travels to establish credentials as a credible Senate candidate. In short, she demonstrated once again—and not for the last time—a capacity to translate setback into success.

SENATOR AND PRESIDENTIAL CANDIDATE

Unlike the extensive attention Clinton (2003, 2014) devotes in her memoirs to her time as first lady and secretary of state, she reflects relatively little on the years dedicated to elective office. That silence is likely attributable to the controversies of her Senate career, notably a vote in October 2002 to authorize the invasion of Iraq. That decision attracted close scrutiny during the 2008 presidential primaries. As Lawrence and Rose (2010, 116 italics in original) observe, Clinton's slogan of "Ready on Day One" became useful cannon fodder for her main opponent: Barack Obama told cheering audiences that "it is important to be *right* on Day One."

Although Clinton's 2002 vote may seem inconsistent with her background as a critic of the Vietnam War, it resonated with her long-standing pragmatism. The Methodist values she had absorbed at home and at church drew Hillary Rodham toward practical opportunities to fix problems and reform structures—not toward revolutionary politics. As a campus leader in the late 1960s and early 1970s, for instance, she regularly listened to many points of view in order to identify commonalities and, ultimately, to reach consensus in a group.

That same search for workable solutions figured heavily in her legislative career. First, in the immediate aftermath of the al-Qaeda attacks, Clinton worked to channel public rage in institutional directions. In particular, her rhetoric captured the visceral sense of vulnerability and anger that permeated the streets of New York City. She promised the next day, on September 12, that those who were found to have assisted the 9/11 attackers would confront what she termed America's "wrath" (Clinton, as quoted in Gerth and Van Natta 2007, 241). Second, Clinton adopted a bipartisan approach in the subsequent days and months. On September 13, she met President Bush at the Oval Office to request $20 billion more than he had offered to that point in emergency aid to New York City. Once Bush approved the additional federal assistance, Clinton (as quoted in Gerth and Van Natta 2007, 232) announced to reporters that she would stand behind him "for a long time to come."

Clinton's language, as well as her support for Bush's policies, served multiple purposes. Both stances helped to undermine claims that in the eight years prior to the attacks, her husband's administrations had underestimated the threat posed by al-Qaeda (see Gerth and Van Natta

2007, 234). They reminded voters that the Clinton presidencies had indeed featured strong military action, notably under the aegis of NATO in the Balkans (see Gerth and Van Natta 2007, 251). Moreover, Hillary's approach directly challenged public views of women leaders as weak on matters of defense (see Gerth and Van Natta 2007, 241; Lawless 2004). By her third year in elected office, Clinton was rewarded with a seat on the Senate Armed Services Committee—which further reinforced her national security credentials (see Bernstein 2007, 550–551).

When Senator Clinton (as quoted in Bernstein 2007, 549) spoke on October 10, 2002 about Bush administration plans for Iraq, she portrayed her vote as "probably the hardest decision I have ever had to make . . . but I cast it with conviction." She said her thinking was grounded in eight years of living in the White House, which gave her firsthand knowledge of the pressures facing the president and the importance of a bipartisan foreign policy. Clinton sought to demonstrate American unity in the face of three factors: the threat posed by Saddam Hussein, the difficulty of using UN diplomatic channels, and the need for men and women in the US military to know "our country will stand resolutely behind them" (Clinton, as quoted in Bernstein 2007, 549).

Documents indicate that prior to voting, Clinton had not read the detailed intelligence briefing on Iraq that was available to senators (see Gerth and Van Natta 2007, 244). Relying instead on her husband and his foreign policy advisors, Clinton maintained that the Iraqi leadership had given "aid, comfort, and sanctuary to terrorists, including Al Qaeda members" (Clinton, as quoted in Gerth and Van Natta 2007, 245; see also Bernstein 2007, 549–550). Even though public opinion polls at the time showed that about two-thirds of Americans believed Saddam Hussein had been involved in the attacks of 9/11, few other Democrats in the Senate were prepared to assert the connection that Clinton alleged (see Gerth and Van Natta 2007, 246).

Bernstein (2007, 549) notes that Clinton recognized the invasion of Iraq as a mistake "later than many of her Democratic colleagues." She then justified her 2002 vote as an attempt to press President Bush to use other levers. As Clinton (as quoted in Bernstein 2007, 549) explained in 2006, "this was not a vote for preemptive war; this was a vote, I thought, that would enable diplomacy to succeed."

Within five years of the attacks of 9/11, Hillary Clinton had developed a divergent and explicitly partisan interpretation of those events. Before the 2006 mid-term elections, both Clintons rejected the view that Republicans were better equipped than Democrats to protect national security (see Gerth and Van Natta 2007, 336–338). On September 23, for example,

Hillary encouraged reporters to read the report of the 9/11 commission in order "to know what [Bill] and his administration did to protect Americans and prevent terrorist attacks against this country." As she continued, "I'm certain that if my husband and his national-security team had been shown a classified report entitled *Bin Laden Determined to Attack Inside the U.S.*, he would have taken it more seriously than history suggests it was taken by our current president and his national-security team" (Clinton, as quoted in Gerth and Van Natta 2007, 338; italics in original).

In campaigning for the Democratic presidential nomination in 2008, Barack Obama focused on the Iraq vote as evidence that Hillary Clinton was correct in asserting she had lots of decision-making experience. The problem, he repeatedly underlined, was that she had shown poor judgment in reaching the most significant of those choices. Clinton's usual rebuttal during the primary season was to depict Obama's approach to foreign policy as "naïve" and lacking in toughness (Clinton, as quoted in Lawrence and Rose 2010, 116).

Although her initial bid for a presidential nomination failed, Clinton's 2008 effort was effective on multiple levels. It eroded centuries of symbolic association between one gender and chief executive office in the United States. The campaign drew almost 18 million votes in state-level primaries and caucuses, an accomplishment that directly challenged views that women's candidacies for top office were not viable (see Lawrence and Rose 2010, 223). Clinton's team raised large sums of money—reaching about $252 million by the end of 2008, compared with roughly $287 million for Obama during the same period (see Federal Elections Commission 2008a, 2008b). Analyses of US media reports found Clinton received "as much or more positive coverage than her main rival" during the nomination race (Lawrence and Rose 2010, 230).

Clinton (2014, 6) displayed stubborn optimism when she addressed supporters in June 2008: "Although we weren't able to shatter that highest, hardest glass ceiling this time, thanks to you, it's got about 18 million cracks in it. And the light is shining through like never before, filling us all with the hope and the sure knowledge that the path will be a little easier next time." Once again, Clinton saw new prospects on the horizon—and, in this case, she found them in a "team of rivals" cabinet.

THE HILLARY DOCTRINE

More than winning a Senate seat or even the presidency, becoming secretary of state offered an international advocate for the rights of women and girls the best possible opportunity to realize her vision. In preliminary discussions about serving as America's top diplomat during the fall of 2008, Clinton (2014, 18) writes, Obama "guaranteed that I would have direct access to him and could see him alone whenever I needed to. He said I could choose my own team, though he would have some suggestions." The two worked together closely from the time Clinton (2014, 19) accepted Obama's offer, as reflected in the fact that she "was at the White House more than seven hundred times during [her] four years" in the cabinet.

The tenor of American policy changed markedly once her appointment was confirmed by the Senate Foreign Relations Committee in January 2009. In particular, the emphasis which Obama (2007) placed on global partnerships and the importance Clinton had accorded civil society interests since her years as first lady meant that the new administration was committed—at least in theory—to a more cooperative, multilateral stance than had been typical of the George W. Bush years. Clinton (2014, 33) spoke extensively about what she called "smart power," for example, in highlighting the need to employ tools in the US arsenal besides armed force. According to Bunting (2011), Clinton's preferred approach to international affairs deeply implicated matters of gender such that she "mentioned women 450 times in speeches in the first five months in office."

In addition to rhetoric, actions taken by Obama and Clinton contrasted with those of the George W. Bush administrations. Like his Democratic predecessor Bill Clinton, Obama reversed the "gag rule" dating from 1984 that prohibited overseas aid for women's reproductive health (see Finkle and Crane 1985; Obama 2009b, 44–45). The Office of International Women's Initiatives, created during the first Clinton term in 1994, was renamed the Office of Global Women's Issues. The unit moved from an offsite location into the State Department headquarters, received a tenfold budget increase, and saw the lead position of Global Women's Issues ambassador made permanent (see Clinton 2014, 572; Hudson and Leidl 2015, 51–52). Clinton began a planning process known as the Quadrennial Diplomacy and Development Review that placed gender at the forefront of both streams. According to Hudson and Leidl (2015, 53), in the first review report, dated 2010, "women and girls are mentioned a total of 133 times in its 242 pages."

The effects of Clinton's presence were also measurable with respect to diplomatic appointments. Under her leadership, more than 50 percent of new US foreign service recruits were women, as were 30 percent of chiefs of mission overseas (see Hudson and Leidl 2015, 57).

Other countries began to see the advantage of sending a female ambassador to Washington. Within a year of Clinton's swearing in, the US capital had become home to twenty-five women emissaries, including ambassadors from Bahrain, Burundi, and Mozambique. Those numbers represented a record level that was five times higher than in the late 1990s (see Jordan 2010).

Clinton also worked to introduce distinctive policies. American programs that dealt with international health and food security began to prioritize initiatives related to women and girls. For example, Clinton promised $50 million toward a UN project that aimed to distribute 100 million cooking stoves by 2020. The new stoves would not use wood or biological waste—thus reducing exposure to smoke, as well as the need to cut trees or gather firewood in places where physical security was already problematic (see Bunting 2011).

Clinton highlighted the accomplishments of women in the global South who operated as change agents and were not awaiting "rescue" by either wealthier nations or men in their own countries. She met, for instance, with South Africans who had created their own housing cooperative, and with women facing a long civil war in the Democratic Republic of the Congo, "who, after they had recovered from being raped and beaten, went back into the forest to rescue other women left to die" (Clinton 2014, 282; see also Bunting 2011). Once she returned to Washington, Clinton tried to focus policies and budgets on women's security. After visiting Africa in 2009, for example, Clinton (2014, 282) "announced that the United States would provide more than $17 million to combat sexual violence in the DRC" (see also Hudson and Leidl 2015, 54–56). She ensured unanimous support in the UN Security Council for Resolution 1888, which made the protection of women and girls from sexual violence a priority for international peacekeeping (Clinton 2014, 282).

What distinguishes Clinton's record, however, is that she perceived the rights of women and girls as foundational to not just international relations, but also US national security. Building on momentum from the Beijing Conference and Vital Voices initiative of the 1990s, Clinton merged her concern for the educational, health, and legal rights of half the world's population with the same strong defense of American interests that had characterized her career in the Senate. By stating in 2010 that "the subjugation of women is a direct threat to the security of the United States," Clinton (as quoted in Hudson and Leidl 2015, 35) elevated gender equality to unprecedented prominence as a potential provocation for war. While what was termed the Hillary doctrine may have seemed to some listeners like a humanitarian trope, it was not, as Hudson and Leidl (2015, 35) argue, "by definition a pacifist doctrine."

Instead, much like Albright's willingness during the 1990s to address rape and murder in the Balkans via the use of NATO firepower, Clinton demonstrated as secretary of state that direct threats to human rights would hold measurable and not just diplomatic consequences. This approach contrasted with the Bush administration's use of pro-women rhetoric to justify military action in Afghanistan and to deepen public support for it—when that intervention was already well underway and had been initiated for different reasons. The most glaring problem in applying Clinton's idea after 2009 was that the new Democratic administration sought to reverse the legacy of the Bush years by limiting the use of US ground troops. As a result, the main military intervention of the first Obama administration was unable to defend Libyan civilians as well as assist rebels seeking to overthrow the Gaddafi regime and, at the same time, ensure an orderly transition to democratic rule that would uphold the rights of women and girls. As a result, the "feminist hawk" position adopted by Clinton, Susan Rice, and Samantha Power in administration debates seemed to produce more conflict than equality outcomes (Hudson and Leidl 2015, 34).

The question of how women have fared since 2011 in Libya implicates not just the Hillary doctrine, but also Obama's foreign policy legacy. His stress on avoiding the aggressive and unilateralist ways of the Bush years included a corollary to the effect that the United States would resist imposing democracy in other parts of the globe, including via military means (see Obama 2007, 14). Obama's focus on "soft power" as opposed to coercive force meant that American decision-makers would help liberalizing interests but not create new regimes.

Did Libyan rebels who benefited from international support demonstrate either an inclination or capacity to uphold democratic values? In particular, how did the rights of women and girls figure in their plans for a post-Gaddafi future? The evidence to date suggests that the breakdown of civil order and influx of arms after the rebel victory were so severe that by August 2016, the United States had initiated military action against Islamic State forces operating in Libya. With respect to gender, according to Hudson and Leidl (2015, 102), "the very first legal change the head of the brand new interim government proposed after the ouster of Muammar Gadhafi was the re-legalization of polygamy. In February 2013, that proposal became law."

Reports from NGO sources indicate that as dismal as circumstances were prior to the end of the dictatorship, they remained more promising than the "disastrous" situation afterward (Madiha al-Naas, as quoted in Hudson and Leidl 2015, 106). One report concludes that the transitional government neither created an inclusive electoral system nor investigated cases of sexual violence that may have occurred before, during, and after the regime change; moreover, external actors failed to uphold their stated commitments to women's security (see ICAN 2013). Given the growth of not just Islamic fundamentalism but also ethnocultural and regional divisions in Libya, the ICAN (2013, 10) authors write, "The post revolution euphoria is turning to fear, and there is growing mistrust and scepticism towards the international community."

On the implementation side, at least initially, Obama's focus on partnerships and Clinton's doctrine concerning women's security fell short in Libya. During the seven years after the end of Gaddafi's regime, no unified, friendly, democratic government that was prepared to adopt and enforce basic liberal rights emerged in its stead. The reputation of the United States thus became imperiled by a gap between official rhetoric about cooperation and the need to protect civilians from an erratic dictator, on one side, and the lives of people in Libya after he had been deposed, on the other. Since American leaders were unwilling to send ground troops and believed that democracy could not be enforced militarily, liberal interests in Libya remained fearful or, in the words of one NGO report (ICAN 2013, 10), "acutely aware of the dangers that rising sectarianism poses to them and to their society at large."

EVALUATING THE RECORD

Among the closest observers of Hillary Clinton has been her husband, who remarked in 2006 that she resembled "all the great female leaders in history [who] were battle-tested, possessed nerves of steel, and owned an indomitable will to win" (Bill Clinton comment to a friend, as paraphrased in Gerth and Van Natta 2007, 344). His description dovetails the trajectory examined in this chapter. As secretary of state, Clinton secured presidential support for a key military intervention in Libya despite opposition from the vice president, CIA director, and chairman of the Joint Chiefs of Staff. Ignoring the controversy that surrounded it, her foreign policy doctrine defined empowering women and girls around the world as integral to American national security.

Using the categories developed by Kirkpatrick (1974, 174), Hillary Clinton seemed to operate as a flexible and "electric" leader who avoided the moralizer tendencies of Jeane Kirkpatrick and Condoleezza Rice. Like Madeleine Albright, she was practical in her approach to public life in general and foreign policy in particular—as demonstrated by an unwillingness to place all bets on any single instrument in the international toolkit. Consistent with the "smart power" approach, for example, she worked with China as well as Russia on negotiations to contain Iran's nuclear program (see Ghattas 2013, Chapter 8; Sharma 2016).

Similar to her predecessors, Clinton dedicated significant energy to building political networks. Given the votes she won as a candidate for the Democratic presidential nomination in 2008, however, Clinton stood out because she commanded the most formidable electoral base of any woman in US diplomatic history. This popular visibility meant that unlike Kirkpatrick, Albright, or Rice, Clinton did not need to develop a "personalizer" repertoire to retain Obama's confidence; rather, a robust national and global profile solidified her standing with the chief executive. Nor did she need to rely on personal closeness to the wife or family of a president to solidify her status within the political executive, as had benefited Albright and Rice but eluded Kirkpatrick.

Clinton reached this point by dedicating sustained time, energy, and concentration to political engagement. Since her teenage years, Hillary Rodham showed exceptional self-assurance. She appeared on TV in high school, commanded a large audience as the first student orator at a Wellesley College commencement, and moderated campus debates on the Vietnam War at Yale. As Hillary Clinton, she refused to let barriers stand in her way: the fact that her husband's electoral career unfolded in a socially traditional Southern state did not prevent her from working to advance children's rights and women's rights. Health-care reform after the 1992 presidential election may have been an impossible task, but as first lady she embraced it with enthusiasm and determination.

The fact that Republicans won major victories across the country in 1994 seemed only to put more wind in her sails. In substantive terms, Clinton recovered by exploring new but related policy interests. From learning about schools in Arkansas as the governor's wife, she reached out as first lady to girls in South Asia whose only opportunities to study ended after elementary school (see Clinton 2003, 274–275). Having served as a legal advocate for children across the United States, she tried to stop the trafficking of young girls in Thailand (see Clinton 2003, 389–390). Clinton drew on these experiences in a series of high-impact speeches to international forums, most notably the Fourth World Conference on Women in 1995.

Clinton's growing familiarity with global politics was helpful on many levels. The travels she undertook connected her domestic starting points to important international policy domains. She developed an urbane cosmopolitanism after years of limited exposure to places outside the United States. Above all, voyages abroad fostered a public profile that was overwhelmingly positive; unlike domestic media stories, news reports from her trips described a hard-working first lady who aimed to advance American interests.

The main upshot of Clinton's travels in the mid-1990s and following was that she became a logical choice for major public office. The positions of senator from New York, secretary of state, and president would have been inconceivable without her journeys as first lady. In turn, reaching each of those posts depended on the confidence and focus she had developed as the eldest child of parents with high expectations. Given the influence of her mother and Don Jones in particular, Hillary had a fulcrum for her ambitions: she made moderate social reform a lifelong passion.

In her adult years, Hillary Clinton became a firm defender of both American national interests and international human rights. Her response to the attacks of 9/11 included a 2002 Senate vote to approve plans to invade Iraq, which revealed her capacity to adopt hawkish positions. That same inclination was clear in Clinton's forceful response as secretary of state to popular uprisings in the Arab Middle East; although she won support for military intervention in Libya, she was unable to convince Obama to arm opponents of the Assad regime in Syria.

Direct links to the past can be discerned as well in her record on the rights of women and girls. Clinton did not deviate after her top diplomatic appointment in 2009 from the path of performing "critical acts" on behalf of women as a group (Dahlerup 1988). As a young law professor, she had worked to establish a rape crisis center in an Arkansas college town. Although the Hillary doctrine represented a significant extension of those earlier activities, it was nevertheless embedded in the same commitment to empowering women.

Did the Obama administration's multilateral approach to foreign policy hold different implications than Bush's more unilateral doctrine? Future analysts will be able to probe this question with the benefit of a longer time horizon. As of this writing, military action both in Iraq under Bush and in Libya under Obama seemed neither to assure women's security in what had been intact countries, nor to advance US national interests in a region of the world with significant ongoing conflicts. Despite Hillary Clinton's policy priorities as secretary of state, therefore, circumstances facing many women appeared to stalemate or slide backward, rather than improve (see Mason 2017).

Chapter 7 returns to the themes presented in earlier parts of the study in order to explore these comparative dimensions in greater detail.

CHAPTER 7

Conclusion

What perspectives does this study shed on women's engagement in international affairs? How do findings from this account square with work in the field of feminist diplomatic historiography, much of which addresses the early modern era through the 1970s? Did the leadership practices of elite appointees diverge from their earlier repertoires? Can we conclude that women leaders made a substantive difference to US foreign policy? How did they act on matters of war and gender politics?

Jeane Kirkpatrick invokes an unusual metaphor in the following commentary:

> The Situation Room was in the basement of the White House and it has special security protection and heavy doors and special locks. We were in the middle of an NSPG [National Security Planning Group] meeting when someone said "it's a mouse." I said: "A mouse in the Situation Room?" We all looked and there was indeed a mouse in the Situation Room. The mouse was sitting across the room and he looked at us, walked across the floor, and disappeared. Now someone else said "it must be the first time there has ever been a mouse in the Situation Room." For some reason something clicked in my head and I thought to myself that day that the mouse was really no stranger a creature to find in the Situation Room than I was. It must have been about the first time that a creature such as I had ever been in the Situation Room too. (Kirkpatrick interview in McGlen and Sarkees 1993, 53–54)

Did women elites operate as mice-like creatures who appeared and then disappeared with barely a trace? This discussion considers each question with an eye toward identifying promising directions for future research.

The literature of feminist diplomatic historiography highlights the treatment of female leaders from the early modern through postwar periods. As detailed in Chapter 1, applying a feminist lens shows the extent to which mainstream analysts have tended either to ignore women diplomats or, alternately, present them as underpowered or overpowered actors in world politics. The discussion in this chapter extends this analytic stream in order to examine the presentation of contemporary elite legacies.

Writings about the 1980s discussed in Chapter 3 reveal a pattern of neglect, at the same time as they demonstrate the persistence of underpowered narratives. Kirkpatrick is missing from Gaddis's (2005) influential study of Cold War foreign policy, even though her ideas guided American international relations during the twilight of that era. The autobiography of Caspar Weinberger (1990), Reagan's defense secretary who was seen as a close ally of Kirkpatrick, omits her entirely. Alexander Haig (1992), a secretary of state whom Kirkpatrick challenged from time to time, does not mention her in his memoir.

George Shultz (1993, 320), who succeeded Haig as secretary of state and also had his differences with Kirkpatrick, describes a "capacity for passionate advocacy" that prevented her from being a "dispassionate broker." Shultz fails to consider whether his own strong commitment to competing points of view constituted "passionate advocacy." Shultz's (1993) account thus echoes an outlook dating from early international diplomacy, when it was assumed that women were overly emotional and that only men could be properly rational and deliberative decision-makers (see Sluga and James 2016).

Studies of the Clinton, Bush, and Obama administrations tend to acknowledge the presence of Albright, Rice, and Clinton, respectively. Yet they also depict women's characteristics as misaligned with international leadership. As noted in the introductory sections of Chapters 4 through 6, analysts alternate between claims that the senior female diplomat in each presidency (a) lacked core attributes necessary to perform her role well, or (b) possessed requisite features in excess. The narrative of underpowered leadership can be found, for instance, in portrayals of Albright as emotional and impatient (see Hyland 1999, 163), of Rice as "overly eager" to retain her personal status (Charles-Philippe 2010, 54), and of Clinton as an ineffectual outsider who never reached "the president's inner circle" (Dueck 2015, 146). At the same time, accounts of these administrations suggest that women were overly endowed with the necessary attributes. Albright showed "excessive self-certainty" (Dumbrell 2009, 168). Rice was caricatured as a "warrior princess" (Alexander-Floyd 2008, 440). Clinton ranked among the few "big hitters" (Milne 2012, 940) who had "international rock star qualities" (Bader 2013, 11). Her assertive influence and that of other female advisors was so pronounced that they were called "militaristic muses" and "Furies" (Dowd 2011).

The contradictions contained in these varied tropes suggest a neglect versus underpowered versus overpowered dynamic that resembles the leadership binds discussed in Jamieson (1995). In the foreign policy field, female elites tend to be ignored by scholars and peers, or dismissed as either lacking the requisite traits or possessing an oversupply of them— rather than being assessed systematically for their decision-making contributions. By focusing on leader images in the field of international relations, future researchers can examine conflicting narratives in accounts of one or multiple countries. How are women in positions of international responsibility presented at the level of expert (including insider) commentary? Do treatments change over time? Are female leaders willing to contest accounts that demean their accomplishments? Does the historical record change once they intervene in this way? How are male leaders depicted in the same narratives?

Above all, this assessment highlights the role of precedent in shaping the actions of foreign policy leaders. Contrary to the thesis proposed by Koch and Fulton (2011), this study finds little evidence that women leaders adopt different decision-making styles or new substantive positions toward national security or women's rights when they reach executive office. Rather than acceding to pressures to conform to masculine norms at that level, materials presented in Chapters 3 through 6 indicate that Kirkpatrick, Albright, Rice, and Clinton arrived in top posts with well-developed repertoires and worldviews that altered little after their appointments. The legacies of their previous work, in fact, likely made them attractive candidates to the presidents who appointed them.

Kirkpatrick's publications from the 1970s, for instance, foreshadow her hawkish approach to international relations, as well as her limited support for progressive feminism in the Reagan years. Albright's record from the 1980s suggests that she saw boldness and strength as crucial assets for American leaders, and viewed feminist causes as integral to international politics. The doctrine of "beyond containment" that Rice articulated in the George H. W. Bush years, along with her unswerving commitment to individual merit as Stanford University provost, stand on the public record as markers of her national security and gender outlooks. Clinton's belligerent response as a senator to the attacks of 9/11 and her sustained advocacy of women's rights anticipate her actions during the first Obama term.

This discussion recalls one additional theme from Chapter 1, namely the changing status of institutions and their leaders. Sluga and James's (2016) work on the decline of informal statecraft in Europe demonstrates how privileged women wielded diplomatic influence in salons and dynastic families prior to the rise of more formal and professionalized structures that were dominated by upper-class men. A similar narrative about the unsettling of older practices applies to the context considered in this book. Kirkpatrick, Albright, Rice, and Clinton all served as foreign policy elites at a time when US military spending vastly overshadowed funds directed toward diplomacy—to the point that Rice (2011, 216) remarks, "there were as many people in military bands as in the Foreign Service" (see also Clinton 2014, 24). The difference between the relative permanence of the two communities was also clear: while senior diplomats like those considered in this study were shuffled with each presidential administration, military commanders tended to remain in place for longer periods. In the field of foreign affairs, the dominance of military over civilian leadership became increasingly clear (Stevenson 2011).

Disparities in human capital are laid out clearly by Clinton (2014, 26), who compares the roughly 70,000 worldwide employees of the State Department and Agency for International Development with the approximately three million working for the Defense Department. As Clinton (2014, 24) writes, "for every dollar spent by the federal government, just one penny went to diplomacy and development" (see also Albright 2003, 642). Albright (2003, 643) expresses particular concern for the steep decline in diplomatic investment since the late 1940s: she observes that "we are spending only about one-tenth as much for these purposes, in real terms, as we did when George Marshall was Secretary of State half a century ago."

The loss of State Department primacy suggests a corollary to Sluga and James's (2016) argument about the negative consequences for women of diplomatic institutionalization. The careers of female elites chronicled here unfolded as the standing of Foggy Bottom weakened, especially relative to that of the Pentagon. The view that women's arrival in top posts signals organizational decline or that they reach the apex of formal power after authority and influence have largely left the building may sound cynical, but accurately captures the pattern of more female elites but less heft at the State Department. This perspective renders the transforming contributions of Kirkpatrick, Albright, Rice, and Clinton that much more remarkable—since it underlines the capacity of forceful, confident individuals to wield clout even as they preside over structures in sustained decline.

Given patterns of institutional change, future analysts will need to pay particular attention to foreign policy activity that happens outside the usual diplomatic channels. For instance, military bureaucracies, supranational organizations, civil society groups, private-sector contractors, and charitable foundations constitute significant sites of financial investment and international decision-making that affect the lives of women and girls in many part of the global South. It is time to train additional analytic spotlights in each direction, following from the work of Caglar, Prügl, and Zwingel (2013), Jain (2005), Meyer and Prügl (1999), Montoya (2013), and others.

MAKING A DIFFERENCE

In assessing four elites who served in the national security teams of US presidents since 1981, this discussion shows that each woman was successful under the terms of Genovese and Thompson's (1993, 1; emphasis in original) rubric: "Leadership is a complex phenomenon revolving around *influence*—the ability to move others in desired directions. Successful leaders are those who can take full advantage of their opportunities and their skills." Simply reaching cabinet rank in the field of foreign policy was, in and of itself, a sign that Jeane Kirkpatrick, Madeleine Albright, Condoleezza Rice, and Hillary Clinton could emerge on top in the highly competitive appointment process for such posts as UN ambassador, secretary of state, and national security advisor. In so doing, they proved that since the 1980s, American women with academic training as well as well-developed networks in the fields of political science, international relations, and law could command the confidence of not just a president and his advisors, but also a group of legislators who vetted executive nominees.

Beyond holding elite office, all four demonstrated a capacity to transcend the characteristics of routine leadership such that they changed in meaningful ways the directions of the presidential administrations in which they served. Given Burns's (2003) distinction between "transformational" versus "transactional" elites, as well as Hook's (1943) account of individuals who make events versus those whose influence could have been replicated by others, we find that each leader shaped decision-making in ways that altered the course of US foreign policy during a given era, and hence measurably acted upon world politics. Kirkpatrick envisioned, articulated, and set in play the international doctrine of the first Reagan mandate. Albright was crucial to the conception, defense, and implementation of foreign policies during the Clinton years, notably the pursuit of multilateral intervention in the Balkans. Rice served as a close advisor to George W. Bush and as the main architect of his foreign policy, including the preemption doctrine used to justify the "war on terror." Hillary Clinton advanced a distinctive view that empowering women and girls around the globe was critical to US national security, and employed that perspective to shape Obama-era responses to the Arab Spring uprising in Libya.

As noted in Chapter 1, all four presidents who appointed these women had limited international experience at the point of their election as chief executive, and each faced major global challenges while in office. None could claim the depth of international knowledge and experience that had accrued to George H. W. Bush as a retired CIA director or, going back to the 1960s, Lyndon Johnson as a veteran member of the Senate Armed Services Committee. Ronald Reagan, Bill Clinton, George W. Bush, and Barack Obama all relied heavily on advice from their foreign policy advisors— although this shared pattern neither predicts whose counsel would be followed, nor to what extent.

During the first Reagan mandate, Kirkpatrick's (1979) argument about the need to restore American primacy and her prescription for attaining that goal served as road maps for the new administration. Among the clearest visual representations of the muscularity and assertiveness of the early Reagan doctrine is the image of Kirkpatrick at the UN Security Council in 1983, when she introduced the radio communications of Soviet fighter jet pilots in order to condemn the Soviet Union for shooting down a civilian airliner over the Sea of Japan. From a longer term perspective, developments that unfolded after she resigned as UN ambassador in 1985 shed light on the consequences of her absence from the national security team. From the point of Kirkpatrick's departure, the foreign policies of the second Reagan administration veered in more conciliatory directions— which confirms the centrality of her first-term contributions (see Dueck 2010, 222–223; Nau 2015, 185).

Albright's willingness to champion the use of multilateral force to protect civilians in the Balkans created major foreign policy legacies of the Clinton years. Her central role in organizing administration responses to conflicts in the former Yugoslavia is reflected in the fact that prominent journalists applied the phrase "Madeleine's War" to the Kosovo conflict (see Dobbs 1999, 422, 424; Isaacson 1999). Previous Clinton-era policy failures in locations including Somalia and Rwanda, where Albright's influence was more limited, suggest that her presence in debates over the Balkans made the difference between America's demonstrating a capacity to take charge of what Albright (2003, Chapter 10) terms the "New World (Dis)Order," on one side, and proving itself unable to do so, on the other (see also Hannay

2008). The strategy she employed of seeking consensus among allies who often disagreed with each other, securing presidential consent despite opposition from senior members of his team (all of them men), and then coordinating military intervention under the aegis of NATO established a model of post–Cold War foreign policy under Democratic presidents that was later emulated by Hillary Clinton in the Obama years.

As Bush's main foreign policy tutor from the time he considered becoming a presidential candidate through his election in 2000, Rice commanded exceptional proximity to power through two executive mandates. Many observers, including administration colleagues, identify Rice as the closest confidante of George W. Bush (see Kessler 2007). She outlined the contours of what would become the Bush doctrine (see Rice 2000) and, following the attacks of 9/11, elucidated a preemption argument that said the United States was obligated to defend itself before enemies struck. In turn, this thesis served as a core justification for invading Iraq in 2003.

While Bush's international relations team contained other members who supported the overthrow of Saddam Hussein, it was Rice who situated that priority inside a policy scaffolding that she had designed—which in turn guided group decision-making. Above all, Rice was instrumental in guiding Bush from a potential White House bid toward the Oval Office. Absent Rice, one might ask, could Cheney, Rumsfeld, or Wolfowitz have systematically prepared a Texas governor with limited knowledge of the larger world for the prime time spotlight? In particular, would Bush have acquitted himself as well as he did in the debate with Gore without the intense, careful preparation she provided? Above all, lacking the preemption rationale, would Powell's 2003 speech at the United Nations have swayed domestic and world opinion such that the United States could construct a "coalition of the willing" to intervene in Iraq?

Hillary Clinton's track record as first lady, senator, and presidential candidate directly foreshadowed the foreign policies of the first Obama mandate. After the 2008 election, her emphasis on the centrality of women's rights to international politics merged with an assertive defense of American interests and a willingness to employ military means when necessary to meet that objective. In the wake of ferment across the Middle East beginning in 2010, Clinton advocated and won support for armed intervention in Libya. Parallel with Albright's actions in response to events in the Balkans during the 1990s, Clinton sought common ground among US allies and secured approval for a NATO mission that the president's top male advisors opposed. Although Clinton was unable as secretary of state to convince Obama either to adopt an interests-based approach to circumstances in Egypt or to intervene militarily in Syria, her views seemed to hold greater sway as time passed. The fact that the United States used force in Syria during his second term in office indicates that Clinton's views had a lagged effect but were nevertheless transforming with respect to Middle East policy.

Taken together, this evidence suggests that the influence exerted by Kirkpatrick, Albright, Rice, and Clinton was sufficiently pronounced in degree and significant in substantive terms that it transcended the routine. Each woman effectively shaped a presidential legacy in ways that altered the foreign policy trajectory of the United States at a time when American decision-making exerted meaningful sway in international politics. Considered as a group, Kirkpatrick, Albright, Rice, and Clinton molded in measurable ways the behavior of a global superpower from the Cold War twilight through the subsequent era of "new world disorder." None of the four, to invoke the language used in Kirkpatrick's statement in the introduction to this chapter, would qualify as a mouse-like creature that left nary a trace in the inner sanctums of executive power.

LEADERSHIP TRAITS

What personal characteristics assisted each woman in reaching these heights? The examination of their backgrounds suggests that particular strengths, including team-building skills, mattered. All four were first-born children whose parents challenged and, at the same time, nurtured their daughters. Kirkpatrick, Albright, Rice, and Clinton grew up in households where politics was in the air in the form of discussion, debate, and, in Rice's case, an annual election race for family president. From an early age, all four were involved in activities that fostered confidence but also entailed obvious risk, notably solo piano performance, public speaking, figure skating, or taking responsibility for younger children.

These pursuits unfolded alongside sustained immersion in activities that made each young girl comfortable in the company of boys and men. Kirkpatrick, Rice, and Clinton were all tomboys who learned about sports and participated in sports that were typically for boys of their generations. Kirkpatrick climbed trees and rode horses on the dusty frontier. Expecting a son, Rice's father bought her a football before she was born and then schooled her in the details of NFL competition. Clinton learned to fish and target shoot near her family cabin in the Poconos. Albright, who grew up in very different circumstances, witnessed lengthy conversations between her father and his fellow political leaders over the future of Czechoslovakia— both during years of exile and afterward. In short, all four observed at close range the dynamics of men and boys, and felt capable of understanding and participating in activities that men engaged in.

Childhoods such as these seemed to impart a combination of individual determination and interpersonal skill. As students, Albright, Rice, and Clinton assumed leadership positions in their respective schools and universities. Kirkpatrick became a star in the neoconservative political constellation. All four were insightful advisors to politicians in the major US political parties and, in Clinton's case, a serious presidential candidate in her own right in 2008 and 2016. These patterns speak to success in groups, whether that effectiveness entails knowing how to counsel nominees for senior public office and interact with other members of the team, or creating a campaign organization of one's own.

The inner strength each woman developed was on clear display in periods of personal travail. Kirkpatrick suffered the slow but steady loss of her eldest son to alcoholism. Albright experienced exile twice by the age of eleven, and the collapse of her marriage in middle age. Condoleezza Rice was very young when firebombs rocked Birmingham, and a teenaged only child when her mother was first diagnosed with breast cancer. Hillary Clinton, whose father practiced what Bernstein (2007, 13) terms "ritual authoritarianism," faced repeated challenges in her marriage. Although the problems they dealt with and the support systems they developed varied widely, these leaders demonstrated remarkable resilience in the face of difficulty.

Moreover, these women shared a set of academic and professional credentials that helped to compensate for the military experience that men such as Al Haig, Colin Powell, and John Kerry brought to public service. Kirkpatrick, Albright, Rice, and Clinton built wide-ranging reputations in the disciplines of political science, international relations, and law. Kirkpatrick distinguished herself as a scholar of US and Latin American politics who applied that knowledge as a high-profile public intellectual. Albright was an expert on Central Europe who built a pioneering program for women diplomats at Georgetown University. Rice studied civil/military relations in the Soviet bloc and led a major administrative overhaul of Stanford University. Clinton contributed significantly to the emerging field of children's rights when she was still a law student and then applied what she knew as an activist, law professor, and litigator.

Each of these patterns points toward an ability to diffuse intellectual work beyond the classroom such that it becomes publicly visible and valued. In particular, all four women leaders did much more than consume information generated by others and then offer incremental steps forward. Instead, they stood out by virtue of knowing how to transform, apply, or popularize scholarship such that the perspectives they offered shone a spotlight on their contributions. Whether we consider the articles prepared by Kirkpatrick and Rice that framed the foreign policy doctrines of Republican presidents, or the feminist perspectives on international affairs advanced by Albright and Clinton that distinguished Democratic administrations, it is clear that these women excelled as knowledge translators. In turn, their ability to shepherd ideas into practice meant that they stood out from other women, as well as men, who held the same degrees.

The communication styles of all four women considered in this book were crucial to that knowledge translation process. While Kirkpatrick, Albright, Rice, and Clinton came from different geographic and ideological starting points, they shared a capacity to speak forcefully, argue with conviction, and persuade other people of their points of view. All four used sharp, direct syntax that perhaps originated in their early careers as university teachers. Kirkpatrick's pronouncements about the need to curtail Soviet influence, Albright's responses to events including the Cuban attack on a civilian aircraft, Rice's preemption rationale for invading Iraq, and Clinton's connection of women's rights to national security were all phrased in bold, uncompromising terms. Wedded to a strong work ethic and a determination to succeed no matter the odds, their oratory was consistently punchy and spirited—which made them in many instances the public faces of the administrations they served.

The fact that all four women reached elite foreign policy positions means that they merged these personal attributes with a capacity to build solid political networks. Unlike many scholars who are content to write books and articles, teach their courses, and comment occasionally in the media, these four consistently stretched beyond their disciplines and beyond the academy. Kirkpatrick participated extensively in Democratic Party as well as neoconservative movement politics. Albright built her early reputation as a Democratic Party fundraiser and foreign policy advisor. Prior to becoming George W. Bush's tutor on international affairs, Rice served as a fellow at the Joint Chiefs of Staff and special assistant at the NSC. Clinton, who volunteered for the Republicans in Chicago when she was still an adolescent, was deeply involved in Democratic campaigns dating back to Eugene McCarthy's presidential bid in 1968.

Given how few women have reached the status of UN ambassador, secretary of state, or national security advisor, it was critical that these high-profile nominees won and retained the confidence of not just the president, but also the people who surrounded him. In terms of relations with presidents, Kirkpatrick and Rice appeared to be closer to Reagan and Bush, respectively, than Albright and Clinton were to the chief executives who appointed them. This suggests a partisan variation such that Republican nominees operated with somewhat different currency inside US administrations than their Democratic counterparts. For Kirkpatrick and Rice, fostering deep personal ties not only consumed significant time and energy, but also placed them at risk of being presidential enablers rather than analysts or advisors. At the same time, closeness to a chief executive was potentially unsettling—notably to other team members and to the first lady, as Jeane Kirkpatrick learned.

Three of the four decision-makers examined in this study faced first ladies who could either advance or block their careers. Nancy Reagan seemed to operate as a gatekeeper who, along with others, closed the door on Kirkpatrick's promotion from the rank of UN ambassador. During the 1990s, Albright benefited from a warm relationship with Hillary Clinton and from Hillary's willingness to endorse her promotion to secretary of state. Rice had long-standing ties to Barbara and George H. W. Bush, which in turn formed the basis for personal closeness to Laura and George W. Bush. In the case of the Obama administration, however, Hillary Clinton's nomination as secretary of state followed from efforts to create a highly accomplished "team of rivals," rather than from ties to Michelle Obama (see Baker and Cooper 2008).

Although traditional views of gender and leadership posit a dichotomy between typically masculine tendencies toward conflict and individualism versus stereotypically feminine emphases on collaboration and interpersonal skill, these four cases suggest that such a bifurcation is misleading. Consistent with Eagly and Carli (2007, Chapter 10), our analysis indicates that becoming a senior foreign policy leader in the United States since 1980 demanded both the "I" elements of confidence and ambition, as well as the "we" dimension that facilitates effective work with others. This conclusion reinforces Kirkpatrick's (1974, 174–175) argument that for female leaders, well-developed interpersonal skills connoting warmth and flexibility are valuable traits.

In terms of relations with first ladies, Albright and Rice were able to apply this lesson better than Kirkpatrick—perhaps because they had more gregarious personalities, more skill at strategic networking, or simply did not face the same formidable adversaries as Kirkpatrick confronted in the Reagan years. Yet it remains clear that all four women examined here were well-endowed with not just individual determination, but also the crucial abilities to argue, persuade, and foster alliances. To use a musical metaphor, each played her own instrument well and, at the same time, demonstrated that she could excel as a performer inside the larger orchestra.

Future researchers will be able to probe the personal traits of additional leaders from the United States and other countries. Are they typically first-born children from politically engaged families? Were they tomboys or girls who felt comfortable for other reasons in the company of men and boys? What types of educational and occupational experiences did they bring to public service, and how personally close were they to the chief executive who appointed them? Were first ladies or their equivalent relevant to the upward mobility of these leaders? Did decision-makers demonstrate a mixture of "I" and "we" attributes that lead us to question the split posited by the leadership literature between masculine and feminine attributes?

ASSESSING PEACE AND CONFLICT

Among the most durable assumptions dating from classical political thought is one that posits women's influence will promote peace and serenity, rather than war and bloodshed. The portrayal that Elshtain (1995) terms "beautiful souls," however, finds little empirical support in the foreign policy records examined in this study. Kirkpatrick's posture toward the Soviet Union and its allies in the 1980s, Albright's willingness to challenge dictators, including in Serbia, during the 1990s, Rice's strategy of using preventive force to attack enemies after 9/11, and Clinton's response to Arab Spring events each reflected a highly assertive approach to international relations. All are inconsistent with stereotypical notions of female passivity, consensus-seeking, and conflict avoidance (see Keohane 2010, 128–134).

Even though the shared tenor of these contributions was decidedly hawkish, the partisan distinctions among them remain notable. As Republican administration appointees, Kirkpatrick and Rice were less invested in and less patient than their Democratic counterparts with supranational institutions including the United Nations, NATO, and international war crimes tribunals. By contrast, Albright and Clinton served Democratic presidents who, like themselves, embraced a more multilateral than unilateral approach to world politics. What remains noteworthy about the cases examined here is that despite the divergent international problems each administration faced and regardless of the varied left/right placement of each presidential team, the women leaders inside them consistently pressed for interventionist foreign policies.

How these records are evaluated in normative terms depends on the starting point of the assessor. Advocates of an unabashedly autonomous US foreign policy will find more to endorse in the contributions of Kirkpatrick and Rice than those of Albright and Clinton. Conversely, proponents of a liberal internationalist outlook will tend to favor the efforts of Democratic over Republican appointees. Yet drilling down more deeply reveals attributes of these decision-makers that defy simple partisan dichotomies. In particular, it is arguable that the more regionally informed, contextualized understandings of world politics demonstrated by Kirkpatrick and Albright better served the interests of the United States than the less area-grounded approaches of Rice and Clinton.

Although Jeane Kirkpatrick was a high-profile neoconservative at the time she joined the Reagan administration, her actual foreign policy engagement defied rigid categories. For example, Kirkpatrick's response to the Falklands War showed her capacity to resist a kneejerk right-of-center view which said that Western powers should rally around Margaret Thatcher's embattled United Kingdom. As a student of Latin American politics during the 1960s and following, Kirkpatrick believed that US presidents could not construct sufficiently sturdy and expansive international alliances if they restricted their purviews to elected governments in North America, Western Europe, Japan, Israel, and a handful of other countries. She was in this sense a realist's realist: a compelling writer and decision-maker who insisted, despite strong pressures to the contrary, that military clout should only be marshalled prudently and that national interests best trump idealistic motives.

Critics of the Reagan legacy can identify many dimensions of Kirkpatrick's record with which to disagree—whether her staunch opposition to communism, support for the Contras in Central America, or loyalty to Israel. My point here is to suggest that far from supporting reckless military undertakings on the global stage, Kirkpatrick promoted a more constrained approach to world politics than her reputation might suggest. In this respect, the brakes she placed over the accelerator called American power would have proven helpful twenty years later in the George W. Bush years.

While Madeleine Albright commanded less cachet as a public intellectual and abstract thinker than Jeane Kirkpatrick, she held a valuable edge in the domain of lived experience. Albright applied her firsthand knowledge of Central European politics—reinforced by years of studying that region—to the conflict zone that was the former Yugoslavia in the 1990s. Few other decision-makers outside the Balkans grasped the complex history, competing ethnocultural cleavages, and potential for humanitarian disaster that underpinned the breakdown of civil order in Bosnia and later Kosovo. Albright used her insights to shape not just Clinton administration policy, but also the decisions of often divided NATO allies. Finally, she used strong personal diplomacy skills to ensure that multilateral avenues for engagement were not blocked by Russian leaders. In this way, Albright's actions embodied effective leadership in an age of "new world disorder."

As with the Reagan legacy and Kirkpatrick's role in creating it, opponents of Clinton-era foreign policy have ample bases for criticizing Albright. States that emerged from the Balkan wars in some cases remain poor and fragile, as noted in Chapter 4. American intervention in Somalia was by most accounts unsuccessful, and the failure to stop genocide in Rwanda deeply tragic. Yet the insights that Albright brought to bear on the region she knew best, Central Europe, bore fruit in that they employed American leadership not only to build a coalition to curtail atrocities against civilians, but also to prosecute the perpetrators of those crimes via international tribunals. As suggested later in this chapter, the intimate cultural and historical familiarity with a troubled geographic area that Albright brought to deliberations over the former Yugoslavia would have been invaluable a decade and a half later, when the Obama administration faced popular uprisings in the Middle East.

Condoleezza Rice's academic research addressed relations between political and military authorities in Soviet bloc regimes of the late 1940s and following. As evidenced by her work on the Czechoslovak army and the Soviet Union, Rice (1984) was not well equipped in scholarly terms to comprehend circumstances in the Middle East and especially Saddam Hussein's Iraq—where the fusion of authoritative personal and state leadership, firm controls over the economy and military, and uncontested governing party hegemony kept a lid on explosive internal differences that burst into the open after he was deposed. Although Rice's childhood in Birmingham, Alabama meant that she had seen social conflict firsthand, her worldview and that of her immediate family conceived of individuals in a liberal democratic society (rather than governments or protest movements) as best able to solve problems. Once she became George W. Bush's closest advisor, Rice in effect permitted a fierce commitment to ideals of individual freedom to overtake what could have been, following the terms of the core argument presented in Rice (2000), a more rigorously interests-based calculus on Iraq (see also Rice 2017).

The problems inherent in Rice's counsel concerning Iraq emerge clearly in a biographical account of how Kirkpatrick responded to the events of 9/11. As Collier (2012, 200) writes, while Kirkpatrick had impulsively joined other neocons right after 9/11 in calling for Saddam Hussein to be removed from power, she became deeply troubled by the prospect of a major land war in Iraq as it actually approached. Trying to remake that country, she feared, would not cure the deep disorder and chaos that infected it; and launching a full-scale invasion would be even more destructive of American national interests than the tepid, ill-conceived multilateral adventures she had criticized during the Clinton years for having bled US sovereignty and sense of purpose drop by drop.

Collier (2012, 201) notes that when Kirkpatrick was asked by the Bush administration to participate in a UN human rights conference in Geneva in 2003, "she refused to use the idea of preemptive self-defense" (see also Kirkpatrick 2007b, 281). According to Alan Gerson, who traveled with her to Geneva, Kirkpatrick (as quoted in Collier 2012, 201) said of the preemption doctrine: "It will never sell. No one will buy it."

Given that prominent legislators including Senator Hillary Clinton, along with about two-thirds of the American public, were prepared to link Saddam with the attacks of 9/11, one could argue that the preemption thesis resonated quite widely (see Gerth and Van Natta 2007, 246). Eliminating an enemy who had ostensibly sponsored the strikes on New York and Washington offered, from this perspective, a more compelling reason to invade Iraq than seeking to destroy weapons of mass destruction that might or might not exist. Kirkpatrick's prediction that the concept of preventive defense would go nowhere proved incorrect. Instead, as Kirkpatrick (2007b, 279) reflects in the wake of the Iraq intervention, "we have helped to create the chaos that has overtaken the country, and we may have slowed rather than promoted the pace of democratic reform." Members of the Bush team, in her view, "did not seem to have methodically completed the due diligence required for reasoned policy-making because they failed to address the aftermath of the invasion" (Kirkpatrick 2007b, 300).

Kirkpatrick (2007b) dissects the assumptions underpinning Bush-era policies. She argues that democracy is imperilled by the absence of social tranquillity. In her view, after 9/11 "our attention to national security was subsumed by a desire to promote democracy, as if democracy alone could imbue chaotic societies and unstable governments with a respect for what we respected: the rule of law, basic human rights, and a peaceful world order" (Kirkpatrick 2007b, 273). If Rice (2000) had titled her foreign policy manifesto for the Bush administration "Promoting the National Interest," then Kirkpatrick's (2007b) assessment of its practical application in Iraq posits that neither the interest nor the political values informing it was advanced.

Optimists, including Rice (2011, 730–733), suggest the benefits of invading Iraq will take time to manifest themselves. This same invocation of promising future developments as a justification for past actions might also characterize assessments of the decision to intervene in Libya, a place that had never figured in Hillary Clinton's educational or research background. Yet one of the signature actions of the first Obama term that Hillary Clinton strongly advocated soon attracted acerbic criticism from, of all people, Obama himself. Speaking to journalist Jeffrey Goldberg (2016) at the end of his second term, Obama said of the Libya intervention: "It didn't work . . . we actually executed this plan as well as I could have expected: We got a UN mandate, we built a coalition, it cost us $1 billion—which, when it comes to military operations, is very cheap. We averted large-scale civilian casualties, we prevented what almost surely would have been a prolonged and bloody civil conflict. And despite all that, Libya is a mess."

Goldberg (2016, italics in original) presents Obama's explanation for the downward spiral in North Africa as follows:

> *Mess* is the president's diplomatic term; privately, he calls Libya a "shit show," in part because it's subsequently become an ISIS haven—one that he has already targeted with air strikes. It became a shit show, Obama believes, for reasons that had less to do with American incompetence than with the passivity of America's allies and with the obdurate power of tribalism.

Besides blaming European allies for failing to follow through on their commitments, Obama saw social circumstances inside Libya as deeply problematic. As he told Goldberg (2016), "The degree of tribal division in Libya was greater than our analysts had expected. And our ability to have any kind of structure there that we could interact with and start training and start providing resources broke down very quickly." According to Goldberg (2016), Obama's outlook on regional intervention was so dark that he told a former colleague from his days in the Senate, "There is no way we should commit to governing the Middle East and North Africa."

Since this study ranks among the first comparative accounts of women leaders in the contemporary period, the questions posed here invite further analysis. Future assessments will be well placed to consider not just elites in other countries, but also successors to the four pioneers examined in these pages, notably Susan Rice, Samantha Power, and Nikki Haley. Susan Rice's roles as UN ambassador during the first Obama term and national security advisor in his second mandate placed her at the center of decision-making on many issues, including the pivot to Asia and responses to the Arab Spring. Power's actions in the National Security Council after 2009 and as UN ambassador beginning in 2013 are worth probing given her background in academia and foreign policy writing (see Power 2013). Haley's appointment as UN envoy in the Trump administration provides an opportunity to study five women from two major parties in that role.

Whether they consider leaders in the United States or their counterparts in other countries, future scholars will be able to assess not only how decision-makers shaped foreign policy, but also what, in normative terms, stand as the consequences of women's engagement in positions of international decision-making. With more cases, researchers can address questions including how perspectives on world politics that were articulated outside the corridors of power were reversed, refined, or reinforced in the course of addressing actual events. Were female elites any more or less consistent in their migration from the abstract to the practical than the men who preceded or succeeded them? What criteria for evaluating leaders' normative success shed the sharpest light on their policy impact? Were pioneering elites more likely to make transforming contributions than those who reached office later?

In future studies of the United States, analysts can ask if it matters whether force was used unilaterally by a Republican versus multilaterally by a Democratic president, in the relative absence versus presence of progressive feminists on his leadership team. Following from Fernandes (2013, 58), researchers might probe how American military action has assisted or, alternately, harmed women. Scholars have yet to undertake a systematic comparison of the implications for women on the ground of intervention in Bosnia, Kosovo, Afghanistan, Iraq, and Libya—where social and legal conditions before external force was applied widely diverged, and where the stated purposes of armed engagement at the point it was undertaken also differed.

To the extent that conclusions have been drawn about US involvement in the Middle East, they suggest that multilateralism and the involvement of critical actors in a presidential team can produce the same results as unilateralism and the absence of such actors. As Hudson and Leidl (2015, 328) write, "the consequences for women of the overthrow of Libya's Muammar Gadhafi, Iraq's Saddam Hussein and other autocratic but secular tyrants caution against destroying state power—even authoritarian state power—without seriously considering the long-term ramifications. This is because it is usually women who come out the worst." In their view, one cannot assume that foreign policy actors in Democratic administrations were any more knowledgeable and aware than Republicans of the erosion of rights that would accrue from regime change.

This conclusion recalls our discussion of Kirkpatrick's (2007b) pessimistic commentary on the fallout from invading Iraq. As well, it echoes President Obama's remarks to Goldberg (2016) on what the departing chief executive termed the "mess" in Libya. Similarly, an expert poll conducted by the Thomson Reuters Foundation in 2011 identified Afghanistan as the most dangerous country in the world for women (Anderson 2011). Future researchers will be able to reflect after the passage of more time on precisely how feminist outcomes fared in the wake of military action. Did the United States or its allies follow through on commitments to women's empowerment in any recent case of armed intervention, beginning with Bosnia? How, if at all, were the effects of conflict minimized for women and girls? What preexisting conditions at the site of intervention appear most conducive to advancing gender equality?

GENDER POLITICS

Just as some decision-makers in the early twentieth century rejected the extension of the franchise while others advocated the right to vote, we find that contemporary elites and the administrations in which they served diverged in important ways—notably along partisan lines. These patterns reinforce the findings of feminist diplomatic historiography. As argued in Chapters 1 and 2, no single narrative captures the varied directions of women leaders with respect to gender politics.

On matters of women's equality, Republican appointees considered in this study operated less as critical actors than their Democratic counterparts. Neither Kirkpatrick nor Rice advanced progressive feminist positions to a significant degree while they held top executive office, particularly when compared with the focused women's rights agendas championed by Albright and Clinton (see also Bloch 2007, 143–144). Moreover, Republican administrations adopted policies that aimed to erode the gains made by pro-equality groups.

This section advances a more finely grained interpretation, however, in showing how the gender records of Kirkpatrick and Rice coincide with the preferences of electoral constituencies that brought Reagan and Bush, respectively, to presidential office. Following from Celis and Childs's (2012) expansive view of political responsiveness, I argue that Republican appointees proved as capable as Democrats of "acting for" women, even though the content of their substantive representation was quite different, and I develop a thesis grounded in normative democratic theory to the effect that linkages between leaders and citizens are not just legitimate, but also valuable no matter where they occur along a political spectrum.

As discussed in Chapter 3, Kirkpatrick (1974, 1976) was critical of radical feminist and women's liberation politics prior to serving in the Reagan cabinet. As a middle-of-the-road liberal feminist, she endorsed the Equal Rights Amendment and opposed a constitutional ban on abortion (see

Collier 2012, 173). Once in office, Kirkpatrick seemed keenly aware of how few women reached senior foreign policy posts—as revealed, for example, in the quotation from an interview that appears in the introduction to this chapter.

Under the terms of the Mexico City policy, the Reagan administration blocked funding for abortion and family planning initiatives in developing countries—an approach that was repeated by successive Republican presidents and was rejected by Democrats. If we consider what she said and did regarding the Mexico City policy in light of her forceful interventions on other foreign policy matters, it seems that Kirkpatrick was muted in her response. Although she described foreign aid that denied support for reproductive services as "pouring water into a bucket with a hole in it" (see Fornos 1988; Gupte 1984), Kirkpatrick did not directly condemn the Mexico City proposal. Instead, she prioritized the articulation and implementation of other ideas above efforts to block the inroads made by social traditionalists.

As a political scientist, Kirkpatrick likely understood better than most cabinet members the motives for administration action against abortion and inaction on the ERA. Reagan had won in 1980 with the support of 55 percent of men and 47 percent of women (see Roper Center 1980). As Bolce (1988) reports, the GOP position against reproductive choice diverged sharply from that of Democratic candidate Jimmy Carter. Republicans went on to enjoy significant success that year among anti-abortion voters (see Bolce 1988, 826). By contrast, Republican opposition to the ERA did not create significant problems for the party (see Mansbridge 1985). Moreover, the hawkish foreign policy views expressed by Reagan that were largely a popularization of Kirkpatrick's (1979) ideas gave him a considerable advantage in 1980 among male voters (see Frankovic 1982; Gilens 1988; Mansbridge 1985).

The fact that, in electoral terms, Republicans benefited from opposing abortion rights, incurred few costs for rejecting the ERA, and solidified their male support base with an aggressive international posture helps to illuminate the gender politics environment of 1981 and following (see Chappell 2012). At a normative level, Kirkpatrick as the sole woman in Reagan's first cabinet could not legitimately behave as a progressive feminist actor given that the administration in which she served had won executive power (a) with considerable support from anti-abortion voters and (b) without paying a measurable price for rejecting the ERA. At the same time, Kirkpatrick's disparaging comment about the Mexico City policy may have helped to moderate the image of the Reagan team by showing that it contained viewpoints other than strong social traditionalism. In effect,

Kirkpatrick's remark flagged the presence of less ideological, perhaps Malthusian views about contraception and abortion inside the cabinet. Yet the statement was as far as Kirkpatrick was prepared to go in voicing what might have been construed as a liberal feminist perspective inside a Republican political executive.

As a conservative African American in the George W. Bush administration, Rice was uncomfortable with the collective demands of civil rights as well as feminist campaigners. She emphasized the primacy of the individual above group claims for either racial or gender equality, and rejected what she viewed as misguided narratives about "victims" (Rice 2010, 48). Like Kirkpatrick, her ideas concerning abortion were more centrist than those of social conservatives; she was "mildly pro-choice" given beliefs that abortion was at times justified but that "some restrictions were wholly appropriate" (Mabry 2007, 85; Rice 2010, 274). Rice resembled her predecessor in that she held a senior post in an administration that imposed the Mexico City policy, thus creating an international family planning regime that was less liberal than her own opinion.

A key difference between the Reagan and George W. Bush years, however, rested in the use of women's rights rhetoric. As discussed in Chapter 5, Republican leaders tried after 9/11 to win support for the war against the Taliban using feminist-sounding language. The first lady, president, and appointed elites, including Rice, invoked a set of arguments that stressed the limitations facing women and girls in Afghanistan; their statements criticized, for instance, Taliban controls over access to education, work, and health care. At the same time, members of the Bush administration glossed over the role US policy had played both in installing the mujahedeen regime and restricting women's reproductive choices in the global South.

Feminist writers are particularly critical of the Bush administration's willingness to justify the "war on terror" as a liberalizing initiative. They view American decisions to intervene militarily in Afghanistan and Iraq as unrelated to gender equality and ultimately damaging for women and girls in both countries. This literature argues that pro-equality rhetoric permitted US leaders to present a humanitarian face for fundamentally inhumane policies; rather than disrupting the core directions of the "war on terror," women such as Rice were integral to making the Bush doctrine more politically palatable (see Al-Ali and Pratt 2009; Faludi 2007; Finlay 2006; Flanders 2005; Hawkesworth 2007).

Public opinion data provide a useful context in which to interpret administration actions. Bush won the presidency in 2000 with the support of 54 percent of men and 44 percent of women (see Roper Center 2000). According to Brians and Greene (2004), Bush avoided taking straightforward positions on feminist issues—notably abortion. In their words, "Governor Bush was more successful in obscuring his, and his party's, abortion policy position among voters in 2000, than was Senator Dole in 1996" (Brians and Greene 2004, 418). Given that fewer than 20 percent of Americans agreed with the Republican position promising a constitutional ban on abortion, Bush had practical reasons to mask that stance (see Brians and Greene 2004, 413).

The attractions of nuance over clarity were at least as compelling in the domain of foreign policy. Data indicate that about a quarter of Republican and GOP-leaning voters in 2000 believed the United States should not concern itself with world problems, while more than half endorsed higher military spending (ANES 2010). These isolationist and hawkish attitudes in the party contrast with views in the general population, where significant support existed for international engagement and, in particular, supranational institutions such as the United Nations. As Holyk (2010) reports, polls conducted between May 2000 and February 2002 reveal that between 52 and 58 percent of Americans believed the United Nations was doing a good job of solving world problems. Given these results, the Bush administration decision to send Powell to the UN Security Council to present a rationale for invading Iraq is entirely understandable. As noted in Chapter 5, Powell was a secretary of state whose military background and centrist leanings gave him credibility across the US ideological spectrum and among international audiences.

Attitudinal data also shed light on how Rice could assist Bush's campaign and governing strategies. Although she was not a feminist critical actor comparable to Albright or Clinton, Rice's status as an accomplished, relatively young African American woman provided instant diversity in the circle of mostly older white men who surrounded George W. Bush. In particular, her presence served to divert attention from Republican positions on reproductive choice and relations with the rest of the world. For middle-of-the-road voters, the black female political scientist at Bush's side was unlikely to be a rabid social traditionalist, hermetic isolationist, or crazed unilateralist. If the heart of Bush's gender politics rested in reassuring moderates—and especially women voters—that he shared views similar to their own, then Rice's role was crucial to staking out legitimacy with that constituency (see Flanders 2005).

In this sense, Kirkpatrick and Rice can be seen as "acting for" the interests of millions of American women who situated themselves outside the boundaries of progressive feminism and the Democratic Party. These citizens were, from the perspective of normative democratic theory, at least as deserving of political representation as other women who expressed stronger pro-equality views and more limited tolerance for Republican foreign policies. Although neither Kirkpatrick nor Rice meets the feminist critical actor threshold, they were both transforming actors whose gender politics resonated with key segments of the Reagan and Bush electorates, respectively.

By contrast, the records of Albright and Clinton are consistent with what the academic literature defines as a critical actor repertoire. Appointed to Democratic administrations that quickly revoked the Mexico City policy, they arrived in senior office with long legacies of feminist advocacy. Albright served as the inaugural director of Georgetown University's program to prepare women diplomats and was a well-connected member of feminist policy circles in Washington. Clinton devoted significant attention from her time as a law professor in Arkansas through her years as first lady to the advancement of women. The shared commitment of Albright and Clinton to feminist causes was reflected in their joint trip to Beijing in 1995 for the Fourth World Conference of Women, and their advocacy of State Department initiatives, including Vital Voices, that followed from it.

Both as UN ambassador and secretary of state, Albright created networks of female decision-makers who worked together on an identifiably pro-equality agenda. The groups she established pressed states as well as supranational institutions to act on issues including rape as a weapon of war. Albright as a national leader also responded to claims emanating from civil society interests based outside the United States—notably in conflict zones, including the Balkans.

These patterns of behavior are consistent with the views of the political constituency that elected the administration in which she served. In 1992, Bill Clinton won the votes of 45 percent of women and 41 percent of men, with roughly a fifth of both groups endorsing independent candidate Ross Perot (see Roper Center 1992). Poll results in Wattier, Daynes, and Tatalovich (1997) indicate that the pro-equality platform adopted by Democrats in 1992 worked well, since the party benefited from particularly high levels of support among females and pro-choice voters. Data in Huddy, Neely, and LaFay (2000) show that members of the American public perceived both Bill and Hillary Clinton as pro-feminist, such that roughly two-thirds of respondents in a 1993 survey said they expected feminist groups to gain influence while he was president (see also Abramowitz 1995).

In terms of foreign policy, Albright's stress on international cooperation resonated well with public opinion of the era. Figures in Richman (1996) indicate that more than half of Americans polled in 1992 and 1994 identified themselves as multilateralists, with much smaller proportions saying their views were unilateralist or isolationist (see also Sobel 1998).

Richman (1996) notes that more than 60 percent of US respondents in 1993 and 1995 believed their country "should cooperate fully with the United Nations."

These findings inform the normative democracy dimension of Albright's leadership. Stated simply, her critical actor role on women's rights was highly legitimate given the coloration of the US electorate and especially the base that brought Bill Clinton to the White House. Voters anticipated that a Democratic administration would pursue pro-equality directions. Albright's record as UN ambassador and secretary of state realized those expectations in innovative, creative ways that pressed beyond what men holding the same positions would likely have done. Albright's legacy is also normatively resonant if we consider its multilateral element: more than half of Americans in the early to mid-1990s endorsed cooperative engagement with supranational institutions, including the United Nations. Albright endeavored inside NATO and the United Nations to gain support for intervention in the Balkans, and directed attention after those events to the prosecution of war criminals via international tribunals.

Hillary Clinton expanded this trajectory by positing a "smart power" foreign policy that linked US national security and international stability with the global empowerment of women and girls. She raised the status and budget of feminist units inside the Department of State, recruited unprecedented numbers of women to the US diplomatic service, and directed funds toward anti-violence and health programs for women in developing countries. Echoing Obama's (2007) emphasis on cooperative partnerships, Clinton pursued a multilateral approach that sought to engage with supranational institutions, other states, and NGOs. Like Bill Clinton, Obama reversed the Mexico City policy he inherited from his Republican predecessor.

These policy directions are consistent with the electoral mandate that returned Democrats to the White House in 2008. Women voters gave a crucial edge to Obama over John McCain, with 56 percent of females casting ballots for the Democratic and 43 percent for the Republican nominee in 2008. Men split about evenly between them (see Roper Center 2008). The two campaigns diverged sharply over reproductive choice and foreign policy. With respect to the former, Obama's pro-choice stance permitted him to portray McCain as a threat to *Roe v. Wade*, a judicial precedent that most Americans did not want to see overturned (see Saad 2008). On the latter, the Democratic nominee capitalized on opposition to the Iraq War in his party and among independent voters, as well as on more general views that the United States needed to show greater care in defending its national interests (see Jacobson 2010; Skidmore 2011).

By advancing feminist and multilateral approaches to international affairs, Hillary Clinton acted in concert with the views of voters who brought the Obama administration to office in 2008. She was for this reason not just a critical feminist actor inside the US political executive, but also a normatively legitimate representative of citizens who endorsed gender equality and demanded foreign policy change in the wake of the Bush years. Would a man in the same position have acted similarly? The much lower profile of gender equality considerations in US foreign policy after Clinton resigned suggests that he would not have.

Clinton's willingness to operate as a critical actor is especially noteworthy because of chronological considerations. She served in top office at a time when, by some accounts, American feminism was discredited by a highly securitized, post–9/11 worldview in which men assumed the unassailable role of "superior" political leaders (Hawkesworth 2007, 179; see also Lawless 2004). Given the results of the 2016 presidential election, when Clinton lost to Republican candidate Donald Trump, the challenges of operating as a feminist critical actor in American politics deserve close attention. The controversy sparked by Albright's remark at a Clinton campaign rally—to the effect that "[t]here's a special place in hell for women who don't help each other"—underlines just how fraught the concept of women supporting women had become (Reilly 2016). Future research will ideally consider not just the 2016 presidential contest, but also the broader longitudinal and cross-national dimensions of representation work.

What significance, if any, did actions taken by American leaders and the administrations of which they were a part hold for women living outside the United States? It is clear that the Mexico City policy directly affected access to contraception and abortion in the global South, since the United States was a primary source of international family planning aid in the 1980s and following (see Goldberg 2009, 98–99, 161). Were other donor countries or major foundations able to compensate for the presence of Republican administrations in Washington? Did women leaders in other industrialized systems devote particular attention to filling the gap caused by Republican policies?

For readers who wonder what a madam president in the White House might mean for international affairs, this discussion confirms McGlen and Sarkees's (2001, 142) conclusion that female leaders "were not a homogeneous group." Their understandings of national security and gender politics diverged in important ways, including when we control for the party of the president who appointed them. Given this central caveat, it is likely that madam president will pursue American interests in ways that dovetail her earlier track record, and will articulate her priorities in cogent, unwavering terms. She will consider the use of military force, whether unilaterally as a Republican or multilaterally as a Democrat. Her gender politics will tend to vary depending on partisanship: as a Republican, she is likely to be less committed to pro-equality policies than as a Democrat, who is more likely to behave as a feminist critical actor. And regardless of the behavior repertoires and substantive directions she adopts, some analysts will probably ignore her contributions, demean her as underpowered for the job, or condemn her as overpowered for the role.

Overall, this study encourages scholars who seek to understand the foundations of elite decision-making to examine precisely that subject. Using an ethnographic approach, this work has explored experiences and perspectives that individuals bring to executive-level office in order to probe what policies might follow. In this account, pre-recruitment background provides many clues to post-recruitment action. By considering cases from the United States and elsewhere in greater detail, future research will reveal more about not just precedents for leaders' choices, but also breaks with precedent.

As demonstrated by each of the four cases evaluated here, women have made a significant difference to the conceptualization and practice of American foreign policy. Each leader was a determined agent who found points of entry to a set of structures long dominated by men. After crossing that frontier, each shaped history in a measurable way. Two of the four can be considered feminist critical actors who, as True (2003, 382) argues, managed to "'play the state' by inserting their agenda into its myriad agencies and institutional practices." Recovering their voices and contributions constitutes a worthy undertaking for feminist researchers—one that promises to alter the storyline of contemporary international affairs.

NOTES

CHAPTER 3

1. Collier (2012, 139) maintains that a subsequent inquiry showed Haig "had been following the UN debate over an open line from France and had intentionally delayed answering Jeane's urgent request for reconsideration of the no vote in an effort to embarrass her." This contention is confirmed by information presented in Gerson (1991, 128).
2. Collier (2012, 139) suggests Kirkpatrick's remark was correctly construed by Haig as a personal attack on him. Gerson (1991, 144), however, maintains the comment did not constitute a personal attack.
3. According to Reagan (2007, 101), Shultz and Kirkpatrick also agreed in the fall of 1982 on the need for a multinational force to ease tensions in Lebanon.

CHAPTER 4

1. Albright (2003, 33) suggests their discussions were general ones that did not pertain to the impact of European anti-Semitism on the Korbel and Spiegel families.
2. On Kirkpatrick's views concerning Vietnam, see Collier (2012, 63–65). On Albright's perspectives, see Albright (2003, 78). Initially, Josef Korbel strongly endorsed US engagement in Vietnam and opposed withdrawal, but after the 1968 Tet offensive he endorsed negotiations with North Vietnam. See Dobbs (1999, 216–218).
3. Albright (2003, 104) writes that while she suspected her father would have endorsed Carter's concern for international human rights, she doubts Josef Korbel would have ever used those words.
4. Albright's main contact in the Clinton transition team was a former Georgetown student, Nancy Soderberg, who went on to become deputy assistant for national security affairs in the Clinton administration and served on Albright's staff at the United Nations; see Maddow (2012, 180). Warren Christopher (2001, 175) credits Albright's appointment in part to "a strong push from women's groups."
5. Albright (2003, 162) notes she was wise to have followed all the rules that applied to hiring and paying household help. Clinton's initial nominee for the job of attorney general, Zoë Baird, was found to have recruited undocumented immigrants to care for her son. The White House chose not to pursue either Baird's candidacy or that of a likely second choice, New York District Court Judge Kimba Wood, because of public controversy over what became

known as Nannygate. Before the practice was prohibited, Wood had hired an undocumented worker to care for her son. She paid Social Security taxes for the employee.

6. Albright (2003, 518) reports that she traveled to Europe fifteen times between March 1998 and March 1999 to consult with the allies concerning Kosovo.

CHAPTER 5

1. Alexander-Floyd (2008, 446 note 10) criticizes what she terms "Rice's sexualized power dressing," arguing that "Rice, in her performance of racialized phallic power, remains caught in and scripted by the gaze of White masculinist authority."

2. According to Rice (2011, 171), Cheney invited "Scooter" Libby, a close associate of Wolfowitz and Rumsfeld, to make a private presentation to the president of unverified intelligence material concerning ties between al-Qaeda and Iraq. Mabry (2007, 185) reports that Bush met with Powell in August 2002 to learn his objections to invading Iraq.

3. The restaurant was owned by A. G. Gaston, a black businessman who subscribed to the self-help ideas of Booker T. Washington. See Rice (2010, 780); Mabry (2007, 25, 47). Gaston also owned a motel in Birmingham that was bombed by the Ku Klux Klan in May 1963, in an unsuccessful effort to assassinate Martin Luther King, Jr. See Rice (2010, 96).

4. The young people John Rice took under his wing visited local synagogues, won national scholarships, and built careers in fields including law, journalism, and academia. See Rice (2010, 65–68).

5. Carter was far from the first Southern president. Andrew Jackson and Andrew Johnson were born in the Carolinas. Washington, Jefferson, Madison, Monroe, and Wilson came from Virginia, while Lyndon Baines Johnson hailed from Texas.

6. Mabry (2007, 139, 140) quotes some observers who rank the scholarly work Rice produced during her years in the professoriate as far from stellar, describing it as "unimpressive" and "mediocre."

7. The story in *USA Today* on November 5, 1999, was headlined "Bush Fumbles Reporter's Pop Quiz."

8. The full name of the legislation is Uniting and Strengthening America by Providing Appropriate Tools Required to Intercept and Obstruct Terrorism Act of 2001.

9. BBC News (2003) cites pro-Iraq interests based in Gaza as claiming that between 2000 and early 2003, the total payments made to Palestinian families reached $35 million.

CHAPTER 6

1. The poem was written by Nancy "Anne" Scheibner. See Rodham (1969).

REFERENCES

Abramowitz, Alan I. 1995. "It's Abortion, Stupid: Policy Voting in the 1992 Presidential Election." *Journal of Politics* 57 (1): 176–186.

Abrams, Elliot, Richard L. Armitage, William J. Bennett, Jeffrey Bergner, John Bolton, Paula Dobriansky, Francis Fukuyama, Robert Kagan, et. al. 1998. "Open Letter from PNAC to President Clinton." January 26. *Project for a New American Century.* https://web.archive.org/web/20131021171040/http://www.newamericancentury.org/iraqclintonletter.htm.

Al-Ali, Nadje, and Nicola Pratt. 2009. *What Kind of Liberation? Women and the Occupation of Iraq.* Berkeley: University of California Press.

Albright, Madeleine. 1996. "Eulogy for Hon. Edmund S. Muskie." In *Late a Senator from Maine, Memorial Tributes to Hon. Edmund S. Muskie,* 36–38. Washington, DC: US Government Printing Office. http://www.gpo.gov/fdsys/pkg/CDOC-104sdoc17/pdf/CDOC-104sdoc17.pdf.

Albright, Madeleine. 1997. "Statement before the Senate Foreign Relations Committee." January 8. Stockholm, Sweden: United States Information Service. https://www.mtholyoke.edu/acad/intrel/albright.htm.

Albright, Madeleine. 2003. *Madam Secretary.* With Bill Woodward. New York: Hyperion.

Albright, Madeleine. 2006. *The Mighty and the Almighty: Reflections on America, God, and World Affairs.* With Bill Woodward. New York: HarperCollins.

Albright, Madeleine. 2008. *Memo to the President Elect: How We Can Restore America's Reputation and Leadership.* With Bill Woodward. New York: HarperCollins.

Albright, Madeleine. 2009. *Read My Pins: Stories from a Diplomat's Jewel Box.* With Elaine Shocas, Vivienne Becker, and Bill Woodward. New York: HarperCollins.

Albright, Madeleine. 2012. *Prague Winter: A Personal Story of Remembrance and War, 1937–1948.* With Bill Woodward. New York: HarperCollins.

Alexander-Floyd, Nikol. 2008. "Framing Condi(licious): Condoleezza Rice and the Storyline of 'Closeness' in U.S. National Community Formation." *Politics & Gender* 4 (September), 427–449.

Alison Palmer, et al. 1986. *Appellants v. George P. Shultz, as Secretary of State; Marguerite Cooper, et al., Appellants v. George P. Shultz, as Secretary of State,* 815 F.2d 84 (D.C. Cir. 1987) U.S. Court of Appeals for the District of Columbia Circuit – 815 F.2d 84 (D.C. Cir. 1987); Argued September 25, 1986. Decided March 24, 1987. http://law.justia.com/cases/federal/appellate-courts/F2/815/84/22782/.

Alison Palmer Papers. 2010. Archive of Women in Theological Scholarship, The Burke Library, Columbia University Libraries at the Union Theological Seminary, 1937–2010. http://library.columbia.edu/content/dam/libraryweb/locations/burke/fa/awts/ldpd_8628225.pdf.

Allen, Beverly. 1996. *Rape Warfare: The Hidden Genocide in Bosnia-Herzegovina and Croatia*. Minneapolis: University of Minnesota Press.

Alonso, Harriet Hyman. 1993. *Peace as a Women's Issue: A History of the US Movement for World Peace and Women's Rights*. Syracuse, NY: Syracuse University Press.

Altman, Elizabeth C. 1976. "The Philosophical Bases of Feminism: The Feminist Doctrines of the Saint-Simonians and Charles Fourier." *Philosophical Forum* 7 (3): 277–292.

American National Election Studies (ANES). 2010. "Time Series Cumulative Data File." Palo Alto, CA: Stanford University.

Anderson, Lisa. 2011. "Trustlaw Poll—Afghanistan Is Most Dangerous Country for Women." *Thomson Reuters Foundation*, June 15. http://news.trust.org/item/?map=trustlaw-poll-afghanistan-is-most-dangerous-country-for-women/.

Annesley, Claire, Susan Franceschet, and Karen Beckwith. 2014. "Informal Institutions and the Recruitment of Political Executives." Paper presented at the annual meeting of the American Political Science Association, Washington, DC, August 28–31. http://ssrn.com/abstract=2452984.

Annesley, Claire, Susan Franceschet, Karen Beckwith, and Isabelle Engeli. 2014. "Gender and the Executive Branch: Defining a New Research Agenda Workshop." Workshop at the Joint Session of Workshops for the European Consortium for Political Research, Salamanca, Spain, April 10–15. http://www.ecpr.eu/Filestore/PaperProposal/d54dc5c0-5415-4a92-a338-e0e802f0c355.pdf.

Arbour, Louise. 2002. *War Crimes and the Culture of Peace*. Toronto: University of Toronto Press.

Arquilla, John. 2006. *The Reagan Imprint: Ideas in American Foreign Policy from the Collapse of Communism to the War on Terror*. Chicago, IL: Ivan R. Dee.

Association for Diplomatic Studies and Training. 2015. "A More Representative Foreign Service." *U.S. Diplomacy: An Online Exploration of Diplomatic History and Foreign Affairs*. http://www.usdiplomacy.org/history/service/representative.php. Accessed November 18, 2015.

Atchison, Amy, and Ian Down. 2009. "Women Cabinet Ministers and Female-Friendly Social Policy." *Poverty & Public Policy* 1 (2): article 3. doi: 10.2202/1944-2858.1007

Auerswald, David P. 1999. "Inward Bound: Domestic Institutions and Military Conflicts." *International Organization* 53: 469–504.

Bader, Jeffrey. 2013. *Obama and China's Rise: An Insider's Account of America's Asia Strategy*. Washington, DC: Brookings Institution Press.

Baker, Peter. 2015. "Elder Bush Says His Son Was Served Badly by Aides." *New York Times*, November 5. http://www.nytimes.com/2015/11/05/us/politics/elder-bush-says-his-son-was-served-badly-by-aides.html.

Baker, Peter, and Helene Cooper. 2008. "Clinton Is Said to Accept Secretary of State Position." *New York Times*, November 21. http://www.nytimes.com/2008/11/22/us/politics/22obama.html.

Bashevkin, Sylvia B. 1985. "Changing Patterns of Politicization and Partisanship among Women in France." *British Journal of Political Science* 15 (January): 75–96.

Bashevkin, Sylvia. 1996. "Tough Times in Review: The British Women's Movement during the Thatcher Years." *Comparative Political Studies* 28 (January): 525–552.

Bashevkin, Sylvia. 1998. *Women on the Defensive: Living through Conservative Times*. Chicago: University of Chicago Press.

Bashevkin, Sylvia. 2006. *Tales of Two Cities: Women and Municipal Restructuring in London and Toronto*. Vancouver: UBC Press.

Bashevkin, Sylvia. 2014. "Numerical and Policy Representation on the International Stage: Women Foreign Policy Leaders in Western Industrialised Systems." *International Political Science Review* 35 (September): 409–429.

Bastien, Corina. 2016. "'Paper Negotiations': Women and Diplomacy in the Early Eighteenth Century." In *Women, Diplomacy and International Politics since 1500*, edited by Glenda Sluga and Carolyn James, 107–119. London: Routledge.

Baxter, Sandra, and Marjorie Lansing. 1983. *Women and Politics: The Visible Majority*. Ann Arbor: University of Michigan Press.

BBC News. 2003. "Palestinians Get Saddam Funds," March 13. http://news.bbc.co.uk/2/hi/middle_east/2846365.stm.

BBC4. 2002. "Edward Stourton Extended Interview of US National Security Advisor Condoleezza Rice." *With Us or Without Us*. Transcript of radio broadcast, August 1. http://www.bbc.co.uk/radio4/news/withus/rice.pdf.

Beckwith, Karen, and Kimberly Cowell-Meyers. 2007. "Sheer Numbers: Critical Representation Thresholds and Women's Political Representation." *Perspectives on Politics* 5: 553–565.

Beers, Laura. 2016. "Advocating for a Feminist Internationalism between the Wars." In *Women, Diplomacy and International Politics since 1500*, edited by Glenda Sluga and Carolyn James, 202–221. London: Routledge.

Belasco, Amy. 2014. *The Cost of Iraq, Afghanistan, and Other Global War on Terror Operations since 9/11*. CRS Report No. RL33110. Washington, DC: Congressional Research Service. http://www.fas.org/sgp/crs/natsec/RL33110.pdf.

Berkman, Michael B., and Robert E. O'Connor. 1993. "Do Women Legislators Matter? Female Legislators and State Abortion Policy." *American Politics Quarterly* 21 (1): 102–124.

Bernstein, Carl. 2007. *A Woman in Charge: The Life of Hillary Rodham Clinton*. New York: Knopf.

Black, Amy E., and Jamie L. Allen. 2001. "Tracing the Legacy of Anita Hill: The Thomas/Hill Hearings and Media Coverage of Sexual Harassment." *Gender Issues* 19 (1): 33–52.

Blair, Tony. 2010. *A Journey*. London: Hutchinson.

Bloch, Julia Chang. 2007. "Women and Diplomacy." In *Bonds across Borders: Women, China, and International Relations in the Modern World*, edited by Priscilla Roberts and He Peigun, 135–146. Newcastle, UK: Cambridge Scholars.

Blood, Thomas. 1997. *Madam Secretary: A Biography of Madeleine Albright*. New York: St. Martin's Press.

Blumenthal, Sidney. 2006. "Mugged by Reality." *Salon*, December 14. http://www.salon.com/2006/12/14/jeane_kirkpatrick/.

Bolce, Louis. 1985. "The Role of Gender in Recent Presidential Elections: Reagan and the Reverse Gender Gap." *Presidential Studies Quarterly* 15: 372–385.

Bolce, Louis. 1988. "Abortion and Presidential Elections: The Impact of Public Perceptions of Party and Candidate Positions." *Presidential Studies Quarterly* 18: 815–829.

Borrelli, MaryAnne. 2002. *The President's Cabinet: Gender, Power, and Representation.* Boulder, CO: Lynne Rienner.

Bowden, Mark. 1999. *Black Hawk Down: A Story of Modern War.* New York: Grove Press.

Boys, James D. 2015. *Clinton's Grand Strategy: US Foreign Policy in a Post-Cold War World.* London: Bloomsbury Academic.

Bratton, Kathleen. 2002. "The Effect of Legislative Diversity on Agenda Setting." *American Politics Research* 30: 115–142.

Brenner, Alletta. 2009. "Speaking of 'Respect for Women': Gender and Politics in U.S. Foreign Policy Discourse, 2001–2004." *Journal of International Women's Studies* 10 (3): 18–32.

Breuning, Marijke. 2001. "Women's Representation and Development Assistance: A Cross-National Study." *Women and Politics* 23 (3): 35–54.

Brians, Craig Leonard, and Steven Greene. 2004. "Elections: Voter Support and Partisans' (Mis)Perceptions of Presidential Candidates' Abortion Views in 2000." *Presidential Studies Quarterly* 34: 412–419.

Brooke, Senator Edward W. 1969. "Commencement Address Delivered at Wellesley College." May 31. Wellesley College Commencement Archives. http://academics.wellesley.edu/PublicAffairs/Commencement/1969/brooke.html.

Brzezinski, Zbigniew. 1970. *Between Two Ages: America's Role in the Technetronic Era.* New York: Viking.

Buechler, Steven M. 1986. *The Transformation of the Woman Suffrage Movement: The Case of Illinois, 1850–1920.* New Brunswick, NJ: Rutgers University Press.

Bunting, Madeleine. 2011. "Clinton Is Proving That a Feminist Foreign Policy Is Possible—and Works." *The Guardian,* January 16. https://www.theguardian.com/commentisfree/cifamerica/2011/jan/16/hillary-clinton-feminist-foreign-policy.

Burns, James MacGregor. 2003. *Transforming Leadership: A New Pursuit of Happiness.* New York: Atlantic Monthly Press.

Bush, George W. 2001a. "Letter to Members of the Senate on the Kyoto Protocol on Climate Change." March 13. Online by Gerhard Peters and John T. Woolley, *The American Presidency Project.* http://www.presidency.ucsb.edu/ws/?pid=45811.

Bush, George W. 2001b. "Remarks at Emma Booker Elementary School." Sarasota, Florida, September 11. *American Rhetoric.* http://www.americanrhetoric.com/speeches/gwbush911florida.htm.

Bush, George W. 2001c. "9/11 Address to the Nation." Washington, DC, September 11. *American Rhetoric.* http://www.americanrhetoric.com/speeches/gwbush911addresstothenation.htm.

Bush, George W. 2002a. "State of the Union Address." Washington, DC, January 29. The George W. Bush Whitehouse Archive. http://georgewbush-whitehouse.archives.gov/news/releases/2002/01/20020129-11.html.

Bush, George W. 2002b. "Remarks at the UN General Assembly." New York, September 12. The George W. Bush Whitehouse Archive. http://georgewbush-whitehouse.archives.gov/news/releases/2002/09/print/20020912-1.html.

Bush, George W. 2003a. "Text of President Bush's 2003 State of the Union Address." Washington, DC, January 28. *Washington Post.* http://www.washingtonpost.com/wp-srv/onpolitics/transcripts/bushtext_012803.html.

Bush, George W. 2003b. "Address by President George W. Bush." Washington, DC, March 19. Transcribed in CNN, "Bush Declares War." http://www.cnn.com/2003/US/03/19/sprj.irq.int.bush.transcript/.

Bush, George W. 2010. *Decision Points*. New York: Crown.

Bush, Laura. 2001. "Radio Address by Mrs. Bush." Crawford, Texas, November 17. The George W. Bush White House Web Archives. http://georgewbush-whitehouse. archives.gov/news/releases/2001/11/20011117.html.

Butler, Judith. 1990. *Gender Trouble: Feminism and the Subversion of Identity*. New York: Routledge.

Caglar, Gülay, Elisabeth Prügl, and Susanne Zwingel, eds. 2013. *Feminist Strategies in International Governance*. London: Routledge.

Campbell, Beatrix. 1987. *The Iron Ladies: Why Do Women Vote Tory?* London: Virago.

Campbell, John. 2008. *Margaret Thatcher: The Iron Lady*. London: Vintage.

Cannon, Carl M. 1999. "From Bosnia to Kosovo." *National Journal*, April 3, 880–885.

Cannon, Lou. 1991. *President Reagan: The Role of a Lifetime*. New York: Simon and Schuster.

Caprioli, Mary. 2000. "Gendered Conflict." *Journal of Peace Research* 37 (1): 53–68.

Caprioli, Mary, and Mark Boyer. 2001. "Gender, Violence, and International Crisis." *Journal of Conflict Resolution* 45: 503–518.

Carroll, Susan J. 1994. *Women as Candidates in American Politics*. 2nd ed. Bloomington: Indiana University Press.

Carroll, Susan J. 2002. "Partisan Dynamics of the Gender Gap among State Legislators." *Spectrum: The Journal of State Government* 75 (4): 18–21.

Celis, Karen, and Sarah Childs. 2008. "Introduction: The Descriptive and Substantive Representation of Women: New Directions." *Parliamentary Affairs* 61 (3): 419–425.

Celis, Karen, and Sarah Childs. 2012. "The Substantive Representation of Women: What to Do with Conservative Claims?" *Political Studies* 60: 213–225.

Celis, Karen, Sarah Childs, Johanna Kantola, and Mona Lena Krook. 2008. "Rethinking Women's Substantive Representation." *Representation* 44 (2): 99–110.

Chappell, Marisa. 2012. "Reagan's 'Gender Gap' Strategy and the Limitations of Free-Market Feminism." *Journal of Policy History* 24 (1): 115–134.

Charles-Philippe, David. 2010. "How Not to Do Post-Invasion: Lessons Learned from US Decision-Making in Iraq." *Defense & Security Analysis* 26 (1): 31–63.

Childs, Sarah. 2004. *New Labour's Women MPs: Women Representing Women*. London: Routledge.

Childs, Sarah, and Mona Lena Krook. 2008. "Critical Mass Theory and Women's Political Representation." *Political Studies* 56 (3): 725–736.

Childs, Sarah, and Julie Withey. 2006. "The Substantive Representation of Women: The Case of the Reduction of VAT on Sanitary Products." *Parliamentary Affairs* 59 (1): 10–23.

Chollet, Derek. 2016. *The Long Game: How Obama Defied Washington and Redefined America's Role in the World*. New York: PublicAffairs.

Christopher, Warren. 2001. *Chances of a Lifetime: A Memoir*. New York: Scribner.

Churchill, Lindsay. 2007. "Exploring Feminism's Complex Relationship with Political Violence: An Analysis of the Weathermen, Radical Feminism, and the New Left." *Lilith: A Feminist History Journal* 16: 28–43.

Clarke, Richard A. 2004. *Against All Enemies*. New York: Free Press.

Clements, Ben. 2012. "Men and Women's Support for War: Accounting for the Gender Gap in Public Opinion." *E-International Relations*, January 19. http://www.e-ir.info/2012/01/19/men-and-womens-support-for-war-accounting-for-the-gender-gap-in-public-opinion/.

Clinton, Bill. 2005. *My Life*. New York: Vintage.

Clinton, Hillary Rodham. 1995. "Remarks to the United Nations Fourth World Conference on Women." Speech, Beijing, September 5. Clinton White House Web Archive. https://clintonwhitehouse3.archives.gov/WH/EOP/First_Lady/html/China/plenary.html.

Clinton, Hillary Rodham. 2001. "New Hope for Afghanistan's Women." *Time*, November 24. http://content.time.com/time/nation/article/0,8599,185643,00.html.

Clinton, Hillary Rodham. 2003. *Living History*. New York: Scribner.

Clinton, Hillary Rodham. 2004. "No Regret on Iraq Vote." CNN, April 21. http://www.cnn.com/2004/ALLPOLITICS/04/21/iraq.hillary/

Clinton, Hillary Rodham. 2009a. "Senate Confirmation Hearing: Hilary Clinton." *New York Times*, January 13. http://www.nytimes.com/2009/01/13/us/politics/13text-clinton.html.

Clinton, Hillary Rodham. 2009b. "A Conversation with U.S. Secretary of State Hillary Rodham Clinton." *Council on Foreign Relations*, July 15. http://www.cfr.org/diplomacy-and-statecraft/conversation-us-secretary-state-hillary-rodham-clinton/p34589.

Clinton, Hillary Rodham. 2014. *Hard Choices*. New York: Simon and Schuster.

Clymer, Adam, Robert Pear, and Robin Toner. 1994. "The Health Care Debate: What Went Wrong? How the Health Care Campaign Collapsed—A Special Report: For Health Care, Times Was [sic] a Killer." *New York Times*, August 9. http://www.nytimes.com/1994/08/29/us/health-care-debate-what-went-wrong-health-care-campaign-collapsed-special-report.html?pagewanted=all.

CNN. 2002. "Transcript of CNN Late Edition with Wolf Blitzer: Interview with Condoleezza Rice." September 8. http://transcripts.cnn.com/TRANSCRIPTS/0209/08/le.00.html.

CNN. 2011. "CNN Poll: Americans Say Yes to No Fly Zone, No to Ground Troops." March 14. http://politicalticker.blogs.cnn.com/2011/03/14/cnn-poll-americans-say-yes-to-no-fly-zone-no-to-ground-troops/.

Cohn, Carol. 2011. "'Feminist Security Studies': Toward a Reflexive Practice." *Politics & Gender* 7 (4): 581–586.

Cohn, Carol, and Ruth Jacobson. 2013. "Women and Political Activism in the Face of War and Militarization." In *Women and Wars*, edited by Carol Cohn, 102–123. Cambridge, UK: Polity Press.

Collier, Peter. 2012. *Political Woman: The Big Little Life of Jeane Kirkpatrick*. New York: Encounter.

Collins, Patricia Hill. 1991. *Black Feminist Thought*. New York: Routledge.

Commission on Presidential Debates. 1980. "The Carter-Reagan Presidential Debate." October 28. http://www.debates.org/index.php?page=october-28-1980-debate-transcript.

Commission on Presidential Debates. 2000. "The Second Gore-Bush Presidential Debate." October 11. http://www.debates.org/index.php?page=october-11-2000-debate-transcript.

Conover, Pamela Johnston. 1988. "Feminists and the Gender Gap." *Journal of Politics* 50 (4): 985–1010.

Cosgrove, Ben. 2014. "Life with Hillary: Portraits of a Wellesley Grad, 1969." *Time*, February 15. http://life.time.com/history/hillary-clinton-in-1969-photos-of-a-recent-college-grad/#1.

Cotter, David, Joan M. Hermsen, and Reeve Vanneman. 2011. "The End of the Gender Revolution? Gender Role Attitudes from 1977 to 2008." *American Journal of Sociology* 117 (July): 259–289.

Cowell-Meyers, Kimberly, and Laura Langbein. 2009. "Linking Women's Descriptive and Substantive Representation in the United States." *Politics & Gender* 5: 491–518.

Cowell-Meyers, Kimberly B. 2014. "The Social Movement as Political Party: The Northern Ireland Women's Coalition and the Campaign for Inclusion." *Perspectives on Politics* 12 (1): 61–80.

Cox News Service. 1989. "Kirkpatrick's Missing Son Held in Threat on Girlfriend." *Orlando Sentinel*, February 25. http://articles.orlandosentinel.com/1989-02-25/news/8902250443_1_kirkpatrick-kaplan-sheppard-and-enoch.

Crapol, Edward P., ed. 1987. *Women and American Foreign Policy*. Westport, CT: Greenwood Press.

Critchlow, Donald T. 2005. *Phyllis Schlafly and Grassroots Conservatism: A Woman's Crusade*. Princeton, NJ: Princeton University Press.

Crowley, Terry. 1990. *Agnes Macphail and the Politics of Equality*. Toronto: Lorimer.

Crowley, Terry. 1991. "Agnes Macphail and Canadian Working Women." *Labour* 28: 129–148.

Curtin, Jennifer. 2008. "Women, Political Leadership and Substantive Representation: The Case of New Zealand." *Parliamentary Affairs* 61 (3): 490–504.

Daalder, Ivo H., and Michael E. O'Hanlon. 2001. *Winning Ugly: NATO's War to Save Kosovo*. Washington, DC: Brookings Institution Press.

Dahlerup, Drude. 1988. "From a Small to a Large Minority: Women in Scandinavian Politics." *Scandinavian Political Studies* 11: 275–297.

Dallaire, Roméo. 2003. *Shake Hands with the Devil: The Failure of Humanity in Rwanda*. With Brent Beardsley. Toronto: Random House.

Davis, Corey. 2013. "An Inconvenient Vote: Hillary Clinton's Iraq War Image Repair Debate Strategies and Their Implications for Representative Democracy." *Public Relations Review* 39 (4): 315–319.

Davis, Flora. 1991. *Moving the Mountain: The Women's Movement in America since 1960*. New York: Simon and Schuster.

Davis, Natalie Zemon. 1993. "Women in Politics." In *A History of Women in the West: Renaissance and Enlightenment Paradoxes*, edited by Natalie Zemon Davis and Arlette Farge, 167–186. Cambridge, MA: Belknap Press.

Davis, Rebecca Howard. 1997. *Women and Power in Parliamentary Democracies: Cabinet Appointments in Western Europe, 1968–1992*. Lincoln: University of Nebraska Press.

Deseret News (Salt Lake City). 1983. "Shultz Takes a Scolding for Poor Consultations." August 5. http://news.google.com/newspapers?nid=336&dat=19830805&id=EC9TAAAAIBAJ&sjid=DIMDAAAAIBAJ&pg=4611,1158188.

Diebel, Terry L. 1989. "Reagan's Mixed Legacy." *Foreign Policy* 75: 34–55.

Dobbs, Michael. 1997. "Albright Reshapes Role of Nation's Top Diplomat." *Washington Post*, June 17. http://www.washingtonpost.com/wp-srv/politics/govt/admin/stories/albright061597.htm.

Dobbs, Michael. 1999. *Madeleine Albright: A Twentieth-Century Odyssey*. New York: Henry Holt.

Docherty, David. 1997. *Mr. Smith Goes to Ottawa: Life in the House of Commons*. Vancouver: University of British Columbia Press.

Dodson, Debra L., ed. 1991. *Gender and Policymaking*. New Brunswick, NJ: Center for the American Woman and Politics.

Dodson, Debra L. 2006. *The Impact of Women in Congress*. New York: Oxford University Press.

Dorrien, Gary. 1993. *The Neoconservative Mind: Politics, Culture, and the War of Ideology*. Philadelphia: Temple University Press.

Dowd, Maureen. 2011. "Fight of the Valkyries." *New York Times*, March 23. http://www.nytimes.com/2011/03/23/opinion/23dowd.html?_r=0.

Dueck, Colin. 2010. *Hard Line: The Republican Party and U.S. Foreign Policy since World War II*. Princeton, NJ: Princeton University Press.

Dueck, Colin. 2011. "The Accommodator: Obama's Foreign Policy." *Policy Review* 169: 13–28.

Dueck, Colin. 2015. *The Obama Doctrine: American Grand Strategy Today*. New York: Oxford University Press.

Dumbrell, John. 2009. *Clinton's Foreign Policy: Between the Bushes*. New York: Routledge.

Eagly, Alice H., and Steven J. Karau. 2002. "Role Incongruity Theory of Prejudice Toward Female Leaders." *Psychological Review* 109 (3): 573–598.

Eagly, Alice H., and Linda L. Carli. 2007. *Through the Labyrinth: The Truth about How Women Become Leaders*. Boston: Harvard Business School Press.

Ehrman, John. 1996. *The Rise of Neoconservatism: Intellectuals and Foreign Affairs, 1945–1994*. New Haven, CT: Yale University Press.

Eichenberg, Richard C. 2003. "Gender Differences in Public Attitudes toward the Use of Force by the United States, 1990–2003." *International Security* 28 (1): 110–141.

Elshtain, Jean Bethke. 1974. "Moral Woman and Immoral Man: A Consideration of the Public-Private Split and its Political Ramifications." *Politics & Society* 4 (4): 453–473.

Elshtain, Jean Bethke. 1995. *Women and War*. Chicago: University of Chicago Press.

Engels, Frederick. 1970. *The Origin of the Family, Private Property and the State*. Edited by Eleanor Burke Leacock. New York: International.

Englehart, Katie. 2011. "In Bosnia, Divided They Stall." *Maclean's*, December 20. http://www.macleans.ca/news/world/divided-they-stall/.

Enloe, Cynthia. 1989. *Bananas, Beaches and Bases: Making Feminist Sense of International Politics*. Berkeley: University of California Press.

Escobar-Lemmon, Maria, and Michelle M. Taylor-Robinson. 2005. "Women Ministers in Latin American Governments: When, Where, and Why?" *American Journal of Political Science* 49 (4): 829–844.

Escobar-Lemmon, Maria, and Michelle M. Taylor-Robinson. 2009. "Getting to the Top: Career Paths of Women in Latin American Cabinets." *Political Research Quarterly* 62 (4): 685–699.

Evans, Peter B., Dietrich Rueschemeyer, and Theda Skocpol, eds. 1985. *Bringing the State Back In*. Cambridge: Cambridge University Press.

Faludi, Susan. 2007. *The Terror Dream: Myth and Misogyny in an Insecure America*. New York: Henry Holt.

Federal Elections Commission. 2008a. "Details for Candidate ID: P00003392, Hillary Clinton for President." http://www.fec.gov/fecviewer/CandidateCommitteeDetail.do. Accessed August 25, 2016.

Federal Elections Commission. 2008b. "Report of Receipts and Disbursements, Obama for America." http://docquery.fec.gov/pres/2008/M6/C00431445.html. Accessed August 25, 2016.

Ferguson, Michaele L. 2007. "Feminism and Security Rhetoric in the Post-9/11 Bush Administration." In *W Stands for Women: How the Bush Presidency Shaped a New Politics of Gender*, edited by Michaele L. Ferguson and Lori Jo Marso, 191–220. Durham, NC: Duke University Press.

Ferguson, Michaele L., and Lori Jo Marso. 2007. "Introduction: Feminism, Gender, and Security in the Bush Presidency." In *W Stands for Women: How the Bush Presidency Shaped a New Politics of Gender*, edited by Michaele L. Ferguson and Lori Jo Marso, 1–14. Durham, NC: Duke University Press.

Fernandes, Leela. 2013. *Transnational Feminism in the United States*. New York: New York University Press.

Finger, Seymour Maxwell. 1988. *American Ambassadors at the UN: People, Politics, and Bureaucracy in Making Foreign Policy*. New York: Holmes and Meier.

Finkle, Jason L., and Barbara B. Crane. 1985. "Ideology and Politics at Mexico City: The United States at the 1984 International Conference on Population." *Population and Development Review* 11 (1): 1–28.

Finlay, Barbara. 2006. *George W. Bush and the War on Women: Turning Back the Clock on Progress*. London: Zed Books.

Fite, David, Marc Genest, and Clyde Wilcox. 1990. "Gender Differences in Foreign Policy Attitudes: A Longitudinal Analysis." *American Politics Research* 18 (4): 492–513.

Flanders, Laura. 2005. *Bushwomen: Tales of a Cynical Species*. London: Verso.

Fornos, Werner. 1988. "Philippines on a Collision Course with Disaster." *Sunday Telegraph*, May 29. https://news.google.com/newspapers?id=VbZhAAAAIBAJ&sjid=S5QMAAAAIBAJ&pg=6915%2C9041013.

Frankovic, Kathleen A. 1977. "Sex and Voting in the US House of Representatives, 1961–1975." *American Politics Quarterly* 5 (3): 315–30.

Frankovic, Kathleen A. 1982. "Sex and Politics—New Alignments, Old Issues," *PS* 15 (3): 439–448.

Fraser, Antonia. 1988. *The Warrior Queens*. New York: Viking.

Freeman, Jo. 2013. "The Tyranny of Structurelessness." *Women's Studies Quarterly* 41 (3–4): 231–246.

Friedenberg, Robert V. 1994. *Rhetorical Studies of National Political Debates, 1960–1992*. Westport, CT: Praeger.

Fukuyama, Francis. 1998. "Women and the Evolution of World Politics." *Foreign Affairs* 77 (September–October): 24–40.

Fuss, Diana. 1989. *Essentially Speaking*. New York: Routledge.

Gaddis, John Lewis. 2005. *Strategies of Containment: A Critical Appraisal of American National Security Policy during the Cold War*, rev. ed. New York: Oxford University Press.

Gamarekian, Barbara. 1989. "Washington Talk: Women Gain, but Slowly, in the Foreign Service." *New York Times*, July 28. http://www.nytimes.com/1989/07/28/us/washington-talk-women-gain-but-slowly-in-the-foreign-service.html.

Garner, Karen. 2012. "Global Gender Policy in the 1990s: Incorporating the 'Vital Voices' of Women." *Journal of Women's Studies* 24 (4): 121–148.

Gates, Robert M. 2014. *Duty: Memoirs of a Secretary at War*. New York: Vintage Books.

Geertz, Clifford. 1973. *The Interpretation of Cultures: Selected Essays*. New York: Basic Books.

Genovese, Michael A., ed. 1993. *Women as National Leaders*. Newbury Park, CA: Sage.

Genovese, Michael A., and Janie S. Steckenrider, eds. 2012. *Women as Political Leaders: Studies in Gender and Governing*. New York: Routledge.

Genovese, Michael A., and Seth Thompson. 1993. "Women as Chief Executives: Does Gender Matter?" In *Women as National Leaders*, edited by Michael Genovese, 1–12. Newbury Park, CA: Sage.

Gerson, Allan. 1991. *The Kirkpatrick Mission: Diplomacy without Apology: America at the United Nations, 1981–1985*. New York: Free Press.

Gerth, Jeff, and Don Van Natta, Jr. 2007. *Her Way: The Hopes and Ambitions of Hillary Rodham Clinton*. New York: Little, Brown.

Ghattas, Kim. 2013. *The Secretary: A Journey with Hillary Clinton from Beirut to the Heart of American Power*. New York: Times Books.

Ghervas, Stella. 2016. "A 'Goodwill Ambassador' in the Post-Napoleonic Era: Rosandra Edling-Sturdza on the European Scene." In *Women, Diplomacy and International Politics since 1500*, edited by Glenda Sluga and Carolyn James, 151–166. London: Routledge.

Gidengil, Elisabeth. 1995. "Economic Man—Social Woman? The Case of the Gender Gap in Support for the Canada-United States Free Trade Agreement." *Comparative Political Studies* 28 (3): 384–408.

Gilens, Martin. 1988. "Gender and Support for Reagan: A Comprehensive Model of Presidential Approval." *American Journal of Political Science* 32 (1): 19–49.

Gilligan, Carol. 1982. *In a Different Voice: Psychological Theory and Women's Development*. Cambridge, MA: Harvard University Press.

Gladstone, Rick, and C. J. Chivers. 2013. "Forensic Details in U.N. Report Point to Assad's Use of Gas." *New York Times*, September 16. http://www.nytimes.com/2013/09/17/world/europe/syria-united-nations.html.

Glenny, Misha. 2012. *The Balkans: Nationalism, War and the Great Powers, 1804–2011*. New York: Penguin.

Goguel, François. 1952. "Christian Democracy in France." In *Christian Democracy in Italy and France* by Mario Einaudi and François Goguel, 109–224. Notre Dame, IN: University of Notre Dame Press.

Goldberg, Jeffrey. 2016. "The Obama Doctrine." *The Atlantic*, April. http://www.theatlantic.com/magazine/archive/2016/04/the-obama-doctrine/471525/.

Goldberg, Michelle. 2009. *The Means of Reproduction: Sex, Power, and the Future of the World*. New York: Penguin.

Goldstein, Joshua S. 2001. *War and Gender: How Gender Shapes the War System and Vice Versa*. Cambridge, UK: Cambridge University Press.

Gottlieb, Henry. 1987. "Shultz Says He Offered to Resign Three Times." *Associated Press*, July 24. http://www.apnewsarchive.com/1987/Shultz-Says-He-Offered-to-Resign-Three-Times-With-AM-US-Iran-Contra-Rdp-Bjt/id-c15b7b59923c98a48d323d7c4d803a1d.

Gupte, Pranay. 1984. "Family Size: Small Is Beautiful." *New York Times*, August 5. http://www.nytimes.com/1984/08/05/opinion/family-size-small-is-beautiful.html.

Gwertzman, Bernard. 1983. "Shultz Finds He's No Longer Immune to Criticism." *New York Times*, June 7. http://www.nytimes.com/1983/06/07/us/shultz-finds-he-s-no-longer-immune-to-criticism.html.

Haider-Markel, Donald P., and Andrea Vieux. 2008. "Gender and Conditional Support for Torture in the War on Terror." *Politics & Gender* 4 (1): 5–33.

Haig, Alexander M., Jr. 1992. *Inner Circles: How America Changed the World, A Memoir*. With Charles McCarry. New York: Warner Books.

Hannay, David. 2008. *New World Disorder: The UN after the Cold War*. New York: Tauris.

Harford, Barbara, and Sarah Hopkins. 1984. *Greenham Common: Women at the Wire*. London: Women's Press.

Hawkesworth, Mary. 2007. "Feminists versus Feminization: Confronting the War Logics of the George W. Bush Administration." In *W Stands for Women: How the George W. Bush Presidency Shaped a New Politics of Gender*, edited by Michaele L. Ferguson and Lori Jo Marso, 163–187. Durham, NC: Duke University Press.

Hedges, Chris. 1999. "Slaying of Serbs Sets Back Effort for Kosovo Peace." *New York Times*, July 25. http://www.nytimes.com/1999/07/25/world/slaying-of-serbs-sets-back-effort-for-kosovo-peace.html.

Herren, Madeleine. 2016. "Gender and International Relations through the Lens of the League of Nations (1919–1945)." In *Women, Diplomacy and International Politics since 1500*, edited by Glenda Sluga and Carolyn James, 182–201. London: Routledge.

Hill, Anita. 2007. "The Smear This Time." *New York Times*, October 2. http://www.nytimes.com/2007/10/02/opinion/02hill.html?_r=0.

Himmelstein, Jerome L. 1990. *To the Right: The Transformation of American Conservatism*. Berkeley: University of California Press.

Hipperson, Sarah. 2005. *Greenham: Non-Violent Women -v- The Crown Prerogative*. London: Greenham Publications.

Hoff, Joan. 2007. "Madeleine Albright and Condoleezza Rice: The Woman Question and US Foreign Policy." In *Bonds across Borders: Women, China, and International Relations in the Modern World*, edited by Priscilla Roberts and He Peigun, 104–134. Newcastle, UK: Cambridge Scholars.

Holbrooke, Richard. 1998. *To End a War*. New York: Random House.

Holsti, Ole R., and James N. Rosenau. 1988. "The Domestic and Foreign Policy Beliefs of American Leaders." *Journal of Conflict Resolution* 32 (2): 248–294.

Holton, Sandra Stanley. 1986. *Feminism and Democracy: Women's Suffrage and Reform in Britain 1900–1918*. Cambridge: Cambridge University Press.

Holyk, Gregory G. 2010. "The Polls—Trends: U.S. Public Support for the United Nations." *Public Opinion Quarterly* 74 (1): 168–189.

Hoogensen, Gunhild, and Bruce O. Solheim. 2006. *Women in Power: World Leaders since 1960*. London: Praeger.

Hook, Sidney. 1943. *The Hero in History: A Study in Limitation and Possibility*. New York: John Day.

Hopkins, Michael F. 2008. "Ronald Reagan's and George H.W. Bush's Secretaries of State: Alexander Haig, George Shultz, and James Baker." *Journal of Transatlantic Studies* 6 (3): 228–245.

Howell, William. 2003. *Power without Persuasion: The Politics of Direct Presidential Action*. Princeton, NJ: Princeton University Press.

Huddy, Leonie, Francis K. Neely, and Marilyn R. LaFay. 2000. "Trends: Support for the Women's Movement." *Public Opinion Quarterly* 64 (3): 309–350.

Hudson, Valerie M., and Patricia Leidl. 2015. *The Hillary Doctrine: Sex and American Foreign Policy*. New York: Columbia University Press.

Hyland, William G. 1999. *Clinton's World: Remaking American Foreign Policy*. Westport, CT: Praeger.

International Civil Society Action Network for Women's Rights, Peace and Security (ICAN). 2013. "What the Women Say; From Subjects to Citizens: Women in Post-Revolutionary Libya." http://www.icanpeacework.org/wp-content/uploads/2013/12/libya-dec3.pdf.

Idrovo, Alvaro J. 2011. "Three Criteria for Ecological Fallacy." *Environmental Health Perspectives* 119 (8): A332.

Indyk, Martin S., Kenneth G. Lieberthal, and Michael E. O'Hanlon. 2012. "Scoring Obama's Foreign Policy: A Progressive Pragmatist Tries to Bend History." *Foreign Affairs* 91 (3): 29–43.

Inglehart, Ronald, and Pippa Norris. 2000. "The Developmental Theory of the Gender Gap: Women's and Men's Voting Behavior in Global Perspective." *International Political Science Review* 21 (4): 441–463.

Isaacson, Walter. 1999. "Madeleine's War." *Time*, May 9. http://content.time.com/time/magazine/article/0,9171,24446,00.html.

Jacob, Suraj, John A. Scherpereel, and Melinda Adams. 2014. "Gender Norms and Women's Political Representation: A Global Analysis of Cabinets, 1979–2009." *Governance* 27 (2): 321–345.

Jacobson, Gary C. 2010. "George W. Bush, the Iraq War, and the Election of Barack Obama." *Presidential Studies Quarterly* 40 (2): 207–224.

Jain, Devaki. 2005. *Women, Development, and the UN*. Bloomington: Indiana University Press.

Jalalzai, Farida. 2013. *Shattered, Cracked, or Firmly Intact? Women and the Executive Glass Ceiling Worldwide*. New York: Oxford University Press.

Jalalzai, Farida. 2014. "Gender, Presidencies, and Prime Ministerships in Europe: Are Women Gaining Ground?" *International Political Science Review* 35: 577–594.

Jalalzai, Farida, and Pedro G. dos Santos. 2015. "The Dilma Effect? Women's Representation under Dilma Rousseff's Presidency." *Politics & Gender* 11 (1): 117–145.

James, Carolyn. 2016. "Women and Diplomacy in Renaissance Italy." In *Women, Diplomacy and International Politics since 1500*, edited by Glenda Sluga and Carolyn James, 13–29. London: Routledge.

James, Carolyn, and Glenda Sluga. 2016. "Introduction: The Long International History of Women and Diplomacy." In *Women, Diplomacy and International Politics since 1500*, edited by Glenda Sluga and Carolyn James, 1–12. London: Routledge.

Jamieson, Kathleen Hall. 1995. *Beyond the Double Bind: Women and Leadership*. New York: Oxford University Press.

Johnson, Glen. 1999. "Bush Fails Quiz on Foreign Affairs." *Washington Post*, November 4. http://www.washingtonpost.com/wp-srv/aponline/19991104/aponline181051_000.htm.

Jordan, Mary. 2010. "'Hillary Effect' Cited for Increase in Female Ambassadors to U.S." *Washington Post*, January 11. http://www.washingtonpost.com/wp-dyn/content/article/2010/01/10/AR2010011002731.html.

Judah, Tim. 2002. *Kosovo: War and Revenge*. New Haven, CT: Yale University Press.

Kandiyoti, Deniz. 2007. "Between the Hammer and the Anvil: Post-Conflict Reconstruction, Islam, and Women's Rights." *Third World Quarterly* 28 (3): 503–517.

Kathlene, Lyn. 1998. "In a Different Voice: Women and the Policy Process." In *Women and Elective Office*, edited by Sue Thomas and Clyde Wilcox, 188–202. New York: Oxford University Press.

Kaufman, Robert G. 2014. "Prudence and the Obama Doctrine." *Orbis* 58 (3): 441–459.

Kenney, Sally J. 1992. *For Whose Protection? Reproductive Hazards and Exclusionary Policies in the United States and Britain*. Ann Arbor: University of Michigan Press.

Keohane, Nannerl O. 2010. *Thinking about Leadership*. Princeton, NJ: Princeton University Press.

Kessler, Glenn. 2007. *The Confidante: Condoleezza Rice and the Creation of the Bush Legacy*. New York: St. Martin's Press.

Kieval, Hillel J. 2000. *Languages of Community: The Jewish Experience in the Czech Lands*. Berkeley: University of California Press.

Kimball, Jeffrey. 2006. "The Nixon Doctrine: A Saga of Misunderstanding." *Presidential Studies Quarterly* 36 (1): 59–74.

King, Martin Luther. 1963. "Letter from Birmingham Jail." Stanford, CA: Martin Luther King Jr. Research and Education Institute. http://okra.stanford.edu/transcription/document_images/undecided/630416-019.pdf. Accessed July 10, 2016.

Kirkpatrick, Jeane J. 1971. *Leader and Vanguard in Mass Society: A Study of Peronist Argentina*. Cambridge, MA: MIT Press.

Kirkpatrick, Jeane J. 1973. "The Revolt of the Masses." *Commentary* 55 (2): 58–62.

Kirkpatrick, Jeane J. 1974. *Political Woman*. New York: Basic Books.

Kirkpatrick, Jeane J. 1976. *The New Presidential Elite*. New York: Russell Sage.

Kirkpatrick, Jeane J. 1979. "Dictatorships and Double Standards." *Commentary* 68 (5): 34–45.

Kirkpatrick, Jeane J. 1981. "Opening Statement to Members of the Senate Foreign Relations Committee." January 15. *American Rhetoric*. http://www.americanrhetoric.com/speeches/jeanekirkpatrickunambassadorconfirmation.htm.

Kirkpatrick, Jeane J. 1984. "Speech to the Republican National Convention." August 20, Dallas. http://www.cnn.com/ALLPOLITICS/1996/conventions/san.diego/facts/GOP.speeches.past/84.kirkpatrick.shtml. Accessed July 8, 2015.

Kirkpatrick, Jeane J. 2007a. "An American Girlhood." *The Weekly Standard*, February 5. http://www.aei.org/print/an-american-girlhood.

Kirkpatrick, Jeane J. 2007b. *Making War to Keep Peace*. New York: HarperCollins.

Klatch, Rebecca. 1987. *Women of the New Right*. Philadelphia: Temple University Press.

Klausen, Jytte. 2001. "When Women Voted for the Right: Lessons for Today from the Conservative Gender Gap." In *Has Liberalism Failed Women? Assuring Equal Representation in Europe and the United States*, edited by Jytte Klausen and Charles S. Maier, 209–228. New York: Palgrave.

Koch, Michael T., and Sarah A. Fulton. 2011. "In the Defense of Women: Gender, Office Holding, and National Security Policy in Established Democracies." *Journal of Politics* 73 (1): 1–16.

Korbel, Josef. 1951. *Tito's Communism*. Denver: University of Denver Press.

Kraditor, Aileen S. 1965. *The Ideas of the Woman Suffrage Movement*. New York: Columbia University Press.

Krook, Mona Lena, and Fiona Mackay, eds. 2011. *Gender, Politics and Institutions: Towards a Feminist Institutionalism*. Houndmills, Basingstoke, UK: Palgrave Macmillan.

Krook, Mona Lena, and Diana Z. O'Brien. 2012. "All the President's Men? The Appointment of Female Cabinet Ministers Worldwide." *Journal of Politics* 74 (3): 840–855.

Lake, Anthony. 2000. *6 Nightmares: Real Threats in a Dangerous World and How America Can Meet Them*. Boston: Little, Brown.

Landler, Mark. 2016. *Alter Egos: Hillary Clinton, Barack Obama, and the Twilight Struggle over American Power*. New York: Random House.

Lawless, Jennifer. 2004. "Women, War, and Winning Elections: Gender Stereotyping in the Post-September 11th Era." *Political Research Quarterly* 57 (3): 479–490.

Lawrence, Regina G., and Melody Rose. 2010. *Hillary Clinton's Race for the White House: Gender Politics and the Media on the Campaign Trail.* Boulder, CO: Lynne Rienner.

Leader, Shelah Gilbert. 1977. "The Policy Impact of Elected Women Officials." In *The Impact of the Electoral Process,* edited by Louis Maisel and Joseph Cooper, 265–284. Beverly Hills, CA: Sage.

Leffler, Melvyn O. 2013. "The Foreign Policies of the George W. Bush Administration: Memoirs, History and Legacy." *Diplomatic History* 37 (2): 190–216.

Leigh, David. 2010. "Iraq War Logs Reveal 15,000 Previously Unlisted Civilian Deaths." *The Guardian,* October 22. https://www.theguardian.com/world/2010/oct/22/true-civilian-body-count-iraq.

Lemmon, Gayle Tzemach. 2011. "The Hillary Doctrine." *Newsweek,* March 6. http://www.newsweek.com/hillary-doctrine-66105.

Lemons, J. Stanley. 1973. *The Woman Citizen: Social Feminism in the 1920s.* Urbana: University of Illinois Press.

LeoGrande, William M. 1998. *Our Own Backyard: The United States in Central America, 1977–1992.* Chapel Hill: University of North Carolina Press.

Lindsay, James M., and Ivo H. Daalder. 2001. "Revitalizing the State Department." *Foreign Service Journal* 78 (March): 50–55.

Lippman, Thomas W. 2000. *Madeleine Albright and the New American Diplomacy.* Boulder, CO: Westview Press.

Logevall, Frederick. 2010. "Anatomy of an Unnecessary War: The Iraq Invasion." In *The Presidency of George W. Bush: A First Historical Assessment,* edited by Julian E. Zelizer, 88–113. Princeton, NJ: Princeton University Press.

Lovenduski, Joni. 2005. *Feminizing Politics.* Cambridge: Polity.

Lu, Kelan, and Marijke Breuning. 2014. "Gender and Generosity: Does Women's Representation Affect Development Cooperation?" *Politics, Groups, and Identities* 2 (3): 313–330.

Lusane, Clarence. 2006. *Colin Powell and Condoleezza Rice: Foreign Policy, Race, and the New American Century.* Westport, CT: Praeger.

Mabry, Marcus. 2007. *Twice as Good: Condoleezza Rice and Her Path to Power.* New York: Rodale.

Mackay, Fiona. 2008. "'Thick' Conceptions of Substantive Representation: Women, Gender, and Political Institutions." *Representation* 44 (2): 125–139.

Macpherson, Kay, and Meg Sears. 1976. "The Voice of Women: A History." In *Women in the Canadian Mosaic,* edited by Gwen Matheson, 71–89. Toronto: Peter Martin.

Maddow, Rachel. 2012. *Drift: The Unmooring of American Military Power.* New York: Random House.

Major, John. 1999. *The Autobiography.* London: HarperCollins.

Mann, James. 2004. *Rise of the Vulcans: The History of Bush's War Cabinet.* New York: Viking.

Mann, James. 2012. *The Obamians: The Struggle inside the White House to Redefine American Power.* New York: Viking.

Mansbridge, Jane J. 1985. "Myth and Reality: The ERA and the Gender Gap in the 1980 Election." *Public Opinion Quarterly* 49: 164–178.

Mansbridge, Jane J. 1986. *Why We Lost the ERA.* Chicago: University of Chicago Press.

Marini, Mirella. 2016. "Dynastic Relations on an International Stage: Margaret de la Marck (1527–1599) and Arenberg Family Strategy during the Dutch Revolt." In *Women, Diplomacy and International Politics since 1500*, edited by Glenda Sluga and Carolyn James, 46–67. London: Routledge.

Marshall, Susan E. 1991. "Who Speaks for American Women? The Future of American Feminism." *Annals of the American Academy of Political and Social Science* 515 (May): 50–62.

Martin, Janet M. 2003. *The Presidency and Women: Promise, Performance and Illusion.* College Station: Texas A&M University Press.

Marx, Karl. 1969. *The Eighteenth Brumaire of Louis Bonaparte*, edited by C. P. Dutt. New York: International.

Mason, Corinne. 2017. *Manufacturing Urgency: The Development Industry and Violence against Women.* Regina: University of Regina Press.

McCarthy, Helen. 2014. *Women of the World: The Rise of the Female Diplomat.* London: Bloomsbury.

McCarthy, Helen. 2016. "Gendering Diplomatic History: Women in the British Diplomatic Service, circa 1919–1972." In *Women, Diplomacy and International Politics since 1500*, edited by Glenda Sluga and Carolyn James, 167–181. London: Routledge.

McCormick, James M. 2011. "The Foreign Policy of the Obama Administration: Change or Continuity?" Paper presented at annual meeting of the International Studies Association, Montreal, March 16–19.

McGlen, Nancy E., and Meredith Reid Sarkees. 1993. *Women in Foreign Policy: The Insiders.* New York: Routledge.

McGlen, Nancy E., and Meredith Reid Sarkees. 1995. *The Status of Women in Foreign Policy.* New York: Foreign Policy Association.

McGlen, Nancy E., and Meredith Reid Sarkees. 2001. "Foreign Policy Decision Makers: The Impact of Gender." In *The Impact of Women in Public Office*, edited by Susan J. Carroll, 117–148. Bloomington: Indiana University Press.

McKenzie, Beatrice Loftus. 2015. "The Problem of Women in the Department: Sex and Gender Discrimination in the 1960s United States Foreign Diplomatic Service." *European Journal of American Studies* 10 (1): article 1.7. https://ejas.revues.org/10589.

McManus, Doyle, and Stanley Meisler. 1993. "Clinton to Press Active U.S. Role in Bosnia." *Los Angeles Times*, January 22. http://articles.latimes.com/1993-01-22/news/mn-1715_1_foreign-affairs.

Melich, Tanya. 1996. *The Republican War against Women: An Insider's Report from behind the Lines.* New York: Bantam.

Meyer, Mary K., and Elisabeth Prügl, eds. 1999. *Gender Politics in Global Governance.* Lanham, MD: Rowman and Littlefield.

Michels, Robert. 2001. *Political Parties: A Sociological Study of the Oligarchical Tendencies of Modern Democracy.* Translated by Eden Paul and Cedar Paul. Kitchener, ON: Batoche Books.

Milne, David. 2012. "Pragmatism or What? The Future of U.S Foreign Policy." *International Affairs* 88 (5): 935–951.

Mitchell, Silvia Z. 2016. "Marriage Plots: Royal Women, Marriage Diplomacy and International Politics at the Spanish, French and Imperial Courts, 1665–1679." In *Women, Diplomacy and International Politics since 1500*, edited by Glenda Sluga and Carolyn James, 86–106. London: Routledge.

Montoya, Celeste. 2013. *From Global to Grassroots: The European Union, Transnational Advocacy, and Combating Violence against Women*. New York: Oxford University Press.

Murray, Rainbow, ed. 2010. *Cracking the Highest Glass Ceiling: A Global Comparison of Women's Campaigns for Executive Office*. Santa Barbara, CA: Praeger.

Naftali, Timothy. 2010. "George W. Bush and the 'War on Terror.'" In *The Presidency of George W. Bush: A First Historical Assessment*, edited by Julian E. Zelizer, 59–87. Princeton, NJ: Princeton University Press.

Nash, Philip. 2016. "A Woman's Place Is in the Embassy: America's First Female Chiefs of Mission, 1933–1964." In *Women, Diplomacy and International Politics since 1500*, edited by Glenda Sluga and Carolyn James, 222–239. London: Routledge.

National Archives. 1974. "Document for August 9th: Richard M. Nixon's Resignation Letter, 08/09/1974." http://www.archives.gov/historical-docs/todays-doc/?dod-date=809.

National Security Council and National Security Council Records Management Office. 1994. "PDD-25—U.S. Policy on Reforming Multilateral Peace Operations, 5/3/1994." *Clinton Digital Library*. https://clinton.presidentiallibraries.us/items/show/12749.

Nau, Henry R. 2015. *Conservative Internationalism: Armed Diplomacy under Jefferson, Polk, Truman, and Reagan*. Princeton, NJ: Princeton University Press.

Navarro, Coke. 2016. "Why the U.S. Spends More on War Than It Does on Diplomacy." *Newsweek*, June 29. http://www.newsweek.com/2016/07/08/state-department-pentagon-diplomacy-475655.html.

Nevitte, Neil, and Roger Gibbins. 1991. *New Elites in Old States: Ideologies in the Anglo-American Democracies*: Toronto: Oxford University Press.

New York Times. 1982. "Mrs. Kirkpatrick Laughs Off Haig's 'Commander' Remark." June 7. http://www.nytimes.com/1982/06/07/world/mrs-kirkpatrick-laughs-off-haig-s-commander-remark.html.

New York Times. 1983a. "President to Replace Hinton as U.S. Envoy to El Salvador." May 29. http://www.nytimes.com/1983/05/29/us/president-to-replace-hinton-as-us-envoy-to-el-salvador.html.

New York Times. 1983b. "Around the World: Zimbabwean Temperate on US Aid Cut." December 24. http://www.nytimes.com/1983/12/24/world/around-the-world-zimbabwean-temperate-on-us-aid-cut.html.

Niederle, Muriel, and Lise Vesterlund. 2007. "Do Women Shy Away from Competition? Do Men Compete Too Much?" *Quarterly Journal of Economics* 122 (3): 1067–1101.

Norris, John. 2012. "Is America Ready for a Male Secretary of State?" *Foreign Policy* 24 (September). http://foreignpolicy.com/2012/09/24/is-america-ready-for-a-male-secretary-of-state/.

Obama, Barack. 2007. "Renewing American Leadership." *Foreign Affairs* 86 (July–August), 2–16.

Obama, Barack. 2009a. "Remarks by the President at Cairo University, 6-04-09." June 4. Barack Obama White House Archives. https://obamawhitehouse.archives.gov/the-press-office/remarks-president-cairo-university-6-04-09.

Obama, Barack. 2009b. "Development: Obama Rescinds Mexico City Policy on Funding." *Foreign Policy Bulletin* 19 (2, June): 38–59.

O'Farrell, Brigid. 2010. *She Was One of Us: Eleanor Roosevelt and the American Worker*. Ithaca, NY: Cornell University Press.

Okin, Susan Moller. 1979. *Women in Western Political Thought*. Princeton, NJ: Princeton University Press.

O'Neill, William. 1971. *Everyone Was Brave: A History of Feminism in America*. New York: Quadrangle.

Orbinski, James. 2008. *An Imperfect Offering: Humanitarian Action in the Twenty-First Century*. Toronto: Random House.

Osborn, Tracy. 2012. *How Women Represent Women: Political Parties, Gender and Representation in the State Legislatures*. New York: Oxford University Press.

Osborn, Tracy. 2014. "Women State Legislators and Representation: The Role of Political Parties and Institutions." *State and Local Government Review* 46 (2): 146–155.

Padgett, Tim. 2011. "The Interrupted Reading: The Kids with George W. Bush on 9/11." *Time*, May 3. http://content.time.com/time/magazine/article/0,9171,2069582,00.html.

Panetta, Leon. 2014. *Worthy Fights: A Memoir of Leadership in War and Peace*. With Jim Newton. New York: Penguin Press.

Pee, Robert. 2015. *Democracy Promotion, National Security and Strategy: Foreign Policy under the Reagan Administration*. London: Routledge.

Perlez, Jane. 1998. "Massacres by Serbian Forces in 3 Kosovo Villages." *New York Times*, September 30. http://www.nytimes.com/1998/09/30/world/massacres-by-serbian-forces-in-3-kosovo-villages.html?pagewanted=1.

Perry, Matt. 2013. "In Search of 'Red Ellen' Wilkinson: Beyond Frontiers and Beyond the Nation State." *International Review of Social History* 58: 219–246.

Peterson, V. Spike, and Anne Sisson Runyan. 2010. *Global Gender Issues in the New Millennium*, 3rd ed. Boulder, CO: Westview Press.

Pew Research Center. 2013. "Public Opinion Runs against Syrian Airstrikes." September 3. http://www.people-press.org/2013/09/03/public-opinion-runs-against-syrian-airstrikes/.

Phillips, Anne. 1995. *The Politics of Presence*. Oxford, UK: Clarendon Press.

Phillips, Melanie. 2003. *The Ascent of Woman: A History of the Suffragette Movement and the Ideas Behind It*. London: Little, Brown.

Pinker, Steven. 2011. *The Better Angels of Our Nature: Why Violence Has Declined*. New York: Penguin.

Pitkin, Hanna F. 1967. *The Concept of Representation*. Berkeley: University of California Press.

Poggione, Sarah. 2011. "Gender and Representation in State Legislatures." In *Women in Politics: Outsiders or Insiders?* 5th ed., edited by Lois Duke Whitaker, 169–184. Boston: Longman.

Powell, Colin. 1995. *My American Journey*. With Joseph E. Persico. New York: Random House.

Powell, Jonathan. 2016. "Chilcot Mustn't Make Us Afraid to Use Force." *The Times*, July 2. http://www.thetimes.co.uk/article/chilcot-mustnt-make-us-afraid-to-use-force-kv96vzh3v.

Power, Samantha. 2013. *"A Problem from Hell": America and the Age of Genocide*. New York: Basic Books.

Purdum, Todd. 2012. "Team of Mascots." *Vanity Fair*, June 6. http://www.vanityfair.com/news/2012/07/obama-cabinet-team-rivals-lincoln.

Putnam, Robert D. 1976. *The Comparative Study of Political Elites*. Englewood Cliffs, NJ: Prentice-Hall.

Raines, Howell. 1984. "Bush and Ferraro Debate: Disagree about Leadership, Foreign Policy, and Religion." *New York Times,* October 12. http://www.nytimes.com/1984/10/12/us/bush-and-ferraro-debate-disagree-about-leadership-foreign-policy-and-religion.html.

Ranta, Ronald. 2015. *Political Decision Making and Non-Decisions: The Case of Israel and the Occupied Territories.* New York: Palgrave Macmillan.

Raymond, Janice G. 2002. "The New UN Trafficking Protocol." *Women's Studies International Forum* 25 (5): 491–502.

Reagan, Ronald. 1990. *An American Life.* New York: Simon and Schuster.

Reagan, Ronald. 2007. *The Reagan Diaries.* Edited by Douglas Brinkley. New York: HarperCollins.

Regan, Patrick M., and Aida Paskeviciute. 2003. "Women's Access to Politics and Peaceful States." *Journal of Peace Research* 40 (3): 287–302.

Reilly, Katie. 2016. "Madeleine Albright Apologizes for 'Special Place in Hell' Comment." *Time,* February 12. http://time.com/4220323/madeleine-albright-place-in-hell-remark-apology/.

Reingold, Beth. 2000. *Representing Women: Sex, Gender and Legislative Behavior in Arizona and California.* Chapel Hill: University of North Carolina Press.

Reynolds, Andrew. 1999. "Women in the Legislatures and Executives of the World." *World Politics* 51: 547–572.

Rice, Condoleezza. 1984. *The Soviet Union and the Czechoslovak Army, 1948–1983: Uncertain Allegiance.* Princeton, NJ: Princeton University Press.

Rice, Condoleezza. 2000. "Promoting the National Interest." *Foreign Affairs* 79 (January/February). http://www.foreignaffairs.com/articles/55630/condoleezza-rice/campaign-2000-promoting-the-national-interest.

Rice, Condoleezza. 2002a. "Overview of America's International Strategy." National Security Strategy, September. George W. Bush White House Web Archive. https://georgewbush-whitehouse.archives.gov/nsc/nss/2002/nss1.html. Accessed January 22, 2018.

Rice, Condoleezza. 2002b. "Prevent Our Enemies from Threatening Us, Our Allies, and Our Friends with Weapons of Mass Destruction." National Security Strategy, September. George W. Bush White House Web Archive. http://georgewbush-whitehouse.archives.gov/nsc/nss/2002/nss5.html. Accessed June 4, 2014.

Rice, Condoleezza. 2010. *Extraordinary, Ordinary People: A Memoir of Family.* New York: Random House.

Rice, Condoleezza. 2011. *No Higher Honor: A Memoir of My Years in Washington.* New York: Random House.

Rice, Condoleezza. 2017. *Democracy: Stories from the Long Road to Freedom.* New York: Twelve.

Richards, David, and Martin Smith. 2006. "Central Control and Policy Implementation in the UK: A Case Study of the Prime Minister's Delivery Unit." *Journal of Comparative Policy Analysis* 8 (4): 325–345.

Richman, Alvin. 1996. "American Support for International Involvement: General and Specific Components of Post-Cold War Changes." *Public Opinion Quarterly* 60 (2): 305–322.

Riley, Russell. 2015. "Sandy Berger's Washington." *The Atlantic,* December 5. http://www.theatlantic.com/politics/archive/2015/12/sandy-bergers-washington/418812/.

Roberts, Barbara. 1989. "Women's Peace Activism in Canada." In *Beyond the Vote: Canadian Women and Politics,* edited by Linda Kealey and Joan Sangster, 276–308. Toronto: University of Toronto Press.

Robinson, W. S. 1950. "Ecological Correlations and the Behaviour of Individuals." *American Sociological Review* 15 (3): 351–357.

Rodham, Hillary. 1969. "Student Commencement Speech." Wellesley College, May 31. http://www.wellesley.edu/events/commencement/archives/1969commencement/studentspeech.

Rodman, Peter W. 2009. *Presidential Command: Power, Leadership and the Making of Foreign Policy from Richard Nixon to George W. Bush.* New York: Knopf.

Roper Center for Public Opinion Research. 1980. "How Groups Voted in 1980." http://ropercenter.cornell.edu/polls/us-elections/how-groups-voted/how-groups-voted-1980/.

Roper Center for Public Opinion Research. 1992. "How Groups Voted in 1992." http://ropercenter.cornell.edu/polls/us-elections/how-groups-voted/how-groups-voted-1992/.

Roper Center for Public Opinion Research. 2000. "How Groups Voted in 2000." http://ropercenter.cornell.edu/polls/us-elections/how-groups-voted/how-groups-voted-2000/.

Roper Center for Public Opinion Research. 2008. "How Groups Voted in 2008." http://ropercenter.cornell.edu/polls/us-elections/how-groups-voted/how-groups-voted-2008/.

Rosenfeld, Alan. 2010. "'Anarchist Amazons': The Gendering of Radicalism in 1970s West Germany." *Contemporary European History* 19 (4): 351–374.

Rothkopf, David. 2014. "National Insecurity: Can Obama's Foreign Policy Be Saved?" *Foreign Policy* 208: 44–52.

Rothman, Sheila. 1978. *Woman's Proper Place: A History of Changing Ideals and Practices, 1870 to the Present.* New York: Basic Books.

Rousseau, Jean-Jacques. 2005. "A Discourse on a Subject Proposed by the Academy of Dijon: What Is the Origin of Inequality among Men and Is It Authorised by Natural Law." In *A Discourse on the Origin of Inequality and A Discourse on Political Economy*, translated by G. D. H. Cole. Stilwell, KS: Digireads.com.

Ruddick, Sara. 1995. *Maternal Thinking: Toward a Politics of Peace.* Boston: Beacon Press.

Rumsfeld, Donald. 2011. *Known and Unknown: A Memoir.* New York: Sentinel.

Saad, Lydia. 2008. "Will the Abortion Issue Help or Hurt McCain?" *Gallup*, September 3. http://www.gallup.com/poll/110002/will-abortion-issue-help-hurt-mccain.aspx.

Sanbonmatsu, Kira, Susan J. Carroll, and Debbie Walsh. 2009. "Poised to Run: Women's Pathways to the State Legislatures." Centre for American Women and Politics. http://www.cawp.rutgers.edu/sites/default/files/resources/poisedtorun_0.pdf.

Saint-German, Michelle A. 1989. "Does Their Difference Make a Difference? The Impact of Elected Women on Public Policy in Arizona." *Social Science Quarterly* 70 (4): 956–968.

Sang-Hun, Choe. 2015. "Peace Activists Cross Demilitarized Zone Separating Koreas." *New York Times*, May 24. http://www.nytimes.com/2015/05/25/world/asia/peace-activists-cross-demilitarized-zone-separating-koreas.html?ref=topics&_r=0.

Santaliestra, Laura Oliván. 2016. "Lady Anne Fanshawe, Ambassadress of England at the Court of Madrid (1664–1666)." In *Women, Diplomacy and International Politics since 1500*, edited by Glenda Sluga and Carolyn James, 68–85. London: Routledge.

Sanzone, Donna S. 1981. "Women in Politics: A Study of Political Leadership in the U.K., France and the Federal Republic of Germany." In *Access to Power*, edited by Cynthia Fuchs Epstein and Rose Laub Coser, 37–51. London: Allen and Unwin.

Savoie, Donald. 1999. *Governing from the Centre: The Concentration of Power in Canadian Politics*. Toronto: University of Toronto Press.

Sawer, Marian, Manon Tremblay, and Linda Trimble, eds. 2006. *Representing Women in Parliament: A Comparative Study*. London: Routledge.

Schanberg, Sydney H. 1984. "New York: George the Gender Bender." *New York Times*, October 20. http://www.nytimes.com/1984/10/20/opinion/new-york-george-the-gender-bender.html.

Schier, Steven E. 2009. *Panorama of a Presidency: How George W. Bush Acquired and Spent His Political Capital*. Armonk, NY: M. E. Sharpe.

Schreiber, Ronnee. 2008. *Righting Feminism: Conservative Women and American Politics*. New York: Oxford University Press.

Scott, Joan Wallach. 1999. *Gender and the Politics of History*. New York: Columbia University Press.

Sears, David O., and Leonie Huddy. 1990. "On the Origins of Political Disunity among Women." In *Women, Politics and Change*, edited by Louise A. Tilly and Patricia Gurin, 249–277. New York: Russell Sage Foundation.

Senate Select Committee on Intelligence. 2014. "Committee Study of the Central Intelligence Agency's Detention and Interrogation Program." Declassified December 3. Approved December 13, 2012. https://www.amnestyusa.org/pdfs/sscistudy1.pdf.

Sewell, William H., Jr. 1992. "A Theory of Structure: Duality, Agency and Transformation." *American Journal of Sociology* 98: 1–29.

Shapiro, Robert Y., and Harpreet Mahajan. 1986. "Gender Differences in Policy Preferences: A Summary of Trends from the 1960s to the 1980s." *Public Opinion Quarterly* 50 (1): 42–61.

Sharma, Dinesh, ed. 2016. *The Global Hillary: Women's Political Leadership in Cultural Contexts*. New York: Routledge.

Shaw, Robin Ferguson. 2009. "Angela Y. Davis and the Prison Abolition Movement, Part II." *Contemporary Justice Review* 12 (1): 101–104.

Shultz, George P. 1993. *Turmoil and Triumph: My Years as Secretary of State*. New York: Macmillan.

Siaroff, Alan. 2000. "Women's Representation in Legislatures and Cabinets in Industrial Democracies." *International Political Science Review* 21 (2): 197–215.

Sinkkonen, Sirkka, and Elina Haavio-Mannila. 1981. "The Impact of the Women's Movement and Legislative Activity of Women Members of Parliament on Social Development." In *Women, Power and Political Systems*, edited by Margherita Rendel, 195–215. London: Croom Helm.

Skard, Torild. 2014. *Women of Power: Half a Century of Female Presidents and Prime Ministers Worldwide*. Bristol, UK: Policy Press.

Skidmore, David. 2011. "The Obama Presidency and US Foreign Policy: Where's the Multilateralism?" *International Studies Perspective* 13 (1): 43–64.

Sluga, Glenda. 2016. "Women, Diplomacy and International Politics, before and after the Congress of Vienna." In *Women, Diplomacy and International Politics since 1500*, edited by Glenda Sluga and Carolyn James, 120–136. London: Routledge.

Sluga, Glenda, and Carolyn James, eds. 2016. *Women, Diplomacy and International Politics since 1500*. London: Routledge.

Smith, Tom W. 1984. "The Polls: Gender and Attitudes toward Violence." *Public Opinion Quarterly* 48 (1B, Spring): 384–396.

Sobel, Richard. 1998. "The Polls—Trends: United States Intervention in Bosnia." *Public Opinion Quarterly* 62 (2): 250–278.

Solomon, Paul D. 2007. *Paul D. Wolfowitz: Visionary Intellectual, Policymaker, and Strategist*. Westport, CT: Praeger Security International.

Squires, Judith. 2007. *The New Politics of Gender Equality*. Houndmills, Basingstoke, UK: Palgrave Macmillan.

Steans, Jill. 2006. *Gender and International Relations*, 2nd ed. Cambridge, UK: Polity Press.

Steinberg, Blema. 2008. *Women in Power: The Personalities and Leadership Styles of Indira Gandhi, Golda Meir, and Margaret Thatcher*. Montreal: McGill-Queen's University Press.

Steinem, Gloria. 1970. "What It Would Be Like if Women Win." *Time*, August 31. http://content.time.com/time/subscriber/article/0,33009,876786,00.html

Stevenson, Jonathan. 2011. "Owned by the Army: Has the President Lost Control of His Generals?" *Harper's*, May. https://harpers.org/archive/2011/05/owned-by-the-army/.

Stiehm, Judith Hicks. 2005. "Women and the Nobel Prize for Peace." *International Feminist Journal of Politics* 7(2): 258–279.

Stoper, Emily, and Roberta Ann Johnson. 1977. "The Weaker Sex and the Better Half: The Idea of Women's Moral Superiority in the American Feminist Movement." *Polity* 10 (2): 192–217.

Stowe, Harriet Beecher. 1967. *My Wife and I*. New York: AMS Press.

Studlar, Donley T., and Gary F. Moncrief. 1999. "Women's Work? The Distribution and Prestige of Portfolios in the Canadian Provinces." *Governance* 12 (4): 379–395.

Sturrock, Carrie. 2008. "U.S. Ends Bias Investigation of Stanford." *San Francisco Chronicle*, April 3. http://www.sfgate.com/bayarea/article/U-S-ends-bias-investigation-of-Stanford-3219927.php.

Swers, Michele L. 2002. *The Difference Women Make: The Policy Impact of Women in Congress*. Chicago: University of Chicago Press.

Swers, Michele L. 2013. *Women in the Club: Gender and Policymaking in the Senate*. Chicago: University of Chicago Press.

Sykes, Patricia Lee. 1993. "Women as National Leaders: Patterns and Prospects." In *Women as National Leaders*, edited by Michael A. Genovese, 219–229. Newbury Park, CA: Sage.

Talbott, Strobe. 2011. "Thinker, Doer, Mentor, Friend." In *The Unquiet American*, edited by Derek Chollet and Samantha Power, 8–22. New York: Public Affairs.

Thatcher, Margaret. 1993. *The Downing Street Years*. New York: HarperCollins.

Thomas, Clarence. 2007. *My Grandfather's Son: A Memoir*. New York: Harper.

Thomas, Sue. 1994. *How Women Legislate*. New York: Oxford University Press.

Tickner, J. Ann. 2001. *Gendering World Politics: Issues and Approaches in the Post-Cold War Era*. New York: Columbia University Press.

Tickner, J. Ann. 2014. *A Feminist Voyage through International Relations*. New York: Oxford University Press.

Time. 1981. "Letter Bomb." October 26, 24.

Tremblay, Manon. 1992. "Quand les femmes se distinguent: Féminisme et représentation politique au Québec." *Canadian Journal of Political Science* 25 (1): 55–68.

Tremblay, Manon. 1998. "Do Female MPs Substantively Represent Women? A Study of Legislative Behaviour in Canada's 35th Parliament." *Canadian Journal of Political Science* 31 (3): 435–465.

Tremblay, Manon. 2010. *Quebec Women and Legislative Representation*. Translated by Käthe Roth. Vancouver: UBC Press.

Tremblay, Manon, and Daniel Stockemer. 2013. "Women's Ministerial Careers in Cabinet, 1921–2010: A Look at Socio-Demographic Traits and Career Experiences." *Canadian Public Administration* 56: 523–541.

True, Jacqui. 2003. "Mainstreaming Gender in Global Public Policy." *International Journal of Feminist Politics* 5 (3): 368–396.

Warner, Judith. 1993. *Hillary Clinton: The Inside Story*. New York: Penguin.

Warrick, Joby. 2011. "Hillary's War: How Conviction Replaced Skepticism in Libya Intervention." *Washington Post*, October 30. https://www.washingtonpost. com/world/national-security/hillarys-war-how-conviction-replaced-skepticism-in-libya-intervention/2011/10/28/gIQAhGS7WM_story.html.

Wattier, Mark J., Byron W. Daynes, and Raymond Tatalovich. 1997. "Abortion Attitudes, Gender, and Candidate Choice in Presidential Elections: 1972 to 1992." *Women and Politics* 17 (1): 55–72.

Weinberger, Caspar W. 1990. *Fighting for Peace: Seven Critical Years in the Pentagon*. New York: Warner.

Weiner, Tim. 2006. "Kirkpatrick, U.N. Envoy under Reagan, Dies." *New York Times*, December 8. http://www.nytimes.com/2006/12/08/washington/ 09kirkpatrick.html?pagewanted=1&_r=0.

Wibben, Annick T. R. 2011. "Feminist Politics in Feminist Security Studies." *Politics & Gender* 7 (4): 590–595.

Wills, Gary. 1992. "H. R. Clinton's Case." *New York Review of Books*, March 5. http:// www.nybooks.com/articles/archives/1992/mar/05/hr-clintons-case/.

Wilson, Robin. 2008. "Investigation of Gender Discrimination at Stanford U. Is Over." *Chronicle of Higher Education*, April 3. http://chronicle.com/article/ Investigation-of-Gender/40747.

Woerhle, Lynne M. 1995. "Teaching about Women from a Peace Studies Perspective: An Annotated Bibliography of Resources on Conflict, Peace, and Justice." *Women's Studies Quarterly* 23 (3–4): 214–248.

Woodacre, Elena. 2016. "Cousins and Queens: Familial Ties, Political Ambition and Epistolary Diplomacy in Renaissance Europe." In *Women, Diplomacy and International Politics since 1500*, edited by Glenda Sluga and Carolyn James, 30–45. London: Routledge.

Woodward, Bob. 2004. *Plan of Attack*. New York: Simon and Schuster.

INDEX

Figures are indicated by an italic *f* following the page number.

Palmer's sex discrimination case, 7–9
women and diplomatic power, male
    discomfort and negative tropes,
    4, 6–11
women's erasure, 3, 4, 59, 205–206
diplomats, female. *See also specific
    individuals and issues*
male views, 6–7
mixed perspectives, 6
Discourse on Inequality, A (Rousseau), 35
Doar, John, 189–190, 191
Dobbs, Michael, 105, 108, 114
Dohrn, Bernardine, 45
dos Santos, Pedro, 21
Down, Ian, 20
Dueck, Colin, 172, 175
Dukakis, Michael, 97, 114
Dumbrell, John, 96

Eagly, Alice, 26–27, 215
Edelman, Marian Wright, 187
education, 4–5
Education Standards Committee, Hillary
    Clinton, 192
Egypt, Hillary Clinton, 176–177, 180
Eichenberg, Richard, 40
Elshtain, Jean, 35–36, 38, 216
Embrace the Base, 42
enfranchisement, women's, 35–36. *See
    also* suffrage movements
Engels, Frederick, 47–48
equal rights, women. *See* gender equality
Equal Rights Amendment (ERA),
    51, 52, 53
    Kirkpatrick on, 59, 223
essentialism, 31, 55, 57. *See also* women,
    war, and feminism
evaluation, public leadership
    Albright, 129–131
    Clinton, Hillary, 202–204
    Kirkpatrick, 88–94
    Rice, 165–168
executive leadership
    consequences, 12–13, 26–30
    functions, 26
    influence, 3–4, 27, 209
    masculine stereotype, 26–27, 207, 215
    responsiveness and
        representation, 26
    studying, 26–30
    transformational *vs.* transactional
        elites, 27, 209
executive office, women in
    actions, 20–23
    vs. legislative office, 19–23

Falklands War, viii, 81–88
Feminine Mystique, The (Friedan), 51
feminism. *See also* gender (women's)
        equality; *specific organizations*
    Albright, 98, 119–120, 226–227
    Bush, George W., 224–225
    Clinton, Bill, 120
    Clinton, Hillary, 170, 174–175, 227–228
    equal rights, 51
    female elites' views, 2, 33
    first- *vs.* second-wave, 35–36
    Kirkpatrick, 222–226
    left ideology, 47–50
    opinion differences, 4, 5–6
    organized, Thatcher on, 20–21
    progressivism, 16, 47, 50–51
    Rice, 224–225
    splits over, 50–52
    substantive representation, 18, 23–26
feminism, second-wave, 13,
        35–36, 49–50
    attitudinal divisions, 52–55
    state lawmakers on, 53–54
feminist historiography, 2–3, 205–206
feminist institutionalism, 56
feminist international relations
        literature, 15
Feminist Majority Foundation, 161
Fernandes, Leela, 221
Ferraro, Geraldine, 97, 113–114
Finger, Seymour, 79
Finkle, Jason, 89
Finland, 15
Flanders, Laura, 161
foreign aid
    budget, *vs.* Defense Department, 208
    rational humanist strategy, 63
    women parliamentarians on, 20
Fourier, Charles, 47
Fourth World Conference on Women,
        Hillary Clinton, 123, 170, 193–194
Franklin, Ursula, 41
Fraser, Antonia, 11, 43, 46, 68
Freedom Agenda, 142, 167
Freeman, Jo, 16–18, 51
Friedan, Betty, 51
Fukuyama, Francis, 42–43
Fulton, Sarah, 21, 22, 24–25, 42, 207

Gaddafi, Muammar, 176–179, 178f, 201,
        202, 221
Gaddis, John Lewis, 61, 206
Gamarekian, Barbara, 8
Gandhi, Indira, viii, 20
Geertz, Clifford, 27

on women's movements, 11, 135–136
on women's rights, 142, 168
Rice, Susan, 177, 201, 220
Richman, Alvin, 226–227
rights. *See* children's rights;
    gender (women's) equality;
    women's rights
Rodman, Peter, 96, 98–99
Roosevelt, Eleanor, 41
Rose, Melody, 196
Rose Law Firm, Hillary Clinton,
    191–192
Rothkopf, David, 175
Rothman, Sheila, 51
Rousseau, Jean-Jacques, 47
Rousseff, Dilma, 21
Ruddick, Sara, 37
Rumsfeld, Donald, 141, 157, 158
Russia. *See* Soviets
Rwanda, Albright, 100, 119, 131

Sagar, Pearl, 42
Santaliestra, Laura, 3
Sarkees, Meredith, 45, 228
Schier, Steven, 137
Schlafly, Phyllis, 52, 190
Scott, Joan, 3
Scowcroft, Brent, 150, 157
Sears, David, 51
Second Sex, The (de Beauvoir), 51
second-wave feminism, 13
secretary of state. *See also specific*
    individuals
    Albright, Madeleine, 1, 95, 124–129
    Clinton, Hillary, 169, 170, 172,
        198–202
    Marshall, George, 208
    Powell, Colin, 141, 164–165
    Rice, Condoleezza, 132, 133, 134f
sex trafficking
    Albright, 25, 131
    Clinton, Hillary, 194
sexual violence, as crime against
    humanity, 120–121
Shah of Iran, 62–63
Shelton, Hugh, 126
Shultz, George, 59, 85–87, 88,
    138, 206
Sluga, Glenda, 3–4, 11, 208
"smart power", 174, 199, 227
Smith, Charles Howard, 6–7
Smith, Tom, 44
social movement activism, 44–45
social networks, 3–5
social programs, domestic, 40

Soderberg, Nancy, 113
Somalia
    Albright, 96, 100, 117–118, 130,
        210, 218
    Bush, George W., 156
    Rice, 139
Somoza, Anastasio, 62–63, 85
Soviets
    Afghanistan, 61, 62, 64, 78, 112, 149
    containment, 61
    expansionism, 148
    weakening, Kirkpatrick, 77–79
Spain, 17th century, 3
Stanford University, Rice as provost, 136,
    152–154
State Department, loss of
    primacy, 5, 208
state houses, gender in, 56
state legislators, females, 95
    feminine and motherly interests, 19
    League and AAUW
        membership, 51–52
    pro-feminism, 19
    second-wave feminism, 53–54
Steans, Jill, 36
Steinem, Gloria, 37, 41, 72
Stoper, Emily, 37
STOP ERA network, 52
Stowe, Harriet Beecher, 36
strength, inner, 67, 181, 213
structural barriers, 13
structures *vs.* individuals, 17–18
substantive representation, 18, 23–26,
    54, 55, 57
suffrage movements, 35–36, 48
Sweden, 15
Swers, Michele, 54
Sykes, Patricia Lee, 20
Syria, Hillary Clinton, 170, 176, 179

Tatalovich, Raymond, 226
Tenet, George, 141
terror suspects, forceful options, 44
Thatcher, Margaret, 43
    Falklands War, viii, 81–83
    feminism and, 20–21
    on women's liberation movement, 54
    women's rights, 54
Thomas, Clarence, 151
Thompson, Seth, 27
Tickner, Ann, 38
torture of prisoners, Bush and Rice on,
    160, 161
transactional elites, 27, 209
transformational elites, 27, 59, 209